ASSOCIATION FOR SCOTTISH I

CW00536024

Scottish and International Modernisms

Relationships and Reconfigurations

EDITED BY

EMMA DYMOCK

AND

MARGERY PALMER McCULLOCH

To have great poets, there must be great audiences too.
—*Walt Whitman*

Association for Scottish Literary Studies
Occasional Papers: Number 15

Published by
Association for Scottish Literary Studies
Scottish Literature
7 University Gardens
University of Glasgow
Glasgow G12 8QH

www.asls.org.uk

ASLS is a registered charity no. SC006535

First published 2011

© ASLS and the individual contributors

All rights reserved. No part of this book may be
reproduced, stored in a retrieval system, or
transmitted in any form or means, electronic,
mechanical, photocopying, recording or otherwise,
without the prior permission of the
Association for Scottish Literary Studies.

A CIP catalogue for this title
is available from the British Library

ISBN 978-1-906841-07-2

The Association for Scottish Literary Studies
acknowledges the support of Creative Scotland
towards the publication of this book.

Contents

Contents (continued)

Acknowledgements

The cover illustration, *The Birth of Venus* (Edward Baird, 1934), appears by kind permission of Mr Graham Stephen and the National Galleries of Scotland. The photograph on p. 165 of *Portrait of Young Scotsman* (Edward Baird, 1932) appears by kind permission of Mr Graham Stephen and Abbott and Holder Ltd.

Acknowledgement is also made to the Trustees of the National Library of Scotland for permission to use extracts from the Sorley MacLean–Douglas Young correspondence held by the library.

The editors would especially like to thank Duncan Jones of the Association for Scottish Literary Studies for his invaluable work in the publishing process of this book. We are also grateful to the Council of ASLS for their initial support for publication, and to administrative staff in the ASLS office and at Stirling University who made the practical arrangements for the successful conference from which this volume emerged.

Introduction

EMMA DYMOCK AND MARGERY PALMER McCULLOCH

Periods of significant literary achievement in Scotland have most often been related to an increased sense of nationhood in the country. In the late medieval period of Henryson, Dunbar and Gavin Douglas, for example, the literary flowering which took place grew out of a desire to enrich the Scots language and make it an instrument fit to challenge the southern 'rose of rhetoric', as Dunbar characterised Chaucer, and also to translate a classic text such as Virgil's *Aeneid*, as did Douglas in his *Eneados*. And the impulse to enrich and display the language and culture of the country itself grew out of the new political confidence developed by a period of relative peace and prosperity during the reign of King James IV between 1488 and 1513. A sense of nationhood was also the impulse for the period of cultural flowering in the eighteenth century which culminated in the poetry and song-writing of Robert Burns and in the novels of Walter Scott which were so influential, alongside the Ossian texts from the Scottish Highlands, in the development of European Romanticism. This time, however, the cultural flowering was a response to the loss of statehood as a result of the Union of the Parliaments of Scotland and England in 1707, a loss which paradoxically led on the one hand to an increased awareness of a distinctive national culture, and on the other to a rush by the upwardly mobile to learn to speak good English for the purpose of advancement. The early twentieth-century literary and cultural revival, initiated by C. M. Grieve/Hugh MacDiarmid in the immediate post-1918 period, and popularly known in its own time as the 'Scottish Renaissance', fits into this relation-to-nationhood pattern. Its primary aim was to regain a distinctive cultural identity for Scotland through a revival of writing in all three of Scotland's languages, and in the longer term to regain a distinctive political identity also. Scotland's status would no longer be that of a provincial 'North Britain'.

The success of this early twentieth-century Scottish renaissance can be measured not only by the quality and variety of the literary work produced by the writers of the time, but also by the strength and confidence of writing in Scotland in our contemporary period (as well as, one might add, the eventual return of a devolved Scottish parliament at the turn of the century). Yet one could argue that the price paid by the interwar revolutionaries for the future success of their descendants has been an overly nationalistic view of their literary work by later Scottish critics, a view encouraged by the fashion for theoretical studies of nationalisms in the 1990s, and coloured negatively by the suspicion of nationalist positions engendered by the events leading up to and during World War Two. And if in the last few decades the literary work of MacDiarmid (in particular) and his interwar colleagues has been viewed suspiciously as unhealthily nationalistic by critics in the home market, then in the overseas market of modernist studies it has until very recently been mostly ignored. Yet in their own time, internationalism was the inseparable other side of the nationalist coin, and to take Scottish culture back into the mainstream of Europe was a primary objective of the reformers. The innovations of continental European writers, as well as of Anglophone writers such as Eliot, Joyce, Pound and Lawrence, fed into their imaginations and their work and interacted with native Scottish traditions which were simultaneously being transformed and made fit for a new age. These 'Scottish Renaissance' writers were in their own time contributors to what we now call modernism.

This recognition that not only is there a distinctive Scottish literature, but that there was in the post-1918 period a Scottish contribution to literary modernism is gradually making its way into academic discourse, with contributions on aspects of Scottish modernism taking their place in publications emanating from within and beyond Scotland. At the same time there has been over a number of years a change in the way modernism itself is regarded, a move away from the earlier critical idea of a small group of 'high modernist' writers, focusing on form and apparently detached from social or political concerns, towards a recognition of the variety of responses to modernity that took place in different cultures and in different social and political conditions during these early twentieth-century years. The aim of this present collection of essays is to contribute to the ongoing international discourse concerning a more varied and inclusive modernism, while at the same time redirecting potentially inward-looking perceptions of the national revival movement towards the recognition of a Scottish modernism that was itself responding to the challenges of modernity, and through its responses bringing revitalised Scottish traditions into a wider international context.

The essays which form the various chapters of this book have been developed from papers given at a conference on Scottish and International

Modernisms sponsored by the Association for Scottish Literary Studies and hosted by the University of Stirling in the summer of 2009. In accordance with the dual aim of expanding awareness in Scotland and elsewhere of the international and modernist dimension of the Scottish interwar revival movement, and of contributing to the current academic re-examination of transnational modernism itself, the various essays have been consciously designed to bring out relationships between Scottish and non-Scottish writers and contexts. And since, despite the dominance of literature in the post-1918 period in Scotland, there were also other art forms responding to the challenges of the time, two chapters discuss visual art and music.

Roderick Watson's opening chapter 'Scotland and Modernisms' sets the scene with a wide-ranging discussion of the European and Anglophone cultural context to which the Scottish interwar reformers responded and to which they saw themselves as contributing. Watson considers themes of identity and nationalism in terms of subjectivity, which, it could be argued, offers a more unconditional terminology in relation to writers and artists who were exploring worlds – material and imaginative – beyond their immediate home environment and reflecting on how these explorations related to their own lives in personal, aesthetic and political ways. Ritchie Robertson's 'Edwin Muir, Kafka, and German Modernism' provides a specific example of such a philosophical and artistic contact with a new world as well as providing a companion narrative to Watson's previous chapter as it traces the genesis of the modernist movement and reflects on work which 'articulated a need for a radical transformation of society'. It can also be seen as an early case study of German modernism in relation to a Scottish writer, thus adding to the French influences referred to by MacDiarmid at the outset of the revival movement, and which were significant also for Scottish visual artists in the early years of the century as discussed by Watson.

The next three chapters of the book provide an interconnected subsection within the study of modernisms in their discussion of the impact of small magazines in the furtherance of new movements. Alistair McCleery's 'Modernity and Nationhood: "Little Magazines" in Scotland' shows that while certain magazines in the Scottish scene were, both politically and culturally, part of the growth of a more general nationalist movement, they also provided a platform for the kind of experimental work that was to shape a modern, and in the case of *The Modern Scot*, a modernist, sensibility within Scotland. Mark Gaipa's 'Modernism, Magazines, and the Creation of an American Literature' explores a similar topic within the American context, connecting the emergence of little magazines in the United States to a new spirit of cultural nationalism. While Gaipa's chapter is primarily concerned with the American literary context, it implicitly brings to our attention similarities between the Scottish and American scenes, at the same time demonstrating the possibilities that are inherent in a wider study of modernism when borders are open and nationalism gives way to internationalism. Alexander J. Cuthbert's discussion of Edwin Muir's relationship with the influential *New Age* magazine also brings Scotland and the USA together and points to the importance of little magazines in the development of the careers of individual writers. The success of Muir's *We Moderns: Enigmas and Guesses* (1918), initially published as a series of short essays in *The New* Age, gained him the patronage of the American publisher Alfred A. Knopf and the journalist and Nietzschean commentator, H. L. Mencken, who wrote the introduction to the American edition of *We Moderns* in 1920, thus opening up the road to Muir's future international career as poet and critic. In his Scottish chapter, McCleery also mentions the literary magazines that came into being from the late 1970s onwards: magazines such as *Chapman, Cencrastus*, and the *Edinburgh Review*, which have their own stories to tell about the development of Scotland from, as McCleery puts it, a 'stateless nation to devolved nation-state (and beyond?)'. Although Gaelic-medium magazines are not included in this discussion of later twentieth-century periodicals, in the Scottish Gaelic sphere the most prominent comparison would be *Gairm*, a quarterly magazine published through the medium of Gaelic, and with Derick Thomson at its helm, from the 1950s until the late 1990s. Hardly a single Gaelic writer of the second half of the twentieth century was not at some point published in this magazine, with by far its greatest achievement being the first place of publication for Sorley MacLean's 'Hallaig', which could be considered as a late but significant flowering within the Gaelic modernist tradition. This is an area of little magazine publication that needs further study, but it would seem that these later Gaelic publications were playing a role similar to adventurous little magazines at home and abroad in the earlier modernist period.

While it is possible to trace specific landmarks of modernism in the pages of magazines, modernism in Scotland can also be defined by specific figures: those who set about exploring their sense of self against the backdrop of modernism. Thus, in 'Primitivism in the Writing of D. H. Lawrence and Neil M. Gunn', Andrew J. Sneddon discusses how Gunn uses the identity of the

Picts to locate his own sense of cultural and spiritual belonging within a greater whole which spans centuries, and brings Gunn's exploration into contact with Lawrence's writings about the Etruscans and other early peoples. Alan Riach, in 'W. B. Yeats and Hugh MacDiarmid', suggests that MacDiarmid's approach was perhaps less restrained in relation to nationalist identity than that of Yeats, while pointing out that the 'regeneration of the small Celtic nation as a state' was, for both Yeats and MacDiarmid, 'valid ground, the earth from which the poetry arises'. In contrast, Scott Lyall's chapter highlights another reality in Scottish modernist literature: that it is possible, as with Lewis Grassic Gibbon, to be anti-nationalist, yet to succeed in defining a country in a national epic which is simultaneously a work of modernist cosmopolitanism.

While MacDiarmid and Yeats were searching for the soul of their respective nations in the myths and traditions of their respective pasts, and at the same time making these traditions anew (albeit through the medium of Scots and English), another poet in Scotland took up this challenge from the late 1930s onwards but did so under the banner of his own native Gaelic language, the very language which MacDiarmid was viewing as an alternative to Scots in his vision of the modern nation in a poem such as *To Circumjack Cencrastus*. Sorley MacLean is perhaps one of the best examples of a modern internationalist poet because of his ability to span cultures. His awareness of the Irish and Scottish Gaelic tradition is coupled to his understanding of a wider European literature and politics, and his search for his own sense of self and identity is carried out within a landscape which is by turns intensely personal and surreally alien (at least from the perspective of a traditional Gaelic mindset). Emma Dymock's chapter on Sorley MacLean concentrates on *An Cuilithionn*, MacLean's long political poem, composed in 1939. While Gaelic poetry will always benefit from being studied within its own context if the inherently Gaelic subjects and themes are to be understood properly, it is also clear that the Lowland writers of the early twentieth-century Scottish revival movement were more than capable of envisaging Gaelic within the sphere of Scottish and European literature, as Dymock's chapter illustrates through references to the correspondence of the poet and scholar Douglas Young.

As with Scottish writers generally, women writers have been among the marginalised in canonical studies of modernist writing. On the other hand, since the early days of feminist criticism, and during the more recent widening of the field of modernist studies, the contribution of women to modernist writing has increasingly been studied, with a consequent recognition of the significance of gender, thematically and formally, in their work. Aileen Christian's chapter on Willa Muir – too often characterised merely as the wife of the more prominent Edwin – discusses Muir's concerns with gender issues in her fiction and essay writing, together with her exploration of the role of the unconscious in human life through her own experience of dreaming as well as through her awareness of the researches of Freud and Jung. Margery Palmer McCulloch discusses Catherine Carswell and Rebecca West as writers who tested traditional boundaries in society and art in their life experiences and their literary work, and brings both together with D. H. Lawrence who was simultaneously breaking conventional boundaries from a male gender perspective. These three women – two Scottish and one, like Byron, 'half a Scot' through her mother – stand here as exemplars of the many interwar women writers, within and beyond Scotland, who challenged the outdated socially-conditioned roles allotted to women and brought a new female-gendered response to modernity into the themes and formal expression of the writing of the time.

Among the many enjoyable features of the conference from which this collection derives were the visual art and musical presentations of Jonathan Blackwood and John Purser. It is regrettably not possible to reproduce here the sounds of the music of Erik Chisholm and the other classical and folk examples played by John Purser to pull his listeners into the heart of his talk on Scottish music; nor is it possible to reproduce the many visual images through which Jonathan Blackwood introduced us to the little-known work of the artist Edward Baird – a painter from Montrose, the small east-coast town from which MacDiarmid launched his modernist literary revolution in the early 1920s, and who was returning to Montrose from Glasgow School of Art around the time MacDiarmid himself was leaving the town.

The editors are grateful to both contributors for the translations of their rich spoken and illustrated presentations into a written form which we think will remind some readers of the visual and aural enjoyment of the original experience while encouraging those coming freshly to the topics to explore the music and visual art further for themselves.

In his chapter on Scottish music, John Purser considers the structures of the work of his composers from traditional and modernist perspectives, showing, for example, that it is necessary to recognise the influence of both *ceòl mòr* and Hindustani music if Erik Chisholm's compositions are to be fully understood. It is this sort of understanding, the endeavour to move outside rigid categories and identifications, which has inspired discussions throughout this book, and which Carla Sassi celebrates in its final chapter. Sassi's emphasis on the importance of the current re-visioning of modernism in general, and her awareness of the importance in relation to an understanding of Scottish modernism of its transformative dialogue with other world modernisms, thus provide an apt conclusion for the book as a whole. In addition, her willingness to consider theoretically how the movement we now call modernism relates to other twentieth-century concepts such as cosmopolitanism and post-colonialism, points to ongoing reconfigurations in how we characterise the relationship between the local and the global in a continually changing modern world.

Scotland and Modernisms

RODERICK WATSON

Whaur's Isadora Duncan dancin' noo?
Is Mary Garden in Chicago still
And Duncan Grant in Paris – and me fou'?[1]

Isadora Duncan died scarcely a year after these lines were published, having revolutionised modern dance with her free style just as she scandalised polite society, inspiring painters, sculptors and the builders of the Théatre des Champs Élysées, where her image featured in stone over the entrance and on the walls of the auditorium within. Aberdeen-born Mary Garden was brought up in the United States before making her professional debut as a soprano in Paris, going on to fame in New York and Chicago. Duncan Grant was the Scottish post-impressionist painter from Rothiemurchus who came to be a member of the Bloomsbury group, had a relationship with David Garnett (son of Constance and Edward Garnett) and a child by Vanessa Bell, Virginia Woolf's sister. This was quite a cosmopolitan crowd for a drunk man to name-drop in Montrose. But was it any more than name-dropping? Can the modern Scottish Renaissance claim a legitimate connection to Anglo-American and European modernism?

Such is the topic of this chapter, although it can only touch on selected examples from the 1920s to the 1940s, the richest years of modernism in an Anglo-American context. The theme of subjectivity (often dressed as 'identity' or indeed 'Scottish identity') will also be considered, to propose that some of the most significant writers of the period are as true to the problematised and modernist conceptions of subjectivity, as they are to the imperative of nationalism, even if their work does also draw on what are indeed nationalist and even essentialist terms.

There is no doubt that MacDiarmid *wanted* to get into bed with modernism. His 'Theory of Scots Letters' in the issues of the *Scottish Chapbook* in the spring of 1923 cites Lawrence, Proust, Spengler, Dostoevsky, Cherneshevsky, Joyce and Mallarmé, in a transparent bid to establish his modernist and European credentials, as part of his then necessary campaign to get Scottish culture to broaden its horizons. Whether all these figures can be accommodated into any single coherent programme is another question, of course. True to form, MacDiarmid took what he wanted from each figure without worrying too much about consistency. In fact Dostoevsky and Cherneshevsky are incompatible, for Dostoevsky's *Notes from Underground* actually satirised the utopian socialist idealism in Cherneshevsky's *What is to be Done?* (And that novel was a big influence on Lenin – another of MacDiarmid's heroes.) Or again, Mallarmé came to believe that poetry was always and only ever about poetry, and MacDiarmid was fond of quoting his aims for '*une poesie qui fut comme deduite de l'ensemble des propriétés et des caractères du langage*', which he glossed as: 'the act of poetry being the reverse of what it is usually thought to be; not an idea gradually shaping itself in words, but deriving entirely from words and it was [. . .] in this way that I wrote all the best of my Scots poems.'[2] We can certainly see the relevance of this, not least in the specific debt the Scot owed to the phrases and images he found in *Jamieson's Dictionary*. However, Mallarmé's aesthetic quite simply cannot be made to square with MacDiarmid's determination to find a national character and a unique Scottish psychology in the recesses of the Doric.

The fact remains, nevertheless, that one of the factors driving the modern Scottish literary renaissance was indeed a conscious determination to engage with what MacDiarmid saw (however erratically) as 'the newest and truest tendencies in human thought'. Nor was he alone in this, for Sorley MacLean was to pick up the torch in the 1930s and 1940s with *Dàin do Eimhir*. Haunted as it is by division, fragmentation, deep inner crisis and what Christopher Whyte calls 'a violently cerebral quality,'[3] it is not difficult to see MacLean's masterpiece as a strikingly modernist text. His publisher was not slow to make the same point, for the design of the 1943 Maclellan edition made an unequivocally modernist claim for the book via the artwork of William Crosbie with its swirling lines, organic shapes, and Picasso-like perspectival distortions.

In fact the Maclellan publishing house regularly asserted its modernist credentials by way of its graphic art during the 1940s. Thus Sydney Goodsir Smith's *The Deevil's Waltz* from 1946 had a dust jacket and full plate illustrations by Denis Peploe for the sections 'Venus', 'Prometheus' and 'Mars'. Maclellan also recruited the then elderly J. D. Fergusson as art editor and designer for *Scottish Art and Letters* in an annual series that ran between 1944 and 1950, and Fergusson also went on to make a significant graphic contribution to the first edition of MacDiarmid's *In Memoriam James Joyce*. So the desire to signal modernity – especially in those mid-century years – is clear. But how radical and sustained was this engagement? And can it be said to have had a specifically *Scottish* dimension?

Robert Crawford has noted that there is no necessary disjunction between Paris or Chicago and Montrose, for many key figures in the rise of modernism have come from what metropolitan culture would have dismissed as 'the provinces'. (One could start with Wordsworth – but let's settle for Whitman, Joyce, Pound and William Carlos Williams.[4]) Bakhtin's understanding of centripetal and centrifugal cultural forces, and the differing perspectives created by postcolonial criticism have led us to rethink the relationship between 'centres' and 'peripheries'.[5] Cairns Craig puts it succinctly: 'core cultures are not normal: they are by definition, abnormal, since cores are few and peripheries many'.[6] And indeed any history of modernism (or rather of 'modernisms', for many different and contradictory elements can be found under that banner) will make the same point, for the period was characterised by the most eclectic and heterogeneous influences from within and beyond the borders of conventional European culture. (One thinks of Yeats's engagement with mysticism and the cyclical understanding of history in *A Vision*; or of the influence of Ouspensky on many of the writers and thinkers in A. R. Orage's *New Age*; or of Ezra Pound's fascination with Chinese verse and his (mis)understanding of the Chinese written character. So why not a Scottish, or even a Celtic, modernism indeed?)

One aspect of the modern renaissance impulse was a determination to prove that Scottish art was *already* incipiently modernist – to validate the programme, so to speak. Hence the reinvention of 'Celticism' as 'Celtic modernism' especially as realised in the work of J. D. Fergusson and in MacDiarmid's 'Gaelic Idea' in poems from the late thirties such as 'Island Funeral'. If this seems unlikely, we must recognise that many versions of European modernism in the literary, musical and visual arts depended upon an equally impossible hybrid of appropriated and misunderstood 'native' sources, not least in the struggle to reconnect with ethnic authenticity and a vision of 'primitive' energy, in the search to find an aesthetic that did not depend upon the discredited inheritance of bourgeois Christian or humanist realism.

With this in mind, I would argue that to recognise a transparent, or even at times an essentialist nationalism in some of the modernist claims of the Scottish Renaissance need not necessarily disqualify those claims. And by the same token they need not control or limit those claims. Creative texts, after all, frequently deliver meanings that are not compatible with their author's declared position, and can even be shown by later critics to contradict the very programme they set out to prove. The editors of the recent volume of critical essays, *Beyond Scotland*, argue for hybridity and interdependence as the prevailing features of twentieth-century Scottish literature, and claim that the distinctions between 'indigenous versus imported, nationalism versus internationalism, essentialism versus cosmopolitanism – are little more than a series of false oppositions';[7] and it will be helpful to bear this in mind when considering the case for literary modernism in Scottish writing. Indeed we are so used to thinking of the modern Scottish Renaissance in purely *literary* terms, that we often forget that it was the painters and artists who led the way. One thinks of the sisters Margaret and Frances Macdonald in Glasgow, with their links to the Arts and Crafts movement, and of course the architectural work of Charles Rennie Mackintosh with connections to its numerous European variations: *modernisme, modernismo, art nouveau, jugendstil,* and so on. Most notably, perhaps, the Scottish Colourists looked to French post-impressionism and the Fauves in the first decade of the century, and J. D. Fergusson in particular was quick to respond to this challenge.[8] In common with many significant modernist writers and thinkers of the day, Fergusson was much taken with the theories of the French philosopher Henri Bergson whose concept of time, flux, perpetual movement and *la durée* was central to how modernist artists were coming to think about space, perspective, subjective time, and the stream of consciousness. Fergusson came to associate this with what he took to be the spirit of 'Celtic' art, linked to the ideas of his partner, Margaret Morris, about female empowerment and the *jouissance* of movement, dance and colour. Accordingly, Fergusson proposed a sophisticated connection between what he saw as the primal force of the linear movement and intricate patterns in Celtic art, the celebratory 'savagery' of Fauvism, and the modernist Bergsonian flux of all subjective experience. In his writing, and in his book *Modern Scottish Painting* (1943), Fergusson came to see this as a 'Scottish modernism', simultaneously national and international, ancient and modern, primitive and philosophically searching.

Fergusson had worked with John Middleton Murry to found the avant-garde periodical *Rhythm* (1911–13), stressing the importance of 'rhythm', as they saw it, in all art. Katherine Mansfield, for example, longed for the same quality in her writing.[9] 'Rhythm' is, of course the title of one of Fergusson's most famous paintings from 1911, and the journal took this image for its cover, too. When he came to illustrate MacDiarmid's long poem *In Memoriam James Joyce*, (written in the later 1930s but not published until 1955) Fergusson revisited this vision of primal Celtic intricacy, and by then MacDiarmid had his own theories about 'the Celtic idea', which he associated with Cencrastus, the 'curly snake', as an emblem of endless movement, mystery and multiplicity. In the 'Author's Note' to *In Memoriam James Joyce*, MacDiarmid acknowledged a special debt to Fergusson 'my friend, that splendid octogenarian and doyen of Scottish painters, who knew James Joyce in Paris'. And if an oriental aspect can be discerned in Fergusson's designs for the book (along with clear echoes of his 'Rhythm' painting), then MacDiarmid would concur, as he later put it in *Lucky Poet*:

> The oriental element in Celticism [...] has been one of the principal considerations in all my work, literary and political, in recent years, [and] is one of the chief themes in the huge unpublished poem with which I have dealt in another chapter, and seems by far the most important of the lines along which the Scottish Movement must develop henceforward.[10]

In Memoriam James Joyce was dedicated to John Tonge and James H. Whyte, both of whom MacDiarmid knew. Whyte ran a bookshop and art gallery in St Andrews from where he founded and edited the periodical *The Modern Scot* from 1930 to 1936. This was Scotland's most influential journal engaged with modernist art, publishing some of the writers of the New Apocalypse, and reflecting on surrealism through the 1930s.[11] MacDiarmid had been struck by what John Tonge had to say about the Celtic in his 1938 book, *The Arts of Scotland*, and he incorporated these insights into his own programme for a 'Celtic' consciousness and what he called the need for an 'East West synthesis'. The following lines are taken from Tonge's book, as cited by MacDiarmid in *Lucky Poet*:

> Scottish art as a whole [...] is much more involved and restless and dynamic than English art, and these characteristics we find in the asymmetrical, intricate, organic Celtic art. This, I think, is what Hugh MacDiarmid has in mind when he speaks of the Scottish genius as 'in general brilliantly improvisatory'[...] It should not be forgotten, too, when the filigree technique of Celtic brooches, or the patterning of

the Crosses, is under consideration, that precisely the same technique characterizes the consummate and intricate atonal art-music of the composers of pibroch, some of the greatest of whose works date from as recently as the seventeenth century.[12]

MacDiarmid had long had a fascination with restless complexity and movement. It is associated with his vision of the curly snake in *To Circumjack Cencrastus* from 1930 ('There is nae movement in the world like yours')[13] and it goes back to before the 1920s, significantly predating his commitment to a 'Celtic idea' or even to Scots and a Scottish identity. In fact the thread can be traced to MacDiarmid's very first book, the collection of short stories with some poems that he wrote while serving with the Royal Army Medical Corps in Salonika in the closing years of the First World War. *Annals of the Five Senses*, by C. M. Grieve, was not published until 1923, but we know that the early stories date from 1917. This puts it at the heart of modernist writing in Britain and I would argue that these 'psychological studies' as Grieve called them are brilliant explorations of what he saw as a 'cerebral sense', in which he explored the inner workings of his protagonists' minds in the full flow of a stream of consciousness that reveals human subjectivity to be what Roland Barthes would later call a 'tissue of quotations' and a 'mosaic' (that is Grieve's word for it) of dislocated sense impressions:

> Night and day, city and country, sunshine and gaslight and electric blaze, myriad-faceted existences and his own extraordinarily vivid pictorial sense of his own cranial geography and anatomical activities were all co-visible to him, I say, and perfectly composed, without any conflict or strain. Nor were any of the elements permanent or passive. All of them lived, and each in perfect freedom, modifying or expanding, easing off or intensifying continually. They moved freely, each in its own particular whim, and they moved also with the unity of one impression.[14]

The effect is entirely 'Bergsonian', and strikingly similar to Virginia Woolf's experimental writing from 1921 in *Monday or Tuesday* – which contained stories from 1917 exactly contemporaneous with the earliest pieces in *Annals of the Five Senses*. Woolf described her method in 'Modern Fiction' from 1925:

> Let us record the atoms as they fall upon the mind in the order in
> which they fall, let us trace the pattern, however disconnected and
> incoherent in appearance, which each sight or incident scores upon
> the consciousness. Let us not take it for granted that life exists more
> fully in what is commonly thought big than in what is commonly
> thought small.[15]

Edwin Muir was quick to make the connection between such visions of
mental flux with modernism and praised *Annals* accordingly in a review for
A. R. Orage's *The New Age*:

> It is not only accomplished in style, but in almost every way original
> and unusual. It gives one an impression of obstinate and self-distilled
> novelty which is rare in present-day literature, and when met, delight-
> ful; that impression which can only be produced by the entry of a new
> personality, a new potentiality, into literature. [...] Mr. Grieve is not
> unlike Mr. Joyce; and I should say that, except Mr. Joyce, nobody at
> present is writing more resourceful English prose.[16]

In the light of this comment one could argue that *Annals of the Five Senses*
is one of the more significantly forgotten examples of modernist writing in
British cultural history. (And why is MacDiarmid so seldom mentioned in
our histories of modernism?)

The point at issue here is that Grieve had made a significant commitment to modernist writing well in advance of his commitment, as Hugh
MacDiarmid, to the Scots language. And although he did not associate
himself with Imagism at all, it has been argued by several critics that the Scots
lyrics by 'Hugh M'Diarmid' from the early 1920s are among the best poems
to meet the Imagist 'rules' that T. E. Hulme, Ezra Pound, Frank Flint, H. D.
and others first defined in their avant garde writings between 1911 and 1917.[17]
(Note, however, that the Scot may still have been familiar with T. E. Hulme's
poetic, for his poems appeared in *The New Age*, a periodical which Grieve
read closely and to which he himself later contributed.) To pursue the *zeitgeist*
I would further argue that one cannot understand MacDiarmid's Scots lyrics
in the context of their times without also referencing the intensity of literary
and graphic Expressionism, especially German Expressionism, or indeed the
savage colour shock of Fauvism in the visual arts. Nor do we need to cite

the best known of the lyrics to make the point. It is very illuminating, for example, to compare the psychological tension, the physical settings and the vivid and violent weather in poems such as 'The Sauchs in the Reuch Heuch Hauch', 'Moonlight Among the Pines', 'Overinzievar', and 'Ex Vermibus', against the highly coloured, stormy and tortured landscapes of, for example, the paintings of Chaim Soutine in works such as *Le gros arbre bleu* (1920–1), and *View of Ceret* (1919–20). Nor do we understand the final meaning of the Scots lyrics unless we recognise that a significant part of their achievement is a version of what the Russian Formalists saw as 'estrangement' at both an aesthetic and a linguistic level. That is to say, they reflect the modernist poet's suspicion of the apparent transparency of language, matched by a desire to foreground his medium, and to resist any too easy assimilation. I think we can be blinded to this because of the apparent familiarity of MacDiarmid's vernacular language, the frequently rural setting of the poems, and the fact that they were recruited, so to speak, to prove theories about a specifically 'Scottish' sensibility. Yet the estrangement of MacDiarmid's Scots, even to native Scots speakers, is a significant and often underestimated aspect of their semantic and aesthetic impact.

Sydney Goodsir Smith's Scots verse has been similarly underestimated, most especially in his masterpiece *Under the Eildon Tree*, which draws on a wildly fluid literary voice, a Poundian palimpsest of different cultural references, and a Bakhtinian boiling pot of languages and registers within language. We completely miss the point of such writing if we can *only* see this as a 'Scottish vernacular' poem sequence, rather than as a deeply unstable, irreverent, intertextual, modernist and even a postmodern reflection on European culture. Written in the late 1940s, in the terrible shadow of a second world war, the elegies of *Under the Eildon Tree* revisit the literary tradition in a quite different spirit to that of T. S. Eliot's measured tones in 'Tradition and the Individual Talent' from 1919:

> The historical sense involves a perception, not only of the pastness of the past, but of its presence; the historical sense compels a man to write not merely with his own generation in his bones, but with a feeling that the whole of literature of Europe from Homer and within it the whole of literature of his own country has a simultaneous existence and composes a simultaneous order. The historical sense, which is the sense of the timeless as well as the temporal and of the timeless and the

> temporal together, is what makes a writer traditional. And it is at the
> same time what makes a writer most acutely conscious of his place in
> time, of his own contemporaneity.[18]

Swinging between chaos, eroticism, laughter, vulgarity, death and despair
Goodsir Smith's poem sequence is an ironic and irreverent response to this
position, simultaneously supportive and mocking, taking the poem far beyond
any question of 'dialect revival' or 'Scottishness'.

Hugh MacDiarmid's espousal of 'antisyzygy' was specifically tied to
Gregory Smith's understanding of Scottishness in character and influence, but
this, too, goes well beyond questions of cultural or national identity, however
important such matters were to MacDiarmid and the modern Scottish
Renaissance agenda. Notwithstanding his notorious use of it as a 'get out of
jail free' card (as in his borrowing from Whitman, 'do I contradict myself,
very well then I contradict myself') MacDiarmid's antisyzygy is well worth
reconsideration in more overtly modernist, or even postmodernist terms.
Indeed, *pace* the poet, it is deeply contradictory to use antisyzygy as a marker
for what is, in effect, an essentialised Scottishness when the condition is, by
his own definition, antipathetic to:

> all fixed opinions – all ideas that are not entertained just provisionally
> and experimentally – every attempt to regard any view as permanent –
> [. . .] every denial of the relativity and transience of all thought [. . .][19]

With this in mind we might see the quarrel between Muir and MacDiarmid
as a contestation between a vision of culture and subjectivity that is mono-
logical (to borrow Bakhtin's term) and homogeneous (to quote Muir's term)[20]
as opposed to one which is dialogical, not to say fundamentally plural and
heterogeneous. Muir and MacDiarmid play this debate out as if it were *only*
relevant to a Scottish context, but we might do better to consider it instead
as another manifestation of modernism's anxieties about subjectivity, and as
early harbingers of the decentred subject and of postmodern criticism's scepticism about *any* kind of stable and singular identity. So I would argue that *A
Drunk Man Looks at the Thistle* is equally searching about the fluid nature of
being and identity, and also equally provisional in its conclusions – despite
the poem's apparently 'nation-building' agenda. (When MacDiarmid refers to

his poem as Scotland's *Waste Land*, therefore, it is more than just a timely name check.)

As early as 1920, Grieve had argued that the protagonists in *Annals of the Five Senses* 'are discernible almost entirely through a "strong solution of books" – and not only of books but of magazines and newspaper articles and even of speeches'.[21] His method in *Annals* was dense with unacknowledged quotations and he revived it as the operating principle behind the later 'epic' and catalogue verses such as *In Memoriam James Joyce*, and *The Kind of Poetry I Want*. Nor is this just a matter of avant-garde literary technique, for, as Roland Barthes was much later to imply in his famous essay 'The Death of the Author', it has implications for subjectivity, too. In the last analysis, therefore (at least according to Barthes), the author is not necessarily distinguishable from his or her text. They *both* might be no more than what the Frenchman described in 1968 as:

> a multidimensional space in which a variety of writings, none of them original, blend and clash. [...] a tissue of quotations drawn from innumerable centres of culture [...] made up of multiple writings, drawn from many cultures and entering into mutual relations of dialogue, parody, contestation.[22]

Might this not describe MacDiarmid's later poetry? It certainly describes *Annals of the Five Senses*. And might this not also be a fruitful key to the fluid subjectivities that are so evident in poems such as *A Drunk Man* and *Under the Eildon Tree*? There is no doubt that Barthes' account of *all* texts applies with special force to specifically modernist texts, not least because many modernist texts more or less made this their *modus operandi*. (And of course postmodern theories of reading and textuality were much influenced by the experience and the aesthetic impact of reading a previous generation of proto-modernist and modernist writers such as Rimbaud, Mallarmé and Joyce.)

In conclusion, the literary texts, under discussion above (and one could add the prose of Grassic Gibbon, Nan Shepherd and Neil Gunn to the mix) find subjectivity to be a much more fluid, elusive and fragmented thing than Edwin Muir wanted to recognise, with his preference for a homogeneous mind and a homogeneous culture.[23] They may draw on and seek native roots, 'Scottish', 'Celtic', 'Pictish' or otherwise. But their underlying position is modernist because they ask significantly 'modernist' questions about the unstable nature of subjectivity. And this applies equally well to antisyzygy, even when it makes essentialist and paradoxical claims to be an exclusively national factor. To most fully engage with the question of modernism and the aesthetic impact of such works in the modern Scottish literary renaissance, we must read these texts beyond questions of linguistic and cultural nationalism, even if such issues were originally part of their own declared programme. This is not to ignore questions of identity, linguistic difference and cultural hegemony, nor to pretend that similar issues have not motivated modernist writing in other cultures. But it does help us to place key works from the Scottish literary renaissance within the wider contexts of modernism that those early manifestos so ardently longed for.

Notes

1   Hugh MacDiarmid, *A Drunk Man Looks at the Thistle, Complete Poems*, ed. by Michael Grieve and W. R. Aitken (London: Martin Brian & O'Keefe, 1978), vol. 1, p. 84.
2   Hugh MacDiarmid, 'Author's Note' in *Lucky Poet* (London: Jonathan Cape, 1972), p. xxiii.
3   Christopher Whyte, *Modern Scottish Poetry* (Edinburgh: Edinburgh University Press, 2004), p. 68. See also Whyte's edition of *Dàin do Eimhir* (Glasgow: Association for Scottish Literary Studies, 2001).
4   Robert Crawford, 'Modernism as Provincialism' in *Devolving English Literature*, (Oxford: Clarendon Press, 1992) pp. 216–70.
5   See Mikhail Bakhtin, 'Discourse in the Novel' in *The Dialogic Imagination*, ed. by Michael Holquist (Austin: University of Texas Press, 1996); and Tony Crowley 'Bakhtin and the History of Language' in *Bakhtin and Cultural Theory*, ed. by Ken Hirschkop and David Shepherd (Manchester: Manchester University Press, 1989).
6   Cairns Craig, *Out of History: Narrative Paradigms in Scottish and English Culture* (Edinburgh: Polygon, 1996), p. 116.
7   'Introduction', *Beyond Scotland. New Contexts for Twentieth-Century Scottish Literature* (Amsterdam-New York: Rodopi, 2004), p. 13.
8   William Johnstone and William McCance are equally notable as Scottish painters with an early and markedly modernist agenda, but it is fitting to talk about Fergusson in particular, for he was among the first to look to modern art in Europe, and his widow Margaret Morris gifted a remarkable collection of his work to Stirling University in 1968. Morris was a dancer who followed Isadora Duncan's method, later going on to found the Margaret Morris movement, the Celtic ballet and the Scottish National Ballet. During their time in London in the first decades of the century the couple formed connections with the London avant-garde in Chelsea, including the Vorticist Wyndham Lewis, the sculptor Jacob Epstein, and Ezra Pound and Katherine Mansfield.
9   She wanted her writing to match Van Gogh's 'Sunflowers', seeking 'a kind of freedom, or rather a shaking free.' *The Collected Letters of Katherine Mansfield* (Oxford: Oxford University Press, 1984–2008), vol. 4, p. 333.

10 Hugh MacDiarmid, *Lucky Poet* (London: Jonathan Cape, 1972), p. 375. He also cited J. H. Whyte on the same point: 'the fact remains that there are stronger affinities between Celtic art and the art of the east than between Celtic art and English.' J. H. Whyte, 'Highlands and Lowlands' [from *Left Review*], quoted in *Lucky Poet*, p. 374. The long poem was *The Kind of Poetry I Want*, another extensive component (along with *In Memoriam...*) in the projected and never to be completed multi-volume epic *Mature Art* (aka *Cornish Heroic Song for Valda Trevlyn*).

11 See especially the chapter 'The Modern Scot' in Tom Normand, *The Modern Scot. Modernism and Nationalism in Scottish Art 1928–1955* (Aldershot: Ashgate, 2000), pp. 37–46.

12 John Tonge, *The Arts of Scotland* (London: K. Paul, Trench, Trubner, 1938), pp. 16–17, cited in *Lucky Poet*, p. 376.

13 *To Circumjack Cencrastus, The Complete Poems of Hugh MacDiarmid*, vol. 1, p. 181.

14 'Cerebral', in Hugh MacDiarmid, *Annals of the Five Senses and Other Stories, Sketches and Plays*, ed. by Roderick Watson and Alan Riach (Manchester: Carcanet, 1999), pp. 6–7.

15 Virginia Woolf, 'Modern Fiction' in Virginia Woolf, *The Common Reader*, (Harmondsworth: Pelican Books, 1938), p. 149. See also Roderick Watson, 'Introduction', in Hugh MacDiarmid, *Annals of the Five Senses* (Carcanet).

16 Edwin Muir, 'Readers and Writers', *The New Age*, 15 November 1923, p. 32.

17 For details and a discussion of the various Imagist agendas, see the anthology *Imagist Poetry*, ed. and introduced by Peter Jones (Harmondsworth: Penguin Classics, 2001).

18 'Tradition and the Individual Talent' in T. S. Eliot, Selected Essays (London: Faber & Faber, 1969), p. 14.

19 Hugh MacDiarmid, 'The Caledonian Antisyzygy and the Gaelic Idea', *Selected Essays of Hugh MacDiarmid*, ed. by Duncan Glen (London: Jonathan Cape, 1969), p. 68. Originally published in *The Modern Scot*, in 1931–2. MacDiarmid's position had by then become doubly contradictory and darkly disturbing because the essay goes on to talk about *Blutsgefühl* and race solidarity.

20 See especially Edwin Muir, *Scott and Scotland*, (1936: Edinburgh: Polygon Books, 1982), pp. 42–6.

21 'In Acknowledgement', *Annals of the Five Senses*, p. 4. 'A strong solution of books' comes from Oliver Wendell Holmes's *Autocrat of the Breakfast Table* in which the intertextual implications are also present when the author observes that 'We get into a way of thinking as if what we call an "intellectual man" was, as a matter of course, made up of nine-tenths, or thereabouts, of book-learning, and one-tenth himself. But even if he is actually so compounded, he need not read much. Society is a strong solution of books. It draws the virtue out of what is best worth reading, as hot water draws the strength of tea-leaves.' In *Lucky Poet* MacDiarmid was to declare his admiration for Holmes's turns of phrase.

22 See the chapter 'The Death of the Author', in Roland Barthes, *Image, Music, Text*, ed. by S. Heath (London: Fontana, 1977).

23 For a further development of this argument see Roderick Watson, 'The Modern Scottish Literary Renaissance' in *The Edinburgh Companion to Twentieth-Century Scottish Literature*, ed. by Ian Brown and Alan Riach (Edinburgh: Edinburgh University Press, 2009), pp. 75–87.

Edwin Muir, Kafka, and German Modernism

RITCHIE ROBERTSON

What was modernism? We all know roughly what we understand by modernism, and most of us would probably agree in dating its advent around 1910: the year in which, according to Virginia Woolf, human character changed.[1] A few more generalisations can be ventured. Modernism extended across the arts, from poetry to furniture design. It was part of an adjustment of Western consciousness to the new conditions of life when most educated people lived in cities, took advantage of new machinery, including increasingly rapid modes of transport, and attended to new media, including mass-circulation newspapers and the early cinema. This adjustment was painful. The art that expressed, enacted and facilitated it, and advertised its own novelty, had therefore to shake readers, viewers and listeners out of their accustomed responses, to assault their feelings, to change their aesthetic categories by requiring them to assimilate ugliness, discord, discontinuity and fragmentation as crucial elements of art. Past art that sought simply to convey beauty now seemed insipid.

Moreover, modernist art expressed a sense of cultural crisis. Humanity's adjustment to the new conditions of urban and mechanised living involved not only pain but also loss. There was widespread nostalgia for imagined pre-industrial communities in which a more vivid and heroic life was possible, 'before' (as Yeats put it, also in 1910) 'the merchant and the clerk / Breathed on the world with timid breath'.[2] The delusive promise to restore such communities would later make many modernists vulnerable to the allure of Fascism. Well before World War One, modernist writing articulated a need for radical transformation of society.[3]

The atomised modern individual, travelling by underground amid anonymous fellow-commuters, not only felt estranged from this imagined communal life, but also from the religious belief which had provided a framework of cosmic meaning in the past. In modernist literature, past belief systems are present only as memories that retain an emotional charge but no longer cohere into a meaningful order. The harsh, ineluctable fact of death – the dissolution of the body, no longer palliated by any hope of transcendence –

challenged art to confront it anew.[4] But the bleakness of external life could in some measure be compensated for by conceiving the internal self as deep, multilayered, unfathomable, with recesses extending to the fascinating mental world of primitive peoples and to the collective unconscious of humanity.[5] Hence D. H. Lawrence told his publisher not to look in his novels for 'the old stable ego of the character' but for 'another ego, according to whose action the individual is unrecognisable'.[6]

All these tendencies, of course, did not appear suddenly in 1910. Now that we can see modernism in historical perspective, we are sharply aware both of its diversity and of its prehistory. The beginnings of modernism keep being backdated – to the Decadence of the 1890s, to French Symbolism, to Baudelaire – and the assertion that some earlier artist is 'modern' or 'anticipates modernism' has long become stale and unconvincing. We must however acknowledge that there is a range of modernist styles, and each of these styles has its own prehistory. Alongside the fragmentation that governs *Ulysses* and *The Waste Land*, and the jagged, quasi-mechanical, anti-humanist presentation of people in Picasso's 'Demoiselles d'Avignon' or Wyndham Lewis's portraits, we have poetry such as that of Edwin Muir or Georg Trakl which is mellifluous, formally rounded and closed, yet cryptic in deploying a network of semi-private imagery and post-humanist in seeming to speak not from the superficial ego but from deeper layers of the self.[7] If in some respects such poetry seems to express a pre-modernist sensibility, owing much to Romanticism, in others it belongs to modernism, not just chronologically but in its enigmatic character, its refusal to be readily decoded or otherwise assimilated.

In encountering modern German literature, Muir absorbed a number of writers whose relation to modernism was similarly complex. Among these is Franz Kafka, whom Edwin and Willa Muir, as translators, and Edwin as critic, introduced to the English-speaking world. Kafka is now central to the modernist canon and indispensable for the artistic apprehension of modernity. His response to modernity comprehends both its existential uncertainty, conveyed through the evocation of a tram journey in 'The Passenger', and the abuse of power in a world where authority can operate without humane restraints: as Alex Danchev has recently pointed out, his images of humanity degraded to an animal level uncannily anticipate the literal treatment of Iraqi prisoners as dogs by American soldiers at Abu Ghraib.[8] Yet even in texts that present appalling images of violence and humiliation, such as 'In the Penal

Colony', Kafka's prose is quiet, lucid, and measured.[9] It reveals his debt to the classic German prose of Goethe, Kleist, and Grillparzer, and to Flaubert whom he admired as a master of economy and understatement. Here we have pre-modernist modes of expression revitalised by a sensibility that was acutely alive to specific features of the modern world. Something analogous, as we shall see, is true of Muir's writing.

A self-taught intellectual, Edwin Muir before and during the First World War worked as a clerk in various firms in Glasgow and its surroundings, and read, especially the works of Nietzsche, in his spare time. His immersion in Nietzsche, along with numerous other writers, helped to stimulate his first book (published under the pseudonym 'Edward Moore'), the iconoclastic aphorisms entitled *We Moderns: Enigmas and Guesses* (1918). Soon after his marriage to Willa Anderson, the couple moved to London. Muir was already a contributor to the magazine *The New Age*. He easily gained access to London literary circles. In 1921, however, the Muirs felt a need for a change from London life, and found that Edwin's income as a reviewer for the *New Age* and the New York *Freeman* would be enough to support them on the Continent. They went first, at the suggestion of their friends Janko Lavrin and Paul Selver, to Prague, where they spent the winter of 1921–22. In March 1922 they moved to Dresden and stayed there for two months before running into an old friend of Willa's, the educational reformer A. S. Neill, who had just started an international school at Hellerau, a garden suburb of Dresden. At Neill's suggestion the Muirs joined him there around the beginning of June 1922, lodging with the housekeeper, Frau Neustätter, an Australian married to a German doctor. Frau Neustätter was the sister of 'Henry Handel Richardson', the Australian novelist, whose husband, J. G. Robertson, was Professor of German at University College London from 1903 to 1933. Kafka's sister Elli Hermann considered sending her son to school at Hellerau, and paid it a visit where, as we can gather from one of Kafka's letters to her, she met Frau Neustätter and a so-called 'Hilfslehrerin' (assistant teacher) who may well have been Willa Muir.[10]

The language of communication in Hellerau was German, and the Muirs spoke it constantly. Learning German was no problem for Willa, who had a first-class honours degree in classics from St Andrews University. Edwin, however, was not only less of a linguist but also much shyer than his wife. In December 1922 he writes: 'I've met a lot of interesting Germans, have made some progress in German, and read a good deal of German poetry. Minnie

[Willa Muir] speaks the language almost like a native.'[11] A year later he writes: 'Minnie speaks German now as if she had been born to it, but I speak it much worse, although I can converse, and understand easily everything that is said.'[12] From Hellerau they paid a couple of weekend visits to Berlin, but did not like the feverish atmosphere and found the architecture 'pretentious' and the cabarets 'brittle, smart and strikingly immoral'.[13] From May till October 1923 they lived in Italy, in what was then the cheap resort of Forte dei Marmi, near Viareggio, and from October 1923 to July 1924 in various parts of Austria.

Muir explored contemporary German literature and wrote about it in a large number of essays and reviews, mostly for the *Freeman*. Very few of these have been reprinted. The important essay 'North and South' was reprinted in Muir's collection *Latitudes* (1924). There remain, however, essays on '*Sehnsucht* in German Poetry', on Hölderlin and Hofmannsthal, on Hoffmann, Schnitzler, Hauptmann, Wedekind and Spengler. All these amount to a critical response to modern German literature that has no counterpart, to my knowledge, in any critic writing in the English language at that period.[14]

Muir's response to German poetic modernism is complicated by the fact that he appreciated German poetry not as a break with the past but as a continuation of Romanticism – which can be justified by the common use of the term, Neoromanticism, applying to modern German poetry of the turn of the century by Stefan George, Hugo von Hofmannsthal, the early Rilke, and others. Muir explained the meaning he attached to Romanticism in a three-part essay, 'The Meaning of Romanticism', published in the *Freeman* in December 1923 and January 1924. He contrasts classical and romantic art as follows:

> Classical art gives us a realization of human weakness in general and the compensations; a realization consoling, for in its largeness of acceptance it purges us of shame. Romantic art operates personally. It evokes in us a sense not so much of the weakness of human nature as of our own; and it does not still our shame, but rather awakens it to a kind of transcendental life.[15]

Muir goes on to characterise the romantic aspiration:

> The romantics were, as we are, in travail; but in their travail they had gigantic visions; and that is the complementary aspect of romanticism.

> It was these visions which as a background gave romantic poetry its unbearable pathos, a pathos not of men living on the earth, but of fallen spirits striving to climb back into a light which had been lost in a universal calamity.[16]

The romantics had to suffer for their visions. After their glimpse of a world transfigured, they could no longer live without regret in the ordinary world, which now seemed intolerably empty and barren. For Muir, the supreme poetic statement of this experience was Wordsworth's 'Immortality Ode'. But he also found a German counterpart in Friedrich Hölderlin. He learnt about Hölderlin during his stay in Germany, where Hölderlin's poetry had recently been virtually rediscovered, thanks to the edition by Norbert von Hellingrath, a young member of the Stefan George circle who was killed in the First World War. Muir writes about him:

> Like Wordsworth, and with some striking differences, like his countryman Nietzsche, Hölderlin was a mystic of the earth, of nature and of man. He was concerned in his last poems with the gods only when they appeared on the earth, in history and behind the forms of nature. He was no longer tortured by the dualism of a heavenly and a human life, expressed so poignantly in his earlier poems; these were resolved for him in the end, he believed, in a form of being in which, while remaining human, he existed in a state of almost divine ecstasy.[17]

Muir found a mystical atmosphere in much more German poetry, especially poems dealing with childhood. Writing in 1923 about the German poetry of childhood, Muir attributes its peculiar poignancy to the exclusion of intellectual reflection: 'It is almost exclusively a thing of pure personal imagination conditioned by subjective feeling.'[18] He regarded German poetry as pre-eminently romantic by virtue of its association of childhood and nature with the apprehension of a transcendent reality momentarily embodied in the earthly world. This explains why his favourite among contemporary German poets was Hugo von Hofmannsthal, in whose early lyrics Muir finds 'a vision of life, fresh, spontaneous; the vision of a boy passing into youth rather than of a youth.'[19] In his essay on Hofmannsthal he gives a 'rough rendering' of what he calls Hofmannsthal's greatest short poem, the 'Ballade des äußeren Lebens':

And children grow up tall with darkling eyes
Which know of nothing, they grow up and die,
And all men go regardless on their way.

And the sweet fruits come out upon the trees,
And fall at night like death-struck birds below,
And lie a little time, and rot away.

And always wind blows, and for ever more
We learn things, and we utter many words,
And smell desire and weariness of flesh.

And roads run through the grass, and different places
Are here and there with torches, trees and pools,
And threatening, and deathly withered up.

For what were these uplifted there? and like
Each other never? and so countless many?
What alternates this laughing, weeping, paling?

What blessing does it bring us, all this play?
Us who are great and yet for ever lonely?
Who, wandering ever, seek not any goal?

What boots it to have seen all these so often?
But yet the man says much who murmurs 'Evening',
A word from which deep meaning and sorrow run
Like heavy honey from the hollow comb.[20]

Though this conveys some of the poignancy of the original, it includes a number of feeble poeticisms ('darkling eyes', 'What boots it'). In places the exigencies of the metre have forced Muir to embellish the plainness of Hofmannsthal's vocabulary, e.g. 'darkling eyes' for 'tiefe Augen'. Hofmannsthal's simple language, suggesting a depth of meaning behind language, is an essential part of his poetic achievement. By contrast, Muir's rendering suggests that even at this time he retained a decidedly pre-modernist sensibility. Margery McCulloch rightly observes that despite his acquaintance with German poetry, 'this theme of longing is itself however mediated through yet another early influence: that of English Romantic and Victorian poetry'.[21]

It may be argued that modernism really enters German literature with Expressionism circa 1912.[22] The landmark event was the publication late in 1911 of Franz Werfel's first volume of ecstatic hymnic poetry, *Der Weltfreund*. This form of literature, with its efforts to construct and explore a post-Christian and post-humanist world, did not appeal to Muir. He wrote to the editor of the *Freeman* in 1923:

> I have in my mind at present an essay on the assault in modern literature on the humanistic tradition: I mean the new savagery, shallow but powerful, in the works of such people as Kipling, Lawrence, O'Neill, the German Expressionists and so forth.[23]

This essay, 'The Assault on Humanism', appeared in the *Freeman* on 27 June 1923. It condemns the writers just named for their inability to see beyond immediate experience, in contrast to the 'emancipation from the particular aspects of experience which is the mood and the condition of great art'.[24] A week later he wrote: 'There is an extreme ingenuity in the plays of Pirandello; an almost abnormal desire to be real, and brutally real, in the dramas of Hasenclever and Kaiser; but they are all somehow outside the humanistic tradition.'[25] The Muirs saw quite a lot of contemporary drama in the theatre. In Vienna they saw Toller's *Hinkemann*, a play about an ex-soldier who has suffered castration and whose wife therefore leaves him for a brutal rival. Muir found it 'sincerely imagined' and 'written with a burning and indefinite purpose', but 'so savage, so hysterical, that it defeats its purpose'.[26] They also attended a midnight performance of a play by Wedekind 'with a whole cartload of perversions'.[27] Muir in his *Autobiography* describes Wedekind as 'a writer admired by German intellectuals for some reason that I have never been able to discover', but in the 1920s he was more sympathetic, praising the presentation of children in Wedekind's early play *Frühlings Erwachen*.[28] At all events, the aggressive versions of German modernism did not appeal to Muir.

Kafka fits neither category. His prose rarely evokes the child's vision of reality (though he does so in the early text 'Kinder auf der Landstraße').[29] His modernism is radical, but deceptively sober and understated. Muir discovered Kafka via his work as a translator. When the Muirs returned to Britain in July 1924, one of Muir's reviewing journals, the *Freeman*, ceased

publication, so their income shrank, leaving them very glad to take up translation as an additional source of revenue. They received unexpectedly a letter
from Ben Huebsch, publisher of the *Freeman*, asking them to translate three
plays by Gerhart Hauptmann as part of an English version of his complete
dramatic works. This commission started them on a long series of translations which continued with Hauptmann's *The Island of the Great Mother* and
continued with Lion Feuchtwanger's historical novel *Jew Süss*. More than
thirty books eventually appeared with 'Translated by Willa and Edwin Muir'
on the title page. Both must have shared the task, for the translations that
each produced single-handed were acknowledged as his or her own. Muir's
only single-handed translation, of Hauptmann's play *Veland*, contains several
dozen serious errors, mostly resulting from carelessness, ignorance of German
idioms, and that familiar problem, reluctance to consult the dictionary. The
translation indicates that Muir had a considerable passive vocabulary, but so
slight a knowledge of grammar that when perplexed by an obscure passage he
could not analyse it and had to resort to guesswork.

Within a few years the Muirs established a reputation as outstanding translators from the German, especially since their translation of Feuchtwanger's
Jud Süß (*Jew Süss*) proved a bestseller. Publishers were prepared to take their
advice on which books to translate, while the Muirs, who thought poorly of
Feuchtwanger and Hauptmann, wanted to translate a work of literary merit
for a change. In 1929 Muir came across an article on Kafka in a German literary
periodical and was so interested that he procured a copy of *Das Schloss* (*The
Castle*). He recorded his first impression of the work in a letter to a friend
who had asked him if he had discovered any interesting new books. After
recounting his discovery of Rilke's *Malte Laurids Brigge*, Muir went on:

> Kafka's book is still more strange in its atmosphere; it is a purely meta-
> physical and mystical dramatic novel; the ordinary moral judgements
> do not come in at all; everything happens on a mysterious spiritual
> plane which was obviously the supreme reality to the author; and yet
> in a curious way everything is given solidly and concretely.[30]

In 1936 Muir wrote to Stephen Spender, 'We are translating Kafka's second
book, *The Trial*, which should appear in Spring. I admire him more and more;
his fascination is simply endless; and a feeling of greatness comes to me in
every sentence.'[31] Later the Muirs got to know Dora Dymant, the companion

of Kafka's last year of life. Following Kafka's death she had become a noted actress and also a Communist. She left Germany for the Soviet Union and arrived in Britain in 1939. According to her daughter, Marianne Steiner (née Lask), Muir used to argue with her about Kafka's religious beliefs, maintaining that Kafka was a deeply religious person, whereas Dora denied that he had any belief in God.[32] (There need be no contradiction between these two statements.) However, leaving aside the perhaps unnecessary and also irresolvable question of Kafka's religious belief, the important point about his novels for Muir was that they treated religious questions in a new way, not as intellectual problems, but from within a religious mentality. As Muir wrote in 1934:

> They do not aim at an intellectual criticism of religious conceptions, in which religion is accepted merely as one among several worlds of discourse but rather take the main categories of religion as self-evident truths, and concern themselves with what, after full acceptance, remains inexplicable or unresolved within religion.[33]

What impact did Kafka have on Muir's own writing, bearing in mind that he discovered Kafka after he had given up writing novels? Muir writes in his *Autobiography*: 'At one stage Kafka's stories continued themselves in our dreams, unfolding into slow serpentine nightmares, immovably reasonable.'[34] This may suggest how one should approach Muir's literary relation to Kafka: not as 'influence', as though the signs of Kafka's presence could be neatly isolated, but as an imaginative penetration and absorption. This is perhaps most obvious in poems with familiar Kafkaesque images such as the castle and the labyrinth. But the poem 'The Original Place', from *Journeys and Places* (1937), will indicate how Muir took from Kafka (no doubt among other stimuli) a clear image and used it as a vehicle for precise thinking in outwardly cryptic poetry. Willa Muir tells us that her husband 'tried to divine and follow up the metaphysics of Kafka's vision of the universe'.[35] To approach Kafka as a thinker, he necessarily paid particular attention to the aphorisms that Kafka wrote in the winter of 1917–18 when the recent diagnosis of tuberculosis compelled a confrontation with the suddenly looming prospect of death. Kafka himself made a selection from these aphorisms which his friend Max Brod published after his death; the Muirs translated them as 'Reflections on Sin, Hope, Suffering and the True Way'. Muir sometimes quotes these aphorisms, as when he mentions an acquaintance who 'gave me more strongly than anyone else I have ever met the feeling that he had come to a place from which there was no turning back, the place which Franz Kafka says must be reached'.[36] There is not room here for an account of the aphorisms; but the crucial point is that although they are enigmatic, and expressed in simple and recurrent images, close study reveals them to have an intellectual consistency and coherence. They are a way of thinking in images. That does not mean, however, that they can be translated without loss into an intellectual system. As Gerhard Neumann has shown with particular authority, their paradoxical structure is an essential part of their meaning.[37] Much of Muir's poetry, especially in the 1930s, is similarly cryptic but is capable of a coherent interpretation.

'The Original Place' was first published in 1934 under the title 'The Stronghold'. It is presented as a dialogue, with different speakers indicated by an alternation between italic and roman type (in Muir's first printed text, though not in his manuscript). Its dialogic structure expresses what Muir, in a letter to Stephen Spender, called 'the modern historical view of the world, in which there is no reality except the development of humanity – humanity being in that case merely an I and not I, a sort of long and interminable monologue of many'.[38] As a dialogue between two unidentified voices, using the pronouns 'we' and 'you' respectively, the poem articulates the limitations of human life as conceived by the 'historical sense'. It shows the development of humanity as a process in which mankind, by cultivating the 'fields' of its 'native land', gradually realises its destiny (creating a 'giant Fate half-grown'), and hopes ultimately to produce a temporal utopia, a kingdom which will be 'stable and beautiful'. The origins of mankind are mysterious: though this is their native land, human beings were first placed here by 'a hand / strange to you', a power which also 'ordained' the freedom said to be theirs also by 'ancient inheritance'. Despite this freedom, they are confined to 'the turning maze of chance' (the labyrinth is one of Muir's favourite images for merely temporal existence) and unable to transcend time ('You could not leave these fields'), though within time they have 'unquestioned rule'. Besides working on the world, they 'weave' their 'tale of Time', i.e. devise artistic and philosophical explanations for their existence, and are almost convinced 'that nothing else can be / but this one tapestry', that there is no reality outside time.

Their hopes that the human 'kingdom' will ultimately become a utopia, however, however, are countered by the poem's final stanza.

But at its centre stands
A stronghold never taken,
Stormed at hourly in vain,
Held by a force unknown
That neither answers nor yields.
There our arms are shaken,
There the hero was slain
That bleeds upon our shields.[39]

The key to these lines is Muir's essay 'The Natural Man and the Political Man', which discusses Hemingway's portrayal of the purely sensual man, 'the natural man, fighting and lusting'. Muir considered such a reductive view of man the inevitable result of the historical sense. The natural man as seen in Hemingway's later work has acquired the political ideals of liberty, fraternity, and equality, but as he apprehends life only as sensation and not as thought or feeling, he cannot attain these ideals. 'The goal of all men has miraculously risen before him; although he has acknowledged nothing but sensation, three ideas have announced themselves to him; but they are in a different world from his world, and can be reached only in a different way from his way.'[40] The natural man therefore tries to attain his ideals by violence, to batter his way into the kingdom of heaven. This is how Muir understands the strangely brutal sentimentality of Hemingway's later novels: 'this sentimentality of violence is implicit in the work of all writers who conceive Utopia as a kingdom to be taken by storm.'[41] The men of 'The Original Place', therefore, are natural men, whose purely secular worldview cannot enable them to realise their ideals and attain the 'stable and beautiful' Utopia they long for. Frustrated, they try incessantly to batter their way into the stronghold which contains the true secret of how human life might be fulfilled. But since these natural men could not understand the secret, the inscrutable occupants of the stronghold do not communicate with them. The poem shows mankind obscurely dissatisfied with their purely secular existence, yet unable to regain contact with transcendent reality.

This analysis does not mean, however, that the poem can simply be decoded. Its interpretation reveals further enigmas to which there can be no answer. Whose was the strange 'hand' that 'set you here'? What is the 'force unknown' that occupies the impregnable yet obsessively fascinating stronghold? Who is the 'hero' whose fall is commemorated on the shields of the persistent besiegers? Once the surface obscurity of the poem has been clarified by interpretation, therefore, the clarity reveals areas of deeper mystery which must be accepted as unfathomable. Moreover, the subtle verse movement expresses and underlines the ebb and flow of emotions. The incantatory tone of the opening stanza gradually arouses the sense of wandering spellbound through a labyrinth. After the emphasis on 'hope and fear', the sudden profusion of unstressed syllables in the last line suggests a moment of apparent freedom which is ended when we find ourselves still in the 'turning maze'; the final emphasis on 'chance' picks up a long-delayed rhyme with 'inheritance' and evokes the desolating experience of arriving in a maze at the same spot you passed half an hour ago. Where we might hope for the stanza to end with some revelation, the stressed final word merely asserts that life appears to be a matter of 'chance', a force both irrational and trivial. The second stanza, by forming a single sentence, enacts the sense of time as a tight sequence of moments whose relentless succession prevents one from apprehending anything outside time. And in the last stanza, the heavy beats of 'Stormed at hourly in vain', where even 'at' gets more stress than such an insignificant word would normally have, mimes the laborious and regular assaults made by the besiegers.

The poem ends without closure, only with a reminder of the human cost of this futile, self-destructive, and interminable siege. A heavy stress falls on 'bleeds', and the vowel assonance links this word to the final 'shields'. 'Bleeds' reminds us of the vulnerable human body, only for this reminder to be withdrawn by the revelation that the bleeding hero is now a heraldic emblem. Not only are the besiegers engaged in a struggle they can never win, but they have elevated their failure, in the image of the fatally wounded and bleeding hero, into a symbol which paradoxically sustains them in their combat. Faint overtones, not only of a pagan warrior, but even of Christ's crucifixion, can be heard.

This insertion of dimly remembered religious symbols into a post-religious text is characteristic of at least one wing of modernism. In Kafka's 'The Judgement', the son condemned to death by his father – a situation which itself reads like a hostile representation of the central Christian narrative – rushes downstairs, passing a maidservant who cries 'Jesus!', and lets himself drop from a bridge, first hanging from the balustrade like Christ hanging from the cross.[42] In Trakl's great poem of the First World War, 'Grodek', the ghostly fallen heroes are implicitly compared to pagan warriors, assembling in a 'grove' ('Hain') and obscurely subservient to an angry God who suggests both Mars and Jehovah.[43] This creative obscurity conveys a sense of inhabiting the ruins of past belief systems that retain an enigmatic power. Its eclectic references to belief systems recall Eliot's *The Waste Land*, where Christianity (for example, in the quotation from Dante and the references to City churches), Sanskrit scriptures, and the mixture of pagan and Christian myths which Eliot found in Jessie Weston's *From Ritual to Romance*, are all pressed into service as ways of giving at least passing significance to what Eliot considers modern desolation. If one wing of modernism, represented by Wyndham Lewis and the Futurists, stridently embraces a secular modernity, another wing probes, reshuffles, and reinterprets the religious imagery inherited from Western civilisation's multiple pasts. It is to this latter branch of modernism that, despite their obvious dissimilarities, Trakl, Kafka and Muir can all be assigned.

Notes

1 Virginia Woolf, 'Character in Fiction' (1924), in *The Essays of Virginia Woolf*, ed. by Andrew McNeillie and Stuart N. Clarke, 5 vols (London: The Hogarth Press, 1986–2009), iii: *1919 to 1924* (1988), pp. 420–38 (p. 421); Margery Palmer McCulloch, *Scottish Modernism and its Contexts 1918–1959: Literature, National Identity and Cultural Exchange* (Edinburgh: Edinburgh University Press, 2009), p. 3.

2 'At Galway Races', in W. B. Yeats, *The Poems*, ed. by Richard J. Finneran (London: Macmillan, 1983), p. 97.

3 See Richard Sheppard, 'The Problematics of European Modernism', in *Theorizing Modernism*, ed. by Steve Giles (London: Routledge, 1993), pp. 1–51.

4 For a telling contrast between realist and modernist representations of dying, see J. P. Stern, 'The Theme of Consciousness: Thomas Mann', in *Modernism, 1890–1930*, ed. by Malcolm Bradbury and James McFarlane (Harmondsworth: Penguin, 1976), pp. 416–29.

5 See (with reference to German modernism) Ritchie Robertson, 'Modernism and the Self, 1890–1924', in *Philosophy and German Literature 1700–1990*, ed. by Nicholas Saul (Cambridge: Cambridge University Press, 2002), pp. 150–96.

6 Letter to Edward Garnett, 5 June 1914, in D. H. Lawrence, *Selected Literary Criticism*, ed. by Anthony Beal (London: Heinemann, 1956), p. 18.

7 Muir refers only briefly to Trakl: see *Selected Letters of Edwin Muir*, ed. by P.H. Butter (London: The Hogarth Press, 1974), pp. 38, 89. But the epochal parallels between their poetic oeuvres deserve exploration. An excellent translation of much of Trakl's work is available as: Georg Trakl, *Poems and Prose*, tr. by Alexander Stillmark (London: Libris, 2001).

8 See 'Like a Dog, or Animal House on the Night Shift: Kafka and Abu Ghraib', in Alex Danchev, *On Art and War and Terror* (Edinburgh: Edinburgh University Press, 2009), pp. 172–96.

9 New translations of 'The Passenger', 'In the Penal Colony', and other short texts can be found in Kafka, *The Metamorphosis and Other Stories*, tr. by Joyce Crick, Oxford World's Classics (Oxford: Oxford University Press, 2009).

10 Letter to Robert Klopstock, Sept. 1922, in Franz Kafka, *Briefe 1902–1924*, ed. by Max Brod (Frankfurt a.M.: Fischer, 1958), p. 418. Willa Muir seems to have been Neill's principal assistant: see her *Belonging: A Memoir* (London: The Hogarth Press, 1968), p. 72.

11 Letter to Mr and Mrs Thorburn, 15 Dec. 1922, *Selected Letters*, p. 26.

12 To the same, 20 Dec. 1923, ibid., p. 30.
13 *Belonging*, p. 77.
14 See Elgin W. Mellown, *Bibliography of the Writings of Edwin Muir*, 2nd edn (n.p.: University of Alabama, 1970).
15 'The Meaning of Romanticism. I', *Freeman*, 26 Dec. 1923, 368–70 (p. 368).
16 Ibid., p. 369.
17 'A Note on Friedrich Hölderlin', *Freeman*, 1 Aug. 1923, 488–90 (p. 490).
18 '*Sehnsucht* in German Poetry', *Freeman*, 31 Oct. 1923, 178–80 (p. 179).
19 'Hugo von Hofmannsthal', *Freeman*, 24 Oct. 1923, 152–54 (p. 152).
20 Ibid., p. 153.
21 McCulloch, Margery [Palmer], *Edwin Muir: Poet, Critic, and Novelist* (Edinburgh: Edinburgh University Press, 1993), p. 4.
22 See Michael Hamburger, '1912', in his *Reason and Energy: Studies in German Literature* (London: Weidenfeld & Nicolson, 1970), pp. 263–90.
23 Letter to Van Wyck Brooks, 18 Apr. 1923, *Selected Letters*, p. 27.
24 'The Assault on Humanism', *Freeman*, 27 June 1923, 369–71 (p. 370).
25 'The Drama of Transition', *Freeman*, 4 July 1923, 403–04 (p. 404).
26 'A German Letter', *Literary Review of the New York Evening Post*, 19 Apr. 1924, 692.
27 *An Autobiography* (London: The Hogarth Press, 1954), p. 221.
28 Ibid.; 'Frank Wedekind', *Freeman*, 10 Oct. 1923, 114–16.
29 Translated as 'Children on the Highway' in *The Metamorphosis and Other Stories*, pp. 3–5.
30 Letter to Sydney Schiff, 8 July 1929, *Selected Letters*, p. 67.
31 Letter to Stephen Spender, 19 Nov. 1936, ibid., p. 93.
32 Letter to George and Marianne Steiner, 12 November 1978. Mrs Steiner was kind enough to send me a copy of this letter with her own comments. On Dora Diamant, later Dora Lask, see Kathi Diamant, *Kafka's Last Love: The Mystery of Dora Diamant* (London: Secker & Warburg, 2003).
33 'Franz Kafka', *Life and Letters*, June 1934, 341–51 (p. 344). On Muir's critical response to Kafka, see Ritchie Robertson, 'Edwin Muir as Critic of Kafka', *Modern Language Review*, 79 (1984), 638–52. For Muir's place in the anglophone reception of Kafka, see Dieter Jakob, *Das Kafka-Bild in England: Eine Studie zur Aufnahme des Werkes in der journalistischen Kritik (1928–1966)* (Oxford and Erlangen: no pub., 1971). Jakob's introduction, 'Das Kafka-Bild in England', was published separately in *Oxford German Studies*, 5 (1970), 90–143.
34 *An Autobiography*, p. 240.
35 *Belonging*, p. 150.
36 *An Autobiography*, pp. 191–92.
37 Gerhard Neumann, 'Umkehrung und Ablenkung. Franz Kafkas "gleitendes Paradox"', *Deutsche Vierteljahresschrift*, 42 (1968), 702–44.
38 Letter, 4 Sept. 1935, *Selected Letters*, p. 85.
39 *The Complete Poems of Edwin Muir*, ed. by Peter Butter (Aberdeen: The Association for Scottish Literary Studies, 1991), pp. 90–1.
40 *Essays on Literature and Society*, enlarged and revised edn (London: The Hogarth Press, 1965), pp. 156–57.
41 Ibid., p. 157.
42 See Ritchie Robertson, 'Kafka as Anti-Christian: "Das Urteil", "Die Verwandlung" and the Aphorisms', in *A Companion to the Works of Franz Kafka*, ed. by James Rolleston (Rochester, NY: Camden House, 2002), pp. 101–22.
43 See Trakl, *Poems and Prose*, pp. 126–27.

Modernity and Nationhood: 'Little Magazines' in Scotland

ALISTAIR McCLEERY

Introductory

On or about December 1910 in Scotland, nothing much changed. Earlier that year the Scottish Education Department had acceded to lobbying from Home Rule groups and instituted the teaching of Scottish history in Scottish schools, a move much deplored by the Socialist Labour Party as a bourgeois distraction from the wider class struggle.[1] The World Missionary Conference held in Edinburgh in June had brought together most of the Protestant churches in a display of unity that illustrated both the continuing centrality of religion in Scottish life and the links it created to the countries of Empire both settled and administered. In August, Lanark racecourse was the venue of the first Scottish international aviation meeting. The event attracted some 200,000 spectators eager to experience the shock of the noisy and new. Henry Newbolt's new serial, 'The Twymans', began appearing in the December edition of *Blackwood's Magazine* that also featured the 'wonderfully virile and vivid' poetry of Alfred Noyes.[2] Perhaps with some casuistry it could be argued that the muted conflict between nation and class or a fascination with flight prefigured predominant themes of the interwar period. However, the *mentalité* of Scotland remained unaffected in 1910, bathed in a cultural contentment that preempted experiment or change.

The key event for the development of a distinctive Scottish 'modernism' was in fact the war of 1914–18. The savage rupture of the First World War offered a challenge to the prior complacency of orthodoxy on two fronts. Firstly, the rejection of the folly and ways of thinking of the older generation gave licence to the cult of the new. Orwell wrote that 'at that time there was, among the young, a curious cult of hatred of "old men". The dominance of "old men" was held to be responsible for every evil known to humanity, and every accepted institution from Scott's novels to the House of Lords was derided because "old men" were in favour of it.'[3] This led to a sudden growth in the number of literary magazines, in the pages of which rebellion could be expressed and promoted. As John Gross wrote: 'The end of the First World War saw a new crop of little magazines, flauntingly experimental and aggressively anti-traditionalist.'[4] This growth was key in establishing new cultural paradigms. As Mark Gaipa also argues in relation to the American literary scene, the essential characteristics of little magazines lend themselves to a transformational role: they play a key part in the nurturing, through editorial mentoring and peer feedback, of new writers; through that nurturing, and through promotion of particular writers and forms of writing, both through publication and through the powerful agency of their review sections, literary magazines can create a critical momentum that may become a literary movement; and finally, literary magazines can take risks and can afford to be experimental in a manner not open to other forms of publication such as book publishing because of the relative cheapness of production.

However, in Scotland, with its heightened sense of the past (a trait shared with Ireland), the small magazines looked backwards as well as forwards because of the battle on the second front of nationhood. The doctrine of self-determination for small countries preached with fervour by Woodrow Wilson, and anticipated by the Easter Rising in Ireland in 1916, provided new impetus and credibility to a Scottish political nationalism hitherto the obsession of romantic Jacobites with a propensity to blight their sons with the names Charles Edward (and sometimes Charles Edward Stewart). 'Scottish modernism' entailed an assertion of nationalism that other forms of modernism rejected: Joyce and Lawrence, for example, had both turned their backs on post-1918 nationalism; the former explicitly and both through wandering cosmopolitan exile.[5]

The Scottish little magazines contained little that was self-consciously experimental in the sense in which that term is conventionally applied to modernism. The modernist *avant-garde* (*avant* and *après* 1914), as both creators and audience, can be defined in terms of minority challenges to majority culture. In the case of Joyce's *Ulysses* and Lawrence's *Lady Chatterley's Lover*, for example, those challenges were both sexual and, in a manner inextricably linked to that, aesthetic. Indeed, the interlocking of the sexually daring and aesthetically adventurous was characteristic of modernism.[6] The conjunction of these two was typical of little magazines such as the *Little Review*. Yet such challenges sat uneasily with a desire to speak to and for the Scottish nation. John Carey rails against just that aspect of modernism: that it deliberately shut out the common reader. 'The principle around which modernist literature and culture fashioned themselves was the exclusion of the masses'. The paradox of *Ulysses,* a novel that has at its centre a 'common' man whose inner life is rendered in as much intimate detail as any Proustian character, lies in its exclusion of a reader like Bloom himself through 'the complexity of the novel, its avant-garde technique, its obscurity [...] More than any other twentieth-century novel, it is for intellectuals only.'[7] This might be contrasted with *Sunset Song* or *Morning Tide*, the latter a Book Society choice. Scottish writers and editors made it new by going back to Dunbar: this implied a rejection of the couthy and sentimental in language and feeling as well as, in regressing beyond 1707, of a unionist perspective in politics; it did not represent a members-only club from which readers (and voters) were excluded.

Making it New

George Blake stressed in 1932 that 'a "consciousness of Scottishness" came to us all after the War'.[8] This was expressed through this desire for change in the overthrow of the previous paradigm. The post-war generation who instituted the movement which became popularly known as the 'Scottish Renaissance' rebelled with vehemence against the writings of their predecessors, the Kailyarders. (And if there is a Freudian note there, it is worth remarking that one of their number, Lewis Spence, had been a sub-editor on the *British Weekly* from 1906 to 1909, under Robertson Nicoll.) The War itself played a part in that reaction: 'every memoir about the time makes clear that the First World War dominated the lives of these who were children then as much as it did the lives of their elders'.[9] In other words, this was not simply a case of writers turning to their own wartime experience and that of others as a source for poetry and prose, but of a catalyst for a profound change in attitudes and perceptions, of rebellion against what had gone before. For the writers of the Renaissance the establishment to be rebelled against was the Kailyard – not just the 'old men', Barrie, Maclaren, Crockett and company, but also the whole industry associated with it, magazines, editors, publishers – the orthodoxy to be rejected was the Kailyard vision of Scotland.[10] The Kailyard was condemned for its failure to depict the diversity of Scottish life and to highlight the national identity in a political manner. According to George Blake, 'the representative writers of the period went on – and on – representing their coevals as either bucolic philosophers or eagle-plumed gallants in the heather'.[11] William Power looked to the readership to take responsibility: 'the real trouble was in the public to whom these writers mainly appealed, the amiable, the respectable, slightly cosy church folk'.[12] C. M. Grieve (Hugh MacDiarmid) characterised Barrie's achievement as 'the triumph of sugar over diabetes'.[13]

The cure to the ills of Scottish culture and civil society entailed establishing a new industry – of magazines, editors, publishers – more in tune with the spirit of the postwar generation. Not that this was, as stressed above, a purely Scottish therapy. However, this growth of nationalist feeling did give the phenomenon in Scotland a unique objective and an additional strength. William Power stated of the establishment of the *Scots Observer* in 1926: 'A central aim for the paper was suggested by the growth of the national movement in Scotland [. . . by] attempts to make a national, spiritual, intellectual and social synthesis of Scotland'.¹⁴ In a small country, the same people met in the political sphere as well as the cultural. They wrote both creatively – poems, novels, plays – and politically – essays, articles, polemics – and the new magazines published both within their covers. A positive vision was offered in the place of the Kailyard: an honest reflection of Scotland as it was and a programme of what it could be if independent.

The Scottish Renaissance cohered at these two levels, the cultural and the political, and often the same individuals were involved in both, stressing again the impetus of nationalism which lay behind the literary achievement. Those figures who participated in the affairs of the National Party of Scotland, to differing degrees of actual commitment as opposed to moral support, were often those, for example, who participated actively in the formation and organisation of the Scottish branch of PEN. The initial stimulus to the formation of the Scottish branch in 1927 came from C. M. Grieve and William Power, then literary editor of the *Glasgow Herald*. A focus for their activities was provided, however, by Helen Cruickshank in her home in Edinburgh. When Grieve came to Edinburgh on PEN business, it was with Helen Cruickshank that he would stay and, when he moved to London in 1928, it was Helen Cruickshank who took over his role as Secretary of PEN. She drew in many Scottish expatriate writers such as the Muirs and it was her home again which acted as their base when they visited Scotland. During 1931 and 1932, James Whyte (also a PEN member) was a frequent visitor to Helen Cruickshank and it was Whyte, as discussed below, who found accommodation for the Muirs in St Andrews. The Muirs became leading figures in Scottish PEN, representing it at conferences abroad. Beyond PEN, the complex web connected these men and women of letters with musicians, artists and many others of various backgrounds. The relationships were interlocking and interacting. So, Marion MacNeill, author of *The Scots Kitchen*, was the sister of Duncan MacNeill, the Inverness solicitor who co-founded the local branch of the National Party of

Scotland (NPS) with Neil Gunn. William McCance, the painter, was a close friend of Francis George Scott, the composer, who, in turn, strongly influenced his ex-pupil, C. M. Grieve. What is clear is that there was in Scotland in this postwar period a vital and creative section of the population dedicated to the reawakening of Scottish national identity.

However, this was as much a party political movement as it was a cultural one. The *Scots Independent* was established in 1926 as the mouthpiece of the NPS. Lewis Spence founded the Scottish National Movement but joined the NPS in 1928. In January 1929, he stood as the new party's candidate in the by-election at North Midlothian and Peebles. Helen Cruickshank was prevented by her occupation as Civil Servant from any such overt party political activity but, after her retiral in 1944, could show open support for the (by then) Scottish National Party (SNP) in the 1945 East Edinburgh by-election. Eric Linklater, despite the seeming later recantation in fictional form in *Magnus Merriman* (1934), stood as a Nationalist candidate in East Fife. Neil Gunn faced Civil Service restrictions but was instrumental in the formation of the SNP by bringing together George Malcolm Thomson (of the Scottish Party and the Porpoise Press) and Sir Andrew MacEwen (of the Liberal Party, and father of David, editor of *Outlook* discussed below) with Gunn himself acting as representative of the NPS. While the very existence of a 'condition of Scotland' was denied by those on the left such as James Barke, it was actively pursued by these nationalist writers (and others) within the pages of the magazines, new and old.

Looking Backwards (and Forwards)

The *Scots Magazine* drew on a putative history dating back to the eighteenth century but was re-founded in 1924 to provide 'a high-class literary periodical devoted entirely to Scotland and things Scottish', to avoid 'the quagmire of partisan politics' and the disfigurements of 'religious dispute' and to serve as 'the organ of the Scottish societies throughout the world'. Any lack of commitment in this prospectus to 'the new' or to political nationalism seems window-dressing in the light of the record, from April 1924 to September 1926, of its first editor, C. S. Black. Black was a committed nationalist, author of *The Case for Scotland* (1930) and *Scottish Nationalism: its inspiration and its aims* (1933), both published by the NPS, as well as various plays, a brief biography of Mary, Queen of Scots, and *The Silver Cross: a saga of Scotland* (1936). In other words, Black combined in his own career as author and editor both the cultural and the political. This was a balance he attempted to maintain within the *Scots Magazine*; this was a balance he had to maintain with some discretion within a publication produced by D. C. Thomson, Dundee, a company noted then for its 'Tartan Toryism'. This balance was reinforced when J. B. Salmond took over the editorship in 1927. He managed the difficult task of maintaining the conventional readership while introducing into the magazine's contents fiction and non-fiction of a more challenging type. For example, he could publish the fiction of Neil Gunn and the nationalist polemics of the latter's pseudonym, Dane McNeil; he could publish Neil Gunn's often bitter early fiction and his anonymous nature notes. Gunn himself recalled later that Salmond 'would print anything of mine and did'.[15]

The cultural and political agenda of the Scottish Renaissance could be forwarded in the *Scots Magazine* with the luxury of a stable circulation and the capitalisation provided by a large company. Yet that was the exception rather than the norm. When William Power set up the *Scots Observer* in 1926, he too looked to the past and deliberately echoed the title of W. E. Henley's famous periodical in order to signal his ambition to attract contributors of high standing. Like the *Scots Magazine,* a patina of tradition could be instantly acquired. However, the magazine was the unofficial organ of the Presbyterian churches in Scotland and the 'amiable, the respectable, slightly cosy church folk' he had seen as responsible for the Kailyard were also its readership. This tension between readership and editor could not be sustained. 'Certain of the Church leaders [...] were most critical both of the intellectual character of the paper and of my "nationalist" tendencies.'[16] He ceased to be Editor in 1929 after only three years.

Creating a new readership for a new set of cultural values was also the problem of C. M. Grieve (Hugh MacDiarmid). His solution was self-publication without the need to depend on a consistent list of subscribers. The first in a series of magazines, for which Grieve himself often provided the contributions under a variety of pseudonyms, was the monthly *Scottish Chapbook*. William Power, then Literary Editor of the *Glasgow Herald,* wrote a leader extolling Grieve's plans for it in May 1922 and the first issue appeared in August. It lasted until the November/December issue of 1923. The *Scottish Nation* appeared from May 1923 until December 1923. The *Northern Review* had the shortest lifespan of all: from May 1924 until September 1924, a total of four issues. The ability to produce these magazines (with the exception of the *Northern Review*) through the printing facilities of the *Montrose Review,* on which he was at the time a reporter, reduced Grieve's dependence on existing publishers from whom he had little support in his role as periodical entrepreneur. For example, he had failed to persuade Blackwoods in 1925/1926 to support a new magazine, *Scots Art*. Perhaps Blackwoods were lacking in sympathy with his aims, as expressed in the *Northern Review*, of furthering 'literary devolution', of rescuing 'Scottish arts and letters from the slough of Kailyardism', of fostering Scottish drama and promoting a nationalist renaissance. (It is worth noting that where Grieve was most successful in these aims was in the pages of the *Scottish Educational Journal*. The *Scottish Educational Journal* was founded in 1918 as the organ of the Educational Institute of Scotland and, although not strictly speaking a 'little magazine', it does represent another contribution to the cultural dynamism of the interwar period.) Grieve could not maintain this spate of publications without a commercial base of willing subscribers, access to greater funding and professional management. Little of sustained or lasting value was derived beyond three factors, important in themselves: an initial platform for young writers; the appearance of a great deal of activity that drew attention to the new movement in Scottish culture; and, thirdly, the first appearance of Grieve's other self, Hugh MacDiarmid.

The Modern Scot

In fact, the most notable of all the little magazines was the *Modern Scot* which overcame the endemic problems of the other periodicals by guaranteeing its sustainability through an independently wealthy editor and owner: James Whyte. It cost two shillings per issue or eight shillings and sixpence for an annual subscription; in return the reader received a very well produced and illustrated journal to rival most mainstream publications. Until the appearance of Tom Normand's excellent book, *The Modern Scot: Modernism and Nationalism in Scottish Art, 1928–1955* in 2000, James Whyte had been relegated to a mere footnote in the lives of Grieve, Neil Gunn, and Edwin Muir.[17] Muir's biographer merely remarks for example: 'James Whyte was editor and financial supporter of the *Modern Scot*, a quarterly issued from St Andrews from spring 1930 until 1936. Both the Muirs contributed to it.'[18] The texts published have overshadowed those agents, apart from the author, involved in their publication. Yet it is important to stress the contribution Whyte made to the furtherance of the aims of the interwar revival movement through his editorship and proprietorship of the *Modern Scot* –

'the best nationalist journal of opinion since the *Scottish Review* [in which] the Scottish literary renaissance was enjoying its last major flourish.'[19] In January 1936, the *Modern Scot* merged with the *Scottish Standard* (itself only in existence since February 1935) to become *Outlook* under the editorship of David MacEwen (a close friend of Neil Gunn) with James Whyte continuing as its literary editor. The *Modern Scot* was printed by James Foreman in Montrose. Foreman had been Grieve's employer at the *Montrose Review* and had also printed the *Scottish Chapbook*. Whyte had integrated himself within the political and cultural web.

However, Whyte had come to St Andrews from Cambridge by accident rather than by design. He had, according to an interview conducted with the late Wilfred Taylor, been involved in some sort of scrape at Cambridge and an allowance from his mother of some £5,000 per annum was conditional upon his staying out of England.[20] This was a fortune at the time. He converted a flat over his Abbey Bookshop in St Andrews in ultra-modern style – Taylor remembered clearly the black bath – before building two houses near the Cathedral. There he offered hospitality to such as Fionn MacColla who recalled him dismissively as 'the wealthy Jewish-American with accidental Scottish connections'.[21] Exhibitions of sculpture and painting were given of the work of such as William McCance who also contributed to the magazine. McCance's 'From Another Window in Thrums' (discussed in detail by Normand) offered an explicit visual rejection of the Kailyard equivalent to MacDiarmid's poem 'Frae Anither Window in Thrums'.[22] While the outstanding feature of the Abbey Bookshop in Wilfred Taylor's memory was its stocking of magazines such as *American Mercury* and the *New Yorker,* for others it was the satirical murals featuring Lauder, Burns and Knox providing a visual representation of the characteristic rejection of that particular past.

A key element of the *Modern Scot*'s success was its longstanding link with Edwin Muir. Edwin Muir had been in touch with James Whyte from 1931, that is, well before the Muirs' arrival in St Andrews. In a long letter in September of that year, he responded to a communication from Whyte with his assessment at that point of the state of Scottish literature – and its publication: 'I did not think there was much immediate hope of an economically self-supporting Scottish literature – and it may be that there isn't ever any ultimate hope of it [. . .] A Scottish writer is in a false position, because Scotland is in a false position.'[23] This analysis would have found favour with, say, Neil Gunn, a consistent proponent of the interdependence of cultural and political autonomy, but Muir's resultant fatalism, his resignation to the elimination of a distinctively Scottish culture, would not. Yet Muir did bring modern Europe to the *Modern Scot*. Muir published an essay on Hermann Broch in the *Modern Scot* in August 1932 that stemmed from 'the deepest experience I have ever had from an imaginative work, since the time, in my 'teens, when I discovered poetry'.[24] The essay was reprinted in the American magazine, *Bookman*, in the same November. The significance of the essay's inspiration for Muir and its wider re-publication support the contention that at this time Edwin Muir considered the *Modern Scot* an extremely important outlet for his writings. Indeed, the following year, 1933, he was attempting to place one of Broch's short stories in the *Modern Scot* and another in Eliot's *Criterion*. Grieve was to write in 1935: 'The cessation of the *Modern Scot* [which did not happen] is going to make it virtually impossible to secure periodical publication of Scots poems of any considerable length; and there is nothing on the horizon to take its place'.[25] The merger of the *Modern Scot* with the *Scottish Standard* into *Outlook* prolonged its life until January 1937.

The coverage of the *Modern Scot* was broad-based. In 1932, Muir had been praising the songs of Francis George Scott to William Johnstone and noted the inclusion of 'one of the best of them' in the forthcoming issue of the *Modern Scot*.[26] However, a monetary motive was also at work in the magazine's ability to attract writers, composers and artists: 'The *Modern Scot* pays, and pays quite well'.[27] His £5000 per annum enabled James Whyte to act as a key patron to the Renaissance through payment of fees to the contributors to the *Modern Scot*. The magazine was also careful not to become sectarian or insular in its politics. Whyte was very clear in his editorials in defining nationalism as inclusive, distinguishing it from European fascism: 'we should like to see Scotland a free country like, say, Norway; and yet should not like to see our fellow countrymen imitating the frantic insularity of the Fascists or the Hitlerists'.[28] This too echoed contemporary nationalists who, with a few exceptions such as Compton Mackenzie and the remaining Jacobites, embraced a nationalism that was also international in its outlook. The second issue of *Outlook* (May, 1936) included the passing of another old song in the form of several tributes to the recently deceased R. B. Cunninghame Graham. The Editorial Commentary (page 7) read: 'Just before our first issue went to press the news came that Mr R. B. Cunninghame Graham had died in South America. Cunninghame Graham was a director of the Scottish Standard Ltd., the publishers of this magazine. He had taken a great interest in the venture, contributing to it financially and giving, what is to an editor more precious, a meed of encouragement and measured praise.' With such supporters as Cunninghame Graham and Muir, as well as the security provided by its editor, the *Modern Scot* provided an informed perspective and a wide cultural exposure that was unrivalled at the time.

However, the strength in editorial commitment in little magazines can also become the weakness of dependence on an individual. The outbreak of another war in 1939 prompted Whyte to leave St Andrews. Wilfred Taylor confirmed a narrow-minded, wartime hostility to Whyte in St Andrews, fuelling and fuelled by the rumour that the gallery at the North Street houses was used for communication, by flashing lights, with German U-boats. After the war, Whyte set up a new bookshop, specialising in foreign literature and art books, in Washington. He kept in constant contact with the survivors of the Renaissance and with the new little magazines that tried after 1945 to recapture the spirit of the earlier period: 'We appreciated seeing the *Saltire Review* which I found intensely interesting. So many of the old contributors to the MS [*Modern Scot*] seem to be still going strong, and there were some fascinating new names as well'.[29] He welcomed visitors such as W. S. Graham to Washington: 'He reminded us both of a younger version of CMG [Grieve] – but minus CM's all-embracing and unpredictable characteristics'.[30] He reminisced with ease about the period of the *Modern Scot* and his involvement in the interacting web of politics and culture: 'Willie Soutar I remember well [...] those Sunday visits when his father would offer us a glass of sherry, making sure that we had peppermint before leaving the house so as not to disgrace the family'.[31] Both Helen Cruickshank and Wilfred Taylor contributed obituaries to the *Scotsman* when James Whyte died in August 1962.[32]

Conclusion and Circle
Of course, that unity of political and cultural purpose was all to end, and it was a war that ended it as it had been a war that had started it. The Renaissance (and the political and intellectual force of nationalism) petered out as a broad movement and the little magazines, with the exception of the, perhaps not really 'little', *Scots Magazine*, died. However, it was of the utmost importance that these magazines had appeared, some to thrive for years, others to expire after much shorter runs. The *Glasgow Training College Magazine* had written in 1923:

> It has ever been the case with young writers that there is no proper outlet for their writings – they have to work away without recognition. The annals of literature are full of proofs that the path to fame in letters is long and hard to traverse, and while this dreary apprenticeship cannot be without its uses, yet it may be carried to excess. It has been carried to excess in Scotland, for Scotland has no literary and publishing centre of its own, and Scottish writers who wish to get into touch with things literary must migrate to London.[33]

The little magazines acted as a seedbed for new writers and as an outlet for material more experienced writers could not place elsewhere. They also provided a social forum where writers could make a contribution to the development of civil society in their day. In particular, they set out the stall of a nationalism that could transform Scotland from a complacent, provincial backwater.

Cultural transformation or adaptation is indeed the key to the survival of Scottish distinctiveness in the political sphere. There is a constant sense of renewal that links events in that political sphere with change in the cultural powered by little magazines. In particular, it would seem marked by a strong awareness of historical precedents. These precedents are signposted by two of the significant little magazines from the next period of renewal from the 1970s: the *(New) Edinburgh Review,* self-consciously looking back to the eighteenth-century Scottish Enlightenment, and *Cencrastus,* similarly referencing the interwar Renaissance. In the period 1979 to 1999, magazines such as *Cencrastus,* the *Edinburgh Review* and *Chapman,* like their interwar predecessors, were pivotal in encouraging a diverse and lively approach to 'the condition of Scotland' and of Scottishness and Britishness. They broadened and deepened the debate about cultural and political identity in Scotland by providing a focus and distribution network for contemporary writing, fiction, poetry and polemic, that defined, reflected, rebutted and amended those identities.[34]

As in the period after 1746, and again after 1918, the period after 1970 is characterised by the disproportionate influence of a relatively small number of writers and intellectuals, with those having access to the means of publication able, as in the 1920s and 1930s, to draw a number of other writers into their orbit and create a critical mass. However, by way of contrast, there was a greater tolerance, perhaps in a post-modernist spirit, of a diversity of manifestations of Scottish identity including those associated with the past and without regard to class or 'high' and 'low' culture. One theme, in particular, differentiates the little magazines of the 1970s onwards from those of the interwar period: the identification of working-class with national identity effacing the class versus nation conflict of earlier. What they hold in common remains the belief that cultural change can effect political change – or at the very least that cultural confidence, in the sense of a flourishing and internationally recognised arts scene and 'positive', inclusive representations of Scottish identity, created political confidence that could then be translated into support for, if not independence, at least devolution. This belief existed in the cultural sphere, among cultural producers, consumers, students, critics and journalists, in other words, among key agents able to influence the wider public sphere through writing and other art forms, through political activities such as rallies, speeches and protests, and, unlike the interwar period, through the mass media of radio and television. A more settled and assertive sense of Scottish cultural distinctiveness after 1999, sustaining Scotland as an entity moving from stateless nation to devolved nation-state (and beyond?), was based on the endeavours of writers and intellectuals in the previous 80 years in defining and developing cultural and political debate through the little magazines. By December 1999 much had changed.

Notes

1 James D Young, *The Rousing of the Scottish Working Class* (London: Croom Helm, 1979), pp. 174–5.

2 *Scotsman*, 8 December, 1910, p. 4.

3 George Orwell, *The Road to Wigan Pier* (London: Gollanz, 1937), pp. 170–1.

4 John Gross, *The Rise and Fall of the Man of Letters* (London: Weidenfeld & Nicolson, 1969), p. 239.

5 Mark Gaipa argues in his essay in this collection that in the USA to be modern also meant to be American.

6 See for example Joyce Piell Wexler, *Who Paid for Modernism? Art, Money and the Fiction of Conrad, Joyce and Lawrence* (Fayetteville: University of Arkansas Press, 1997) and, in its discussion of the homosexual market for *Ulysses*, Edward Bishop, 'The "Garbled History" of the First-edition *Ulysses*', *Joyce Studies Annual* 9 (Summer 1998), 3–36.

7 John Carey, *The Intellectuals and the Masses: Pride and Prejudice among the Literary Intelligentsia, 1880–1939* (London: Faber, 1992), pp. 21, 20.

8 George Blake in *Scotland in Quest of her Youth* ed. David Cleghorn Thomson (Edinburgh: Oliver & Boyd, 1932), p. 158. Thomson was head of the BBC in Scotland at that time.

9 Samuel Hynes, *The Auden Generation* (London: Faber, 1976), p. 17.

10 See Andrew Nash, *Kailyard and Scottish Literature* (Amsterdam: Rodopi, 2007).

11   George Blake, *Annals of Scotland 1895–1955* (London: BBC, 1956), p. 11.
12   William Power, *Literature and Oatmeal* (London: Routledge, 1935), p. 161.
13   C. M. Grieve, *Contemporary Scottish Studies* (1926: Edinburgh: Scottish Educational Journal, 1976), p. 4.
14   Power, p. 214.
15   Alistair McCleery, 'The Early Novels of Neil Gunn', *The Bibliotheck* 10/4 (1981), 129. Gunn had earlier used this pseudonym under two circumstances. Firstly, when he was still a member of the Customs and Excise, he used it to write articles which might be considered too stridently 'political' by his Civil Servant masters. Secondly, he used it when writing pieces, particularly verse, where he was unsure of their literary merits. The choice of pseudonym was not arbitrary. While the key to his identity lay in 'McNeil', 'Dane' emphasised the Scandinavian background of Caithness.
16   Power (1935), p. 161.
17   Tom Normand, *The Modern Scot: Modernism and Nationalism in Scottish Art, 1928–1955* (Aldershot: Ashgate, 2000).
18   *Selected Letters of Edwin Muir* ed. P. H. Butter (London: Hogarth Press, 1974), p. 70n.
19   H. J. Hanham, *Scottish Nationalism* (London: Faber, 1969), p. 158.
20   Alistair McCleery, unpublished interview with Wilfred Taylor, 4 November 1986.
21   Fionn MacColla, 'Mein Bumpf' in *Essays on Fionn MacColla* ed. David Morrison (Thurso: Caithness Books, 1973), p. 24.
22   Normand, pp. 13–17.
23   Edwin Muir to James Whyte, 10 September 1931, *Letters,* p. 81.
24   Edwin Muir to Hermann Broch, 2 June 1932, in *Letters,* p. 76.
25   C. M. Grieve to William Soutar, 13 December 1935, in Hugh MacDiarmid, *Letters* ed. Alan Bold (London: Hamish Hamilton, 1988), p. 176.
26   Edwin Muir to William Johnstone, 19 July 1932, in *Letters,* p. 78.
27   Edwin Muir to Hermann Broch, 20 November 1933, in *Letters,* p. 8
28   *Modern Scot,* 3, 4 (Winter 1933), 284.
29   James Whyte to Helen B. Cruickshank, 24 December 1958, in Helen Cruickshank Papers, MS1: Correspondence, Stirling University Library.
30   Whyte to Cruickshank, 28 January 1952, MS1, SUL.
31   Whyte to Cruickshank, 24 December 1958, MS1, SUL.
32   *Scotsman,* 12 September 1962, and 14 September 1962.
33   The *Glasgow Training College Magazine* January, 1923.
34   See Linda Gunn and Alistair McCleery, 'Wasps in a Jam Jar: Scottish Literary Magazines and Political Culture 1979–1999' in *Further from the Frontiers: Cross-currents in Irish and Scottish Studies,* eds. Aimee McNair and Jacqueline Ryder (Aberdeen: Aberdeen University Centre for Irish and Scottish Studies, 2009), 41–52.

Modernism, Magazines, and the
Creation of an American Literature

MARK GAIPA

What role, if any, did modernism and little magazines play, early in the twentieth century, in helping to fashion America's national literature? If we were to pose this question of Scottish literature, the answer would be pretty clear: through little magazines like *The Scottish Chapbook* and *The Scottish Nation*, Hugh MacDiarmid forged the Scottish Renaissance by aligning Scottish vernacular and literary identity with modernist experimentation.[1] In American cultural history, however, the connection between modernism and the emergence of a national literature is still very much a matter of debate. Therefore, before I bring these two concerns together in this essay, let us consider each separately.

On the one hand, it is commonly agreed that little magazines, in the United States and abroad, were key to promoting modernism – that great outpouring of avant-garde experimentation, from about 1890 to 1940, when all the arts went haywire. Since about mid-century, modernist literature has been regarded as part of mainstream culture; but when these works appeared at the start of the century, they were mostly too revolutionary or shocking to be printed in respectable publications. Rather, much modernist literature first came into print in little magazines – magazines with shoestring budgets, edited often by artists themselves, and directed at small coterie audiences. According to Frederick Hoffman, Charles Allen and Carolyn Ulrich, little magazines were 'willing to lose money, to court ridicule, to ignore public taste' so they could publish whatever they wanted.[2] Hoffmann et al. estimate that six hundred such magazines in English appeared between 1912 and 1945, with most going bankrupt after a few issues. But somehow during these years, modernism not only survived but flourished with their collective support.

On the other hand, even as American modernist authors began publishing in little magazines, both in America and Europe, another cultural phenomenon was taking place in the United States: Americans were finally winning cultural independence from Britain, the country they had wrested their political independence from some hundred years earlier. Calls for Americans to create their own traditions and discover their own literature could be heard throughout American history, but a colonial mentality persisted when it came to art and culture; and American scholars of literature, as well as American writers, typically deferred to the artistic standards established in Britain and Europe. In the nineteenth century, American literature was not an academic discipline studied in American colleges; and even after English departments emerged on American campuses, the literature taught there was overwhelmingly British – with American literature discounted, by academics and the American public alike, as an inferior and still maturing part of British letters. Yet in the first decades of the twentieth century, a new spirit of cultural nationalism took hold of many Americans, and within only a few decades numerous new anthologies of American literature were published, the study of American literature emerged as a discipline, and scholars of American literature even started their own journal by that name.[3]

So my question boils down to this: what does this new cultural nationalism at the turn of the century have do with little magazines and the appearance of modernism in the same period? One of the chief organs for cultural nationalism in the teens was a short-lived little magazine called *The Seven Arts* – but its contributors, like Waldo Frank and Van Wyck Brooks, expressed little interest in contemporary avant-garde literature.[4] In fact, if *The Seven Arts* community regarded modernism as it is often viewed today – as a cosmopolitan movement of expatriates who pursued their individual visions abroad while creating a difficult art beyond the reach of most people – then American cultural nationalists and American modernists in the teens were probably working, and moving, in opposite directions. Certainly America's best-known modernists, T. S. Eliot and Ezra Pound, seem to support this view: both left America to participate in the transnational avant-garde overseas, with Pound eventually becoming a notorious traitor and Eliot a subject of the Queen.

There is good reason to believe, then, that American modernists were indifferent (or even resistant) to the cultural nationalists' goal of promoting a distinctly American literature. The aim of this essay, however, is to offer a reason to think otherwise. In what follows, I will show how at least one elite, arty, little magazine in America was essential for promoting a distinctively American literature and for laying the institutional foundation for the study of American literature in the US. As we are in the habit of saying at the Modernist Journals Project (MJP), modernism began in the little magazines – and, I would suggest, American literature began there as well.

American Poetry in Two American Magazines

The primary materials I will use to illustrate this claim come from the archive of journals at the MJP, where I work as project manager. The MJP's mission is to produce digital editions of magazines from the early twentieth century which we make freely available to the public on our website; since the MJP began fifteen years ago, we have produced complete or substantial runs of more than a dozen journals, as well as sample issues of twenty-four other journals from around 1910.[5] Most of these journals are British publications, but recently we have completed editions of two significant American journals: *Poetry: A Magazine of Verse* and *Scribner's Magazine*. *Poetry* is a little magazine, first published in October 1912, in Chicago, and edited by Harriet Monroe; it is arguably the first important little literary magazine to appear in twentieth-century America. By contrast, *Scribner's,* which began in 1887 and was published on Fifth Avenue in New York, is a much bigger quality magazine with a national circulation. Where *Poetry* is avant-garde in disposition, *Scribner's* is conservative and commercial – and chock full of wonderful illustrations and colour advertising.

To prepare for this essay, I decided to see what picture of American literature appears in the pages of these two American magazines during the two-year period of 1915 and 1916 – about the time of *The Seven Arts* and just before the US entered the war. Because *Poetry* is devoted to poetry, I focused on the poems in both magazines.

So what impression did I get? The first thing I noticed was that *Scribner's* was no slouch when it comes to poetry. Though *Scribner's* published many different kinds of writing and literature, from 1915 to 1916 it also printed 104 poems by 79 poets, which amounts to an average of four to five poems per issue, with each issue including at least one poem and as many as seven. That makes more poems than appear in each issue of *The New Yorker* today.

The second thing I noticed is that virtually none of the poets that *Scribner's* published during these two years is known today, whereas at least a dozen of the poets who published in *Poetry* during the same two-year period have made it into the American canon. A list of poets whose work appeared in *Poetry* from 1915 and 1916 includes T. S. Eliot, Robert Frost, H. D., Amy Lowell, Vachel Lindsay, Edgar Lee Masters, Marianne Moore, Ezra Pound, Carl Sandburg, Wallace Stevens, and William Carlos Williams – and these are just the most outstanding American names. A talent roster from the same years of *Scribner's* includes such luminaries as Livingston Ludlow Biddle,

Florence Earle Coates, Abbie Carter Goodloe, William H. Hayne, and Sarah Cleghorn: not exactly household names today. Of course I am being selective here, and a closer look at the contributors to both magazines reveals that seventeen of the poets in *Scribner's* during these two years also had poems published in *Poetry* during the ten years of the magazine that the MJP has digitised. But aside from Amy Lowell and maybe Edwin Arlington Robinson and Sara Teasdale, who appeared in both magazines during these two years, one has to look long and hard in anthologies of American literature today to find any of the *Scribner's* poets.

In a moment I will look at some sample poems from the two magazines with the hope of understanding what happened here. But first we ought to marvel at this situation, since it goes to the heart of my essay: how could a little magazine like *Poetry* have made such an oversized impact on the American canon, while a powerhouse in its day like *Scribner's* has left so little impression upon American poetry? By the start of the twentieth century, widely circulating magazines like *Scribner's* had finally reached a national audience in the US and were flush with money from advertising revenue paid by national brands; one would think that they were well-positioned to cultivate a national literature for their readers. Yet it was left to a little magazine like *Poetry* to do that – a magazine that had only 1/100th of *Scribner's* circulation and a tiny fraction of its financial clout.[6] One might conclude that *Scribner's,* unlike *Poetry,* simply was not concerned with publishing quality poetry – but that was hardly the case, since it believed itself to be doing just that. In 1912, *Scribner's* was described as 'representing the best standards' of the day and 'must be counted not only among the publications which belong to periodical literature, but also as an important contribution to permanent literature.'[7] When it comes to poetry, though, it did not turn out that way.

So I would like to begin by comparing two short poems, both by women, one from either magazine: 'The Old Technique' by Margaret Sherwood, which appeared in the March 1915 issue of *Scribner's,* and 'The Wind Sleepers' by H. D. (Hilda Doolittle), which was published, also in March 1915, in the pages of *Poetry.*[8] Unfortunately, this little experiment is complicated by copyright law in the United Kingdom, which makes it prohibitive to reproduce more than a small fragment of either poem in this book. But since the poems are out of copyright protection in the United States, readers may now want to visit the MJP's website (at **www.modjourn.org**) to see what they look like. In fact, thanks to Google Books and other websites, a simple search for the author and title of each poem on the internet will instantly deliver to readers what we cannot display here.

Readers who succeed in tracking down Sherwood's 'The Old Technique' in issue 57.3 of *Scribner's* will encounter a squat poem of just two quatrains that has been tucked into the cozy space at the bottom of page 317, which is otherwise dominated by two columns of prose that mark the conclusion of the preceding item in the magazine. If readers then zoom in on the poem, they will discover that each of its stanzas adheres to an ABAB rhyme scheme and that each of its eight lines resolves into five iambs. This formal reliability is typical of the mostly conservative poetry that *Scribner's* published; but Sherwood's 'Old Technique' does not merely adopt poetic conventions from the past – it also celebrates them, by tracing its own verse technique and poetic order generally to the unchanging motions of the natural world. Listen to this poem, Sherwood seems to say, and you can escape the 'wild piping' of the chaotic modern world by hearing the comforting ancient rhythms of the sun, stars, and waves embodied in the structured verse.

Readers who manage to track down H. D.'s 'The Wind Sleepers' will find something else entirely. Though a short poem of only 97 words (just 38 more than Sherwood's), it occupies an entire page (and a bit of the next) in issue 5.6 of *Poetry*, where it cascades irregularly through space, a few jagged words at a time. Perhaps an instance of that 'wild piping' Sherwood finds so threatening, this poem is composed in free verse – its lines are ordered neither by regular metre nor by rhyme, while a few lines devolve into a single word. Significantly, the poem uses the same imagery of the sea shore that Sherwood employs, but to different effect; where 'The Old Technique' presents itself as a dreamy natural refuge from the world of today, 'The Wind Sleepers' awakens into a world of natural violence – full of stinging, tearing, breaking – which the poet nonetheless seems intent on embracing as the very stuff of poetry: 'chant in a wail', 'pour meted words / of sea-hawks [...] that cry / discords'. It is as though H. D.'s wind sleepers have awakened from the otherworld of Sherwood's poem but have continued their wild piping in concert with the fallen world about them.

Readers are probably familiar already with the kind of comparison I am drawing here. When we move from the *Scribner's* poem to the *Poetry* poem, we are rehearsing the story of how modern poetry arose, catalysed by imagists like H. D. who battled genteel poetry and the way it stood at a hazy distance from the contemporary world. In its first years, *Poetry* magazine was very much identified with both imagism and free verse, publishing this kind of poetry before any other journal did;[9] in March 1913, it also provided the first explication of imagism – F. S. Flint's short essay 'Imagisme', coupled with Pound's 'A Few Don'ts by an Imagiste' – which ever since have famously directed poets to pursue, contrary to Sherwood's example, 'direct treatment of the "thing"', to use only those words that 'contribute to the presentation', and to 'compose in sequence of the musical phrase, not in sequence of a metronome'.[10] These new poetic values were also practised throughout Harriet Monroe's magazine. In an August 1916 review of imagist and Georgian poetry, Monroe, who names H. D. the 'perfect imagist', describes imagist poets generally as having 'stript off many old impedimenta. They are [. . .] more simple and direct in presentation than the Georgians, and their cadenced rhythms are less bound by metrical rules'.[11] But that new simplicity and directness appear in most of the poems in *Poetry*, not just those by imagists and *vers libri*sts.

Americans in 1915 had reason to distrust imagism – especially when it was spelled with an 'e' at the end: *Imagisme* – since it looked like a foreign import,[12] another radical movement, like Futurism or Vorticism, that was deforming art and literature in the early teens. Certainly the editors of *Scribner's* were suspicious – only five of the 104 poems it published in 1915 and 1916 may be counted as free verse, let alone as imagism. Yet far from being a foreign presence in American letters, imagism and free verse – I would claim – opened the door, in the pages of *Poetry* and elsewhere, to America's own literature, while the high-minded genteel poetry from the late nineteenth century had to be sidelined before that could happen – not because it directly imitated British poetry, but because it vaguely oriented itself toward the past, distanced American poetry from actual American experiences and voices, saddled itself with religious duties, and conceived of British literature as the ultimate source of its traditions and values.

The obstacle that genteel poetry posed to a vital American literature can be sensed in the archaic, Biblical language that Edith Thomas uses in her poem 'The Ground-Swell', published in the November 1915 issue of *Scribner's*:

> Child! Heed thou not at all!
>   Thine is yon dimpling sea; [. . .]
> That tempest smites a land
>   Where thou wast never cast.[13]

Thomas apparently came from Ohio, but aside from a handful of Mennonites in the mid-west, few Americans at the turn of the century spoke that way. Of course, such exalted language offered readers yet another vehicle of escape, distancing them, like the child in Thomas's poem, from the pain of the European conflict overseas. But because so much of the real world has been censored in this poem, it is hard to appreciate that – or know what exactly 'The Ground-Swell' is about.

By contrast, we have no trouble deciphering what is going on in Amy Lowell's free-verse poem 'Venus Transiens', which appeared in the April 1915 issue of *Poetry*, since it mostly draws upon a simpler language that could have been spoken by actual Americans of the day:

> Tell me,
> Was Venus more beautiful
> Than you are,
> When she topped
> The crinkled waves,
> Drifting shoreward
> On her plaited shell?
> Was Botticelli's vision
> Fairer than mine;
> And were the painted rosebuds
> He tossed his lady
> Of better worth
> Than the words I blow about you
> To cover your too great loveliness
> As with a gauze
> Of misted silver?
> For me,
> You stand poised
> In the blue and buoyant air,
> Cinctured by bright winds,
> Treading the sunlight.
> And the waves which precede you
> Ripple and stir
> The sands at my feet.[14]

The words 'topped' and 'crinkled' seem too casual or insufficiently literary to be included in a genteel poem; yet there they are in Lowell's poem, alongside the more elevated 'plaited', 'cinctured', and the Latin 'transiens' in the title. In the March 1916 issue of *Poetry*, Alice Corbin Henderson, associate editor of the magazine, would praise such straightforward language as key to modern poetry: 'In its new simplicity of diction, its use of the speech of today, and in its direct approach to life, poetry is once more addressed to a living audience'.[15] And the comparison in Lowell's poem, like its language, points us toward the living present, too: when measured against the classical goddess, Lowell's beloved comes out on top.

The contrast between poems in *Scribner's* and *Poetry* extends as well to how they were printed within the two magazines. While poetry in *Scribner's* occasionally received full-page treatment or even led off an issue, many of the poems the magazine published are short lyrics – like Sherwood's 'The Old Technique' – that appear in the space left over, at the bottom of the page, after an article or story. Monroe complained about this kind of economising of space, noting how 'the older magazines were still using verse as an end-of-the-page decoration' (May 1916). Believing that poetry should stand on its own, she made sure that the poems in her magazine dominated the pages they are printed on, playing second fiddle to no other genre and almost vulnerably exposed, with vast swathes of virgin space all around. Reflecting these same priorities, the first half of *Poetry* always consists entirely of poems, while all other matters composed in prose – like editorials and reviews – are made to wait until the back pages.

Monroe was wrong to conclude, however, that the marginal positioning of poems in *Scribner's* signalled their marginal value as decoration or afterthought; indeed, *Scribner's* thought so highly of its poems that, twice a year, it created one volume index for poetry and another for all the other texts it published. But that segregation of poetry from the rest of the magazine's contents reveals the ideological function the magazine assigned to its poems: as an ideal otherworld suffused with spirituality, poetry offered an uplifting complement to our mundane material lives. On the page, it gave readers a moment of relief – in the form of refined cultural reflection – in the wake of articles that squarely engaged the more immediate demands of the world. It is against this supplemental view of poetry that Monroe's layout of her magazine acquires its true significance. Centered on the page and complementing no other discourse, each poem is freed from serving as spiritual compensation.

It should not be surprising, then, that so much poetry in the non-sectarian *Scribner's* is essentially religious, while so little in *Poetry* is. When a poem escapes marginal placement in *Scribner's* – like Phoebe Hunter Gilkyson's 'The Mother', which provides the basis for the frontispiece illustration in the December 1915 issue, or Marjorie Pickthall's 'Mary Shepherdess', which is the lead item in the same issue – it is often because the poem's religious authority has been foregrounded as well. By contrast, many poems in *Poetry* seem to be self-consciously flouting this expected coupling with the Christian faith – like Edgar Lee Masters' 'Silence' (February 1915), which looks to the stars but finds only silence there, or Alfred Kreymborg's 'Old Manuscript' a year later, which invokes metaphysical realities outside a Christian framework. By freeing aesthetics from religious oversight, these poems seem to be creating a new space in American society in which a poetic culture can stand on its own two feet.

With these few examples, I want to suggest that the poetry that appeared in *Poetry* magazine was more disposed to the project of cultural nationalism than the poetry in *Scribner's*. By breaking with genteel poetry, these poets pursued not only a more robust art but also a more specifically American art: a poetic fog yields to a sharp image, and the indefinite past to the living here-and-now. The simpler language of such poetry brings it closer to the language of the American people; and where the poems in *Scribner's* are typically hemmed in, the new open spaces on the pages of *Poetry* magazine seem ready to chart the open spaces of the American landscape – something that actually occurs in *Poetry* with Carl Sandburg's famous 'Chicago Poems', published in 1914, but also in Howard Mumford Jones' 'November in the Lake Michigan Dunes' (*Poetry* Dec. 1916), Daphne Kieffer Thompson's 'Indiana' (May 1916), and John Gould Fletcher's 'Arizona Poems' (March 1916). By escaping the impoverished space carved out for American poetry by religious discourse, *Poetry* also opened poetry to non-Christian Americans, like Maxwell Bodenheim and Louis Untermeyer. And the open verses in Monroe's magazine seem open as well to the diversity of the American people, as Vachel Lindsay may have illustrated with his 'Booker Washington Trilogy' (June 1916) and Constance Lindsay Skinner with her 'Songs of the Coast Dwellers' (October 1914), spoken in the voice of American Indians. Not content, however, merely to represent such voices, *Poetry* went a step further and published translations of actual Chippewa chants and other aboriginal poetry.

The closed forms and poetic language of *Scribner's* poems also seem to handicap it from addressing seriously the modern reality of war. The title of Olive Tilford Dargan's 'This War' (January 1915) points us directly at the fighting in Europe, but that gesture strikes us as ironic since everything else in the poem is designed to distance us from that unfolding event:

> That Hate shall end what Love began,
> And strip from Life her human boast, –
> The Maker's whitest dream be lost,
> The dream he trusted to the Man,
> The Man who upright rose and stared
> Farther than eagle dared [. . .][16]

A much more successful poem about the war, appearing in *Poetry* (November 1915), is written by Catherine Wells – who happens to be British, the wife of H. G. Wells:

> There was a time
> When there was no war.
> Deep I look into that pool of memory
> And see the things I thought of then, the dreams I dreamed,
> Like strange corals at the bottom of the sea—
> Each, for being so far, so lost,
> Shining with a beauty past its own.
> They lie like jewels that have slipped into the ocean,
> Unattainable and gone;
> A moment of great sweetness, a day of great beauty, a dream,
> a longing, a happy chance.
>
> Never shall I touch them again;
> Never, I believe, shall I see their like again
> In the dark horror of these days.[17]

Lacking the high-mindedness of Dargan's poem, Wells's 'War' strikes me as being more powerful, precisely because it is more direct and personal.
Another poem from *Scribner's* – Clinton Scollard's 'The Ride of Tench Tilghman' (December 1915), a ballad about the American revolutionary war – does a better job than Dargan's of addressing the topic of war, but that is probably because it is safely removed in the past. Recalling Paul Revere's

famous ride, Tench Tilghman – an actual figure plucked from history – rides his horse from city to city, spreading the news about Cornwallis's defeat and the end of British rule in America, all the while chanting the refrain 'The World Turned Upside Down':

> In dreams, Tench Tilghman, still you ride,
>> As in the days of old,
> And with your horse's swinging stride
>> Your patriot tale is told;
> It rings by river, hill, and plain,
>> Your memory to crown; —
> 'Cornwallis' ta'en! Cornwallis' ta'en!
>> *The World Turned Upside Down!*'[18]

Perhaps the American readers of *Scribner's* felt a surge a patriotic pride upon reading this poem, but one has to wonder what the editors were thinking in publishing the ballad, which promotes American identity at the expense of the British, when Britain was currently engulfed in a devastating war across the sea. Perhaps the timelessness of genteel poetry momentarily rendered the editors tone-deaf. But there is more irony for us to appreciate here: for there is nothing revolutionary about Scollard's poem, as it clings to the closed poetic forms that, at this very time, were being identified by other poets with America's British heritage. Indeed, in 1915, Bodenheim's 'The Steam-shovel', a poem about a very unpoetic device for turning up soil, is a far better expression, than Scollard's, of how, in the realm of poetry, the world has been turned upside down.

The Cultural Legacy of the Little Magazine

I have tried so far to show how *Poetry* magazine, with its quest to promote poetry as a major art, helped advance the project of cultural nationalism by publishing a more vital, more diverse, and freer poetry. In particular, once it was divested of religious authority, modern American poetry could help build up the separate institution of literature – which coincided with the effort to build a national literature. But a closer look at the editorial content of *Poetry* reveals that this was no coincidence: the idea of creating an American literature had all along been part of what the magazine wanted to do in giving poetry new life in America. No better (and more surprising!) example of this can be found than in Ezra Pound himself. Though Pound at this time lived

in England, he acted as foreign correspondent for the magazine, directing
talent to it and also publishing poetry and prose in its pages. In the twenty-
four issues of *Poetry* that appeared in 1915 and 1916, Pound had material in
ten of them, while his writing was discussed or advertised in most of the
rest. Of these contributions, one essay in particular stands out, a piece called
'The Renaissance' that was serialised in three issues in 1915. Here, Pound
outlined his plans for orchestrating a poetic reawakening in America; his big
idea is that individual Americans of means – the country's Rockefellers and
Carnegies – should become patrons of the arts, providing life-long endowments to established American artists and short-term endowments to the
country's promising youth, so they may 'follow their highest ambitions
without needing to conciliate the ignorant *en route*'.[19] Such a scheme was as
unlikely as it was elitist, yet it illustrates Pound's interest in bringing about a
new American literature. The following year, he observed in *Poetry* how the
American poetic renaissance had already begun: 'As for the younger generation, in 1912 America had very little wherewith to challenge comparison with
England or France. At the present writing one can select an all-America team
of *les jeunes* to compete with *les jeunes* of either France or England or any
other nation'.[20]

Harriet Monroe would never endorse Pound's top-down vision of culture,
but she also saw *Poetry* as a vehicle to promote a poetic Renaissance in
America. Monroe's editorials championed the great awakening of interest
in poetry (June 1916), while advertisements for *Poetry*, published on its back
pages, quoted reviews from other papers that identified it as 'the magazine
that rightfully stands at the head of the new movement' (*The New York Sun*)
and claimed that *Poetry* 'has been responsible for the Renaissance in that art'
(*The St. Louis Mirror*).[21] Oftentimes it is hard to distinguish Monroe's promotion of modern poetry from her promotion of American poetry, so talk about
a poetic renaissance in *Poetry* magazine bleeds into the cultural nationalists'
rhetoric about a general American Renaissance in the arts – rhetoric which
could be heard, at about this time, in Van Wyck Brooks' 1915 book *America's
Coming-of-Age* and later in Waldo Frank's *Our America* (1919).

But Monroe's efforts on behalf of this awakening went beyond editorial-
ising: she saw, as did Pound, the need to change the material conditions in
America that had stifled poetry. Thus she proceeded, on a number of different
fronts, to construct, with her magazine, an institutional framework for poetry
that had been missing in America. Monroe sought to build up poets, first by

paying her contributors – in defiance of the popular idea that poets do their best work when starving – but also by sponsoring prizes to the best writers, with many of the prizes reserved for poets who were American citizens and for writing that was 'American in subject matter'.[22] Monroe also took pains to build up an American audience and community for poetry; to finance the magazine, she secured 100 guarantors from the Chicago community who volunteered $50 a year for five years, and she also asked subscribers to the magazine to regard themselves as patrons of poetry – playing on their sense of civic duty by suggesting that their subscription would 'encourage [poetry's] creation and publication in the United States' and thus help make poetry an 'art of as much national concern as the arts of painting, sculpture, music and the drama'.[23]

One further battle that Monroe fought was to get poetry recognised as a vibrant discipline, but here she faced a formidable adversary: the 'colonial' mindset of Anglophilic professors of literature, who would ignore and deprecate American literature in their classes and invite British rather than American poets to speak on campus.

> Almost every season [...] there are poets, straight from England, reading or lecturing in these parts. This is as it should be, of course; we can not get too well acquainted. But why a certain added deference toward the Englishmen, as compared with Americans of equal or superior quality? – a deference shown not only by complimentary amenities of one kind or another, but by the greater number of engagements at higher prices than are offered to the native bards.[24]

Monroe was especially indignant when she learned that Yale University had awarded its 'Henry Howland memorial prize of fifteen hundred dollars, for distinguished achievement in literature', to the heirs of the recently deceased Rupert Brooke. It would seem that, for American academics, a dead British poet is preferable to any living American one.

Nonetheless, through Poetry Clubs and Societies, often attended by students but not their professors, Monroe sought, from outside the academy, to extend the influence of *Poetry* magazine over the emerging discipline of American poetry. The fact that American literature was only beginning to be taught in American universities during the first two decades of the century[25] actually proved be an opportunity for both the modernists and cultural nationalists, as they could exercise disproportionate influence upon how the canon turned out. In 1918, Van Wyck Brooks famously argued that if Americans were to free themselves from the deadening influence of their cultural inheritance, they needed to construct for themselves a 'usable past' – to rewrite literary history and install literary figures who have 'desired the things we desire and have encountered the same obstacles' so as to 'make the way straight for us'.[26]

For the modern poets who contributed to *Poetry* magazine, the most notable American poets from the past that they could identify with, and then use to advance their own work, were Walt Whitman and Emily Dickinson. Whitman was widely recognised as an eccentric through the nineteenth century, and Dickinson was mostly overlooked. Yet within a few decades of the twentieth century, both had been installed as central figures in American literature. They first appeared in new anthologies, like Louis Untermeyer's *Modern American Poetry* in 1919, which proclaimed that '"America's poetic renaissance" is no longer a phrase; it is a fact' and led off with poems by Dickinson.[27] But these two figures also appeared, eventually, in the classroom, where the new anthologies and literary histories, composed by cultural nationalists like Untermeyer, were increasingly used to teach American literature to American students. On the back cover of every issue of *Poetry* magazine appears the same quotation by Whitman: 'To have great poets there must be great audiences too'. But it was in Whitman's breaking the poetic line that he made the way straight for so many of the *vers librists* whose work appeared within each issue. And it was with her spare small poems that Dickinson pointed the way forward for so many imagists, whose work uncannily resembles hers. Indeed, according to Monroe, Dickinson was an imagist *avant la lettre*.[28]

When students today open the first volume of the *The Norton Anthology of Modern and Contemporary Poetry* and discover that modern poetry begins with Whitman (1819–1892) and Dickinson (1830–1886), they are thus experiencing, unbeknownst to them, a sort of legacy afforded them by Harriet Monroe and the other modernists who contributed to her little magazine. And when those students then go on to discover, in that anthology, that the next five modern poets are all British – Hardy, Hopkins, Houseman, Yeats, and Kipling – they may also conclude, not without some justification, that modern poetry begins in America. That is another legacy of *Poetry* magazine: to make 'modern' and 'American' more or less synonymous, so American poets may now appear not only on the same footing as the British, but also a bit out in front. Such a thing was unthinkable in the nineteenth century – as well as in the pages of *Scribner's* early in the twentieth century. If we take for granted today the importance of Whitman and Dickinson for American literature, it is because *we* have forgotten that before they could appear at the head of the line, the world of poetry in America first had to be 'turned upside down'.

Notes

1   See Margery Palmer McCulloch, *Scottish Modernism and its Contexts 1918–1959* (Edinburgh: Edinburgh University Press, 2009), pp. 15–21.

2   Frederick J. Hoffman, Charles Allen, and Carolyn F. Ulrich, *The Little Magazine: A History and a Bibliography* (Princeton University Press, 1946), p. 2.

3   See, for instance, Charles C. Alexander, *Here the Country Lies: Nationalism and the Arts in Twentieth-Century America* (Bloomington: Indiana University Press, 1980) and Joseph Csicsila, *Canons by Consensus* (Tuscaloosa: University of Alabama Press, 2004). Alexander notes that *American Literature*, the first journal devoted to American literary scholarship, was created in 1929 (p. 149).

4   According to Alexander, 'Paul Rosenfield [...] was the only one of the *Seven Arts* group who really came to terms with European and American avant-gardism' (p. 76).

5   All of the MJP's editions end before 1923 since publications from that year forward in the US are still protected by copyright.

6   Like other little magazines, *Poetry*'s finances were often precarious, and bankruptcy was never far away. Early on, it had a budget of about $10,000 per year, whereas the start-up cost for *Scribner's*, in 1887 when it first appeared, was a half million dollars (Hoffman et al., p.43; Frank Luther Mott, *A History of American Magazines*, volume 4: 1885–1905 (Cambridge: Harvard University Press, 1957), p. 718). In terms of what the two magazines could pay contributors, *Scribner's* also had quite the advantage, as it paid handsomely and attracted the best talent of the day, like Teddy Roosevelt, who received $50,000 in 1910 for his serialised piece on 'African Game Trails' (Mott, p. 724); *Poetry* could hardly compete in that market – though the editors prided themselves on paying authors, unlike most little magazines: 'about fifty cents a line, or ten dollars a small page' (Mott, vol. 5, p. 226). Finally, in terms of exposure, *Scribner's* wins hands down: according to Hoffman et al., *Poetry* had a circulation of 'only 1,400 after the first six years' (p. 44) whereas *Scribner's*, in its peak year of 1910, reached a circulation of 215,000 (Mott, vol. 4, p. 725).

7   *Outlook* 100 (Jan. 13, 1912), p. 65; as cited by Mott, p. 723.

8   Sherwood's poem appears in *Scribner's* 57.3 (March 1915), p. 317, and H. D.'s appears in *Poetry* 5.6 (March 1915), pp. 265–266. Websites: *Scribner's Magazine*: MJP website: **www.modjourn.org**; *Poetry: A Magazine of Verse*: MJP website: **www.modjourn.org**

9   As Pound notes (in the April 1916 issue of *Poetry*): 'Imagism, before it went off into froth, [...] had its first breath of air in these pages' (p. 39).

10 *Poetry* 1.6 (March 1913), p. 199.

11 *Poetry* 8.5 (August 1916), p. 258. Also see Monroe's defence of imagism in the September 1915 issue.

12 Imagists included both Americans and British poets, many of whom lived in London.

13 *Scribner's* 58.5 (November 1915), p. 634.

14 *Poetry* 6.1 (April 1915), p. 9.

15 *Poetry* 7.6 (March 1916), p. 303.

16 *Scribner's* 57.1 (January 1915), p. 89.

17 *Poetry* 7.2 (November 1915), p. 72.

18 *Scribner's* 58.6 (December 1915): p. 760.

19 *Poetry* 6.2 (May 1915): p. 90.

20 *Poetry* 8.1 (April 1916), p. 40.

21 See, for instance, *Poetry* 7.1 (October 1915), p. H [MJP edition].

22 Ibid, p. 52.

23 Advertisement for *Poetry Magazine*, *Poetry* 5.5 (February 1915), p. M [MJP edition].

24 Harriet Monroe, 'Colonialism Again', *Poetry* 10.2 (May 1917), p. 94.

25 Csicsila, pp. 1–4.

26 'On Creating a Usable Past', *The Dial* 64 (April 11, 1918), p. 341.

27 Louis Untermeyer, *Modern American Poetry: An Introduction* (New York: Harcourt, Brace and Howe, 1919), p. vii.

28 Monroe calls Dickinson 'an unconscious and uncatalogued *Imagiste*', *Poetry* 5.3 (December 1914), p. 138.

Edwin Muir and *The New Age*

ALEXANDER J. CUTHBERT

'I do not think there is anything admirable in being up to date, apart from the fact that it is necessary. And to be born outside your age and have to catch up with it and fit into it is a strain.'[1] So wrote Edwin Muir in the first version of his autobiography, *The Story and the Fable*, published in 1940. Yet despite describing himself as having had to 'catch up with' modern life, which he suggests had a hundred and fifty years head start on him (*SF*, p. 263), Edwin Muir did far more than merely 'fit into' the contemporary literary scene. Through his contributions to *The New Age* magazine under its editor A. R. Orage between 1913 and 1924, Muir played an important role in helping to define what it was to be modern for a generation of readers. In addition, the early articles and poems he published in the magazine not only offer early glimpses of the later preoccupations of his mature poetry and prose, but also provide a real sense of the raw intellectual energy which Orage fostered at *The New Age*. As articulations of the period and portents of his later work, Muir's *New Age* writings have a merit which exceeds their literary face value; nevertheless the ephemeral nature and pastiche style of his early verse, and the provocative aphorisms of his Nietzschean inflected prose, are important components of Muir's literary apprenticeship and demonstrate his engagement with contemporary modes of thought. In this, they typify the spirit of immediacy and contention which made *The New Age* such a vibrant talking shop of modernist ideas.

As a young man in Glasgow in the pre-World War One period, Muir had been reading *The New Age* for around three years when he found that his 'faith in the future' was becoming increasingly difficult to live up to.[2] Out of desperation he wrote to Orage seeking some practical advice. Orage responded with a compassionate reply describing his own struggles as a young man and advised Muir to devote himself to the study of a great thinker as he himself had done with Plato. Orage had tentatively advised him to study the *Mahabharata*, the epic Hindu text which he himself was currently working on, but Muir, in need of 'a more drastic stimulus' (*SF*, p. 139) chose Nietzsche with whose ideas he had already come into contact through *The New Age*. Nietzsche's radical and positivist philosophy seemed perfectly suited to his needs; the challenge lay in integrating those ideas with those he had developed previously through his involvement with the Clarion Scouts movement and its associated debating and lecture groups. It was a task that ultimately proved too difficult, but the resulting intellectual maelstrom eventually generated sufficient *New Age* column entries to compile *We Moderns: Enigmas and Guesses* (1918), a publication which gained Muir the patronage of the American publisher Alfred A. Knopf and the journalist and Nietzschean commentator, H. L. Mencken, who penned the introduction to the American edition of *We Moderns* in 1920, a volume which established Muir as a writer of international standing.

In order to suggest something of the influential role *The New Age* and its eclectic form of modernism played in Muir's development, first as a reader, then as a writer, it is worthwhile pausing at this point to offer some background information on Orage himself and his relationship with the magazine. Orage and Holbrook Jackson acquired *The New Age* in 1907, then under the editorship of Joseph Clayton. The magazine was heavily in debt and owed a large sum of money to its printer when they took it on. Orage and Jackson financed the purchase with support from Lewis Wallace, a merchant banker and theosophist, and George Bernard Shaw who, like Orage and Jackson, was a member of the Fabian Society. It had been Jackson who first introduced Orage to Nietzsche's work in 1900 and together they established the Leeds Arts Club in 1903, with the group serving as a breeding ground for the unique mixture of artistic and political considerations, new science, and philosophy which *The New Age* would go on to celebrate. However, following a year of poor sales and numerous differences of opinion regarding editorial policy, Jackson left the magazine in 1908 to pursue an independent career in journalism. Orage became sole editor and continued to transform the magazine in accordance with his own eclectic interests, quickly gaining a loyal following of readers, and committed writers who were keen to articulate their own particular take on what it meant to be modern.

Although its original subtitle was 'An Independent Socialist Review of Politics, Literature, and Art' *The New Age* was far from a mere extension of the Fabian Arts Group that Orage and Jackson had helped found in the January of 1907.[3] By issue 27 (31 October 1907), the words 'Independent' and 'Socialist' had been dropped from the masthead with Jackson's name disappearing by issue 36 (4 January 1908).[4] Despite the change in subtitle, *The New Age* remained socialist in its politics if not always explicitly by name, and under Orage's sole editorship the magazine grew in popularity (its circulation quadrupling under his tenure)[5]. The range of content grew to include articles on guild socialism, theosophy, psychology, science, philosophy, economics, literature, the arts, music, parliamentary reports, social commentary, as well as various forms of literary parody and pastiche. The diversity of its contents was the result of Orage's seemingly inexhaustible enthusiasm for the new, the innovative and, importantly, the divergent.

As Robert Scholes, director of the Modernist Journals Project at Brown University, describes in his 'General Introduction to *The New Age* 1907–1922', Orage had an outstanding ability to identify and foster talent, a skill which resulted in a wide array of emerging and well-established writers becoming regular contributors to the magazine (most of whom went without payment). Notable contributors included Ezra Pound, George Bernard Shaw, H. G. Wells, G. K. Chesterton, Hilaire Belloc, Oscar Levy, Katherine Mansfield, Havelock Ellis, Edith Sitwell, Siegfried Sassoon, Denis Saurat, Patrick Geddes, John Davidson, and James Young (the Jungian therapist who conducted the second phase of Muir's unfinished psychoanalysis), to name but a few of the many whose contributions helped to ensure that the magazine remained an eclectic forum for the presentation and revaluation of ideas. In his *Lives and Letters* of 1978, John Carswell (no doubt reflecting the opinion and recollections of his parents Catherine and Donald Carswell as well as drawing on his own researches while editing Catherine Carswell's *Lying Awake: An Unfinished Autobiography*), comments that *The New Age* 'was as much a journal of ideas as of comment, and it chimed with the aspirations of thousands of individuals and small groups throughout the country who were uncommitted, progressive and for the most part, young.'[6] As Scholes proposes, when reading *The New Age* today it is still possible to get a sense of 'the stir, the buzz, the intellectual energy of an exciting period in our cultural history':

> To read it now is, in a certain way, to envy those original readers, for we live in a time when the phrase 'intellectual journalism' sounds like an oxymoron. For the readers of *The New Age*, however, that phrase was simply a description of what they expected and received – every week.[7]

For many of these readers the magazine also formed the first point of contact with literary culture. As Wallace Martin notes in *The New Age Under*

Orage (1967), many young readers 'like Edwin Muir, having been forced to work for a living after a few years of schooling, obtained their education in contemporary politics and literature from *The New Age*.'[8] Echoing this sentiment, Muir himself recalls how the magazine provided him with a 'picture of contemporary politics and literature, a thing I badly needed, and with a few vigorous blows shortened a process which would otherwise have taken a long time' (*SF*, p. 146). While in retrospect he considered that the tone of the paper could, at times, be 'crushingly superior and exclusive', excluding 'Orage's own political and literary notes' from this criticism (*SF*, p. 145), the magazine nevertheless formed his point of entry into literary culture, first as a reader then, with Orage's patronage, as a promising new writer.

Muir began reading *The New Age* around 1908 while working as an office clerk in a beer-bottling plant in Glasgow. He was already an active member of the Clarion Scouts and the Independent Labour Party and was regularly attending Sunday night lectures on politics, progressive economics and social reform. Everything he read during this period 'were books pointing towards the future', the kind of future envisaged in the works of George Bernard Shaw, Henrik Ibsen, and Edward Carpenter (*SF*, p. 137). His much sought after 'faith in the future' was further bolstered by the prose of Heinrich Heine, via a translation with an introduction by Havelock Ellis, which he read while recuperating in Orkney after a bout of whooping cough saw him signed off from work for a month during the summer of 1908 (*SF*, pp. 137–43). Heine's irreverence and irony enthralled Muir, but he suggests that it also led him to shun sentimentality and encouraged him to adopt an air of superiority which was at odds with his youth and his natural character. The decision to undertake the study of Nietzsche's work had an even more profound impact; and while in retrospect he was dismayed by the effect Nietzsche had both on his fragile psychology and on his literary style (the latter owing more to the stylistics of the translations rather than Nietzsche's actual writings), this decision must also be seen as one of the most significant contributing factors in his development as a writer. Indeed, without his Nietzschean phase, Muir might not have become a writer at all. Looking back over his early contributions in *The New Age* while writing *The Story and the Fable* in 1939, he was without doubt about the problems he had faced both on and beyond the page:

> When I first began to write, some years later, what I produced was
> a sort of pinchbeck Nietzschean prose peppered with exclamation

marks. I should have been astonished at the perversity with which, against my natural inclinations, my judgement, and my everyday experience, I clung to a philosophy so little suited to a clerk in a beer-bottling factory, if I did not realize that it was a 'compensation' without which I should have found it hard to face life at all. (*SF*, p. 151)

This self-assessment is undoubtedly accurate, yet these writings also provide fascinating evidence of his first steps into literary criticism and social commentary. His initial contributions were mostly literary pastiche and polemics, but from the beginning it is clear that he had something significant to contribute to the contemporary debates being conducted in *The New Age*. H. L. Mencken who, as mentioned previously, wrote the introduction to the American edition of *We Moderns*, clearly saw merit in Muir's energetic application of Nietzsche, suggesting that his aphorisms announced the 'emancipation of the modern spirit from its rotting heritage of ingenuous fears and exploded certainties'.[9]

Muir's first published piece of prose took the form of a short dialogue on the subject of 'The Epigram' and appeared in *The New Age* on 29 May 1913 under his chosen pseudonym of 'Edward Moore'. It was included under the regular pastiche section and effectively forms a justification for his subsequent adoption of an epigrammatic style. Through his Socratic debaters, John and Tom, Muir provides a series of arguments for and against the use of the epigram. Berated because it 'denotes a lack of mastery', the epigram is also celebrated for being very effective when used to convey genuine 'conviction'.[10] As John astutely proclaims, it was 'an epigrammatic age',[11] and while ironically applauding writers like Hilaire Belloc and George Bernard Shaw for their triumphs of style over substance, the epigram was a literary mode clearly suited to Muir's needs – having the potential to be pithy and profound or ironic and derisive as he required. When Muir began contributing to *The New Age* he was living in Glasgow and working in a Renfrew shipbuilding office. As a result, he spent a great deal of time travelling on trams and buses, and he used whatever scraps of time he could find to read and compile his own thoughts. 'Whenever I hit upon a paradox which lay conveniently near the surface I took it for the final truth', Muir comments, but he also recognised that his aphorisms were the product of an 'inward excitement' (*SF*, p. 180), the type of untempered intellectual enthusiasm which Orage actively encouraged in his contributors.

As well as being his first publication, 'The Epigram' also typifies Muir's achievements and his limitations in the first phase of his development as a writer. While the self-reflexivity of a dialogue using epigrams both to berate and celebrate the use of epigrams shows a good modernist turn of heel, its haughty tone and contrived nature somewhat undermine its rhetorical playfulness, as Tom and John's closing statements against the misuse of epigrammatic form highlight:

> TOM: The epigram is most vicious, however, when it is a habit. As by excessive drinking one may become that half-human thing a drunkard, so, by force of habit, the journalist or writer ceases to be a journalist or writer, and becomes an epigrammatist. In time he thinks more of how a sentence sounds than of what it means. When I read a new book, I find myself often saying, 'Ah! that is clever!' but very rarely, 'That is true!'
>
> JOHN: The epigram is the mark of an hysterical age. It denotes lack of mastery. Our writers are not serious enough even to write seriously. Their capricious pens lead them a fantastic dance. The epigram is not a weapon which they have mastered, but an obsession which has mastered them. They can resist anything but an epigram.[12]

It is this mixture of ironic posturing, burgeoning talent and genuine engagement which characterises Muir's style at this time. The series of eighteen satirical epigrams which ran over four issues between 23 March and 20 April 1916 provides further examples of this, with the exchange between Muir and the Irish writer and actor James Stephens also unwittingly demonstrating how such a dialogue could descend into public mudslinging. The first volley was Muir's 'To W. B. Yeats' in which he asks the poet to 'Remember, when you rave of mist and bog,/Bog is a name for slush, and mist for fog'; and 'To James Stephens' in which he instructs 'Stephens, from foolish rivalry desist!/Your bog's inferior, second-hand your mist'.[13] Stephens replied swiftly the following week with 'Moore Epigrams': 'Moore: that bog you will not find/Among my books – they must be in your mind./Moore: you snap at Yeats without avail;/To what fool master will you wag a tail?'[14] The following week's issue allowed the final word to go to Muir: 'Stephens, our tails will wag like anything,/When Celtic epigrams have found a sting./Stephens, the bog, at least, I do retract;/Your spleen has made yours mud, to be exact.'[15] Although hardly a demonstration of poetic jousting to match the flytings of the late medieval poets Dunbar and Kennedy, this exchange does demonstrate just how provocative and deliberately inciting *The New Age*'s contributors were encouraged to be, and how swiftly such responses could be shared and returned.

In his book on Orage's *New Age*, Wallace Martin refers to Willa Muir's description of how Muir recalled writing his epigrams quickly in whatever scraps of time he could find during his working day, and how while apparently working on the office accounts, he would be writing aphorisms on slips of paper hidden inside the ledger.[16] As well as being obviously composed swiftly, at times these aphorisms appear a little forced, and yet they also convey a real sense of Muir's fervour in engaging with contemporary literary and social matters. They show a young writer attempting to find his own voice amid the overpowering influence of both his contemporaries and his literary mentors. It is also significant that Muir instinctively chose a verse form to convey his ideas and opinions, and while his poetry after 1921 is clearly of a very different order from these epigrams, his more lyrical *New Age* poems such as 'Metamorphosis' and 'Sleep's Betrayals', with their marriage of classical and Christian imagery, or the sense of longing in 'Utopia' and the world-weariness of 'The Forsaken Princess',[17] all gesture toward the attitudes and themes of the poetry he would later achieve.

Muir had been contributing light verse and prose to *The New Age* for six years by the time the newly wed Muirs moved to London in the autumn of 1919. Within two months he was invited by Orage to be his assistant at *The New Age*, a position Muir gratefully accepted. On the other hand, while Muir had the upmost respect for Orage as a writer and an editor, he did not wish to continue along the groove which he had cut for himself with *We Moderns*. By this point, he was also consciously developing a more balanced and generous critical appreciation of the work of other writers. However, like Orage, Muir continued to be self-conscious about his modernity in his writing; neither of them appears to have taken for granted that the period in which they were living and writing was essentially the most important to their own time. There seems to have been a deliberate effort on both their parts to assimilate the past into the present, to be modern, and to understand what it means to be modern, and by so doing to understand also how the present relates to the past. In literary terms, this search for understanding involved a critical assessment of the prevailing literary styles as well as a re-evaluation of those which were falling from fashion. This is a key element in understanding just how relevant Muir's early writings are in relation to the form of modernism which Orage embraced at *The New Age*, and it is probably best illustrated by an example of their shared concerns regarding the limitations of realism and the nature of representational art. As Scholes summarises: 'the modernism of *The New Age* was not built upon a rejection of romanticism but on a re-examination of it [. . .] nor was it built on a rejection of realism, but on a reconsideration of it.'[18]

This reconsideration of realism was part of the larger discussion taking place within the magazine regarding the nature of artistic representation. Distinguishing between literature which forms a dynamic presentation of ideas and that which merely represents them, Orage demonstrates that a similar distinction can equally be applied to the journals in which such literature is discussed. In an entry from his long-running 'Readers and Writers' series dated 17 March 1921, Orage provides a brief survey of the current journals and magazines available, concluding that *The New Statesman*, *The Spectator*, *The Saturday Review*, *Outlook* and *The Nation* all form varying examples of the 'representative' journal, reflecting the tastes of their respective readers. *The New Witness*, edited by Belloc and Chesterton, by contrast, is placed alongside *The New Age* as being of the 'presentative' form.[19] Wallace Martin elaborates further on Orage's distinction, arguing that while the representative periodical is 'devoted solely to a representation of the interests of the public', being a chronicler 'of taste, fashion, and public opinion',[20] presentative periodicals must create the audience to which they appeal. As Martin identifies:

> As an editor, Orage deliberately attempted to make *The New Age* a presentative periodical which would mediate between specialized fields of knowledge and public understanding, and encourage a vital relationship between literary experimentation and the literary tradition. As a result of the editorial genius he brought to this task, *The New Age* provides a comprehensive record of the emergence of modern culture from its Victorian and Edwardian antecedents.[21]

It is this forward-looking yet historically referential approach which the best of Muir's *New Age* writings reflect. An example of this perspective is voiced in his attack on modern realism in 'We Moderns' from 16 November 1916 in which he lambasts modern realist writers for seeking to reproduce 'life as it is lived' instead of attempting to offer an interpretation of life: 'in their attempt to simplify art, to understand it', the realists have only served to deface its universal value. While classical literature sought 'the interpretation of life' through symbolising its 'deepest questions and enigmas', the modern realists, he argues, have sought only to represent the ordinariness of ordinary life.[22] In this, Muir not only prefigures the criticism of 'realism for realism sake' which Virginia Woolf discusses in her essay 'Modern Novels' (1919) and in more detail in 'Mr Bennett and Mrs Brown' (1924),[23] but also anticipates Katherine Mansfield's criticism of the passivity of writers who 'aim only at representing life'.[24]

What Muir and Orage sought was not the rejection of realism or representational art per se but that such conventions should justify their continued usage; that they should allow readers to see the world continually from new perspectives and, in doing so, discover new truths, however temporary they might turn out to be. In short, they must contribute to the development of a new vision of life for a new age. This is where Muir's *New Age* writings show their true modernist credentials, demonstrating an emerging young writer attempting to re-imagine an image of human life worth celebrating in literature and art, and challenging readers to do likewise. The challenge to his readers is not to be mere spectators, as Mansfield feared so many writers and readers had become, but to see life differently and to make it different. As Muir recalls, at *The New Age* he was far from being a solitary voice in this endeavour: 'in these first years after the War, in spite of the disillusionment elsewhere, in spite of *Ulysses*, *Chrome Yellow* and *H. S. Mauberley* and *The Love Song of J. Alfred Prufrock*, the circle which surrounded Orage still lived in an atmosphere of vast hopes' (*SF*, p. 208).

Many of the 'vast hopes' being expressed in *The New Age*, diverse as they were, articulated, if not an actual faith in the future, then certainly a desire that the future should be very different from the recent past; and that contemporary literature, art and politics should reflect that ambition. While human consciousness or 'character' might not have changed quite so radically or swiftly as Virginia Woolf proposed in 'Mr Bennett and Mrs Brown',[25] there were certainly many, like those whose work appeared regularly in *The New Age*, who sought to hasten its evolution.

It is no overstatement to propose that Muir's relationship with *The New Age* magazine acted as the catalyst to his career as a professional writer. Serving as an invaluable resource for his autodidactic education during his Glasgow years, the magazine provided him with his first publications as a social commentator, literary critic and poet, as well as his first paid literary post. In addition to writing the introduction for the American edition of *We Moderns*, Mencken brought Muir's work to the attention of Van Wyck Brooks, then literary editor of *The Freeman* magazine, who commissioned Muir to provide regular articles at a rate of sixty dollars an article. With the promise of this regular money, the Muirs undertook their first journey to continental Europe in August 1921, a period which led Muir to begin his creative process of 'going against the flow of time',[26] unlocking his poetic imagination and releasing sufficient material to compile his first volume of verse, *First Poems*, published by Virginia and Leonard Woolf at the Hogarth Press in 1925.

Orage played an important personal role in Muir's development as writer. Acting on Orage's advice – albeit not entirely as he had intended – Muir embarked on a sustained study of Nietzsche, which, by his own admission, provided the necessary compensatory antidote against the setbacks which he had endured during his traumatic adolescent years in Glasgow. Orage also played an instrumental role in helping Muir finally to overcome this defensive psychological state by introducing him to Maurice Nicoll who conducted the first phase of Muir's psychotherapy, later handing over to James Young who, alongside fellow Jungian analyst J. A. M. Alcock, published articles on psychology and psychotherapy in *The New Age*.[27] Not only did Muir's therapy hasten his psychological recovery, it also stimulated a wealth of material which would find its way into his poetry for many years after, as he discusses at length in *The Story and the Fable*.

Muir's varied contributions to *The New Age* reflect the divergent and deliberately contentious editorial policy which Orage fostered. While they also provide fascinating glimpses of the more considered and balanced approaches that he would adopt in his later work, what is most striking about these writings (in spite of the awkwardness of his 'parody' of Nietzschean prose) is the way in which they display the type of immediate and highly personal critical engagement that readers of *The New Age* demanded and responded to. In indentifying their contribution to a particularly modern and yet simultaneously ancient debate, Mencken summarises the value of Muir's speculations and assertions for his contemporary international audience:

> The thing he argues for, despite all his fury against the debasement
> of art to mob uses, is not an art that shall be transcendental, but an

art that shall relate to life primarily and unashamedly, an art that shall accept and celebrate life [...] It seems to me that, in more than one way, they illuminate the central aesthetic question – the problem as to the nature and function of artistic representation.[28]

For both Muir and Orage this 'problem' of artistic representation was of the upmost importance to the modern creative imagination, and Muir's engagement with it forms just one of the many reasons why his *New Age* writings constitute such a valuable archive of responses to the literary and political debates of the day. 'To be a modern in the true sense', argues Muir 'is to be a forerunner'; 'to have faith that the "elevation of the type Man" is possible, yes, that the time is ripe to prepare for it; and to write and live in and by that thought: this is to be modern'.[29] It is this 'faith in the future' which excited Muir's imagination as a young reader of *The New Age* and it was a belief he remained committed to as a writer for the rest of his career.

Notes

1   Edwin Muir, *The Story and the Fable* (London: Harrap, 1940), p. 264. Page numbers for subsequent quotations from *The Story and the Fable* will be given in parenthesis in the text.
2   Muir's most positive formulation of this faith is found in 'We Moderns', *The New Age*, Vol. 20, No. 20 (14/03/1917), 470–1 (p. 471). See Muir (1940), p. 149.
3   Wallace Martin, *The New Age Under Orage*, (Manchester: Manchester University Press, 1967), pp. 21–2.
4   'A Socialist Review' would reappear in the masthead in the first issue of 1921 (6 January), but was removed again by 27 October 1921. At this point the words 'Religion and Science' were added to the subtitle, perhaps signalling a change of direction in Orage's own interests at this later date.
5   Robert Scholes, 'General Introduction to *The New Age* 1907–1922'. http://dl.lib.brown. edu/mjp/render.php? id=mjp.2005.00.001&view=mjp_object. Accessed 11/01/2011
6   John Carswell, *Lives and Letters: A. R. Orage, Beatrice Hastings, Katherine Mansfield, John Middleton Murry, S. S. Koteliansky, 1906–1957* (London: New Directions Publishing Corporation, 1978), p. 35. Catherine Carswell, *Lying Awake: An Unfinished Autobiography* (London: Secker and Warburg, 1950); reprinted Edinburgh: Canongate Classics, 1997.
7   Robert Scholes, 'General Introduction to *The New Age* 1907–1922'. http://dl.lib.brown. edu/mjp/render.php? id=mjp.2005.00.001&view=mjp_object. Accessed 11/01/2011.
8   Wallace Martin, *The New Age Under Orage*, (Manchester: Manchester University Press, 1967), p. 7.
9   H. L. Mencken, 'Introduction' to *We Moderns: Enigmas and Guesses* (New York: Knopf, 1920), p. 8.
10 Edward Moore, 'The Epigram', *TNA*, Vol. 13, No. 5 (29/05/1913), p. 124.
11 Ibid., p. 124.
12 Ibid.

13 Edward Moore, 'Epigrams', *TNA*, Vol. 18, No. 23 (06/04/1916), p. 545. Muir is probably alluding to the lines 'Down for me whose fire is clogged,/Clamped in sullen earthy mould,/ Battened down and fogged and bogged/Where the clay is seven-fold ?' from Stephens' poem 'The Nodding Star' (II: 9–12), *Songs From The Clay* (London: Macmillan, 1915), p. 68.

14 James Stephens, 'Moore's Epigrams', *TNA*, Vol. 18, No. 24 (13/04/1916), p. 562.

15 Edward Moore, 'Still More Epigrams', *TNA*, Vol. 18, No. 25 (20/04/1916), p. 595.

16 Martin (1967), p. 278.

17 Edward Moore, 'Metamorphosis'. *TNA*, Vol. 16, No. 1 (11/05/1914), p. 6, 'Sleep's Betrayals', *TNA*, Vol. 15, No. 1 (07/05/1914), p. 20, 'Utopia', *TNA*, Vol. 14, No. 24 (16/04/1914), p. 742, and 'The Forsaken Princess', *TNA*, Vol. 16, No. 17 (25/02/1915), p. 463.

18 Robert Scholes, 'General Introduction to *The New Age* 1907–1922'. http://dl.lib.brown. edu/mjp/render.php? id=mjp.2005.00.001&view=mjp_object. Accessed 11//01/2011.

19 R. H. C., 'Readers and Writers', *The New Age*, Vol. 28 No. 20 (17/03/1921), pp. 235–6, p. 236.

20 Martin, pp. 2–3. John L. Strachey (former editor of *The Spectator*) however, argues that there is a moral responsibility to respond to public opinion, suggesting that 'there are worse things than studying public opinion and endeavouring partly to interpret it honestly and partly to guide it in the right direction'. John L. Strachey, *The Adventure of Living: a Subjective Autobiography* (New York: G. P. Putnam's Sons, 1922), p. 324.

21 Martin, p. 3.

22 Edward Moore, 'We Moderns', *The New Age*, Vol. 20. No. 3 (16/11/1916), pp. 63–4.

23 See 'Virginia Woolf: Unrecorded Times Literary Supplement Reviews', *Modern Fiction Studies*, Vol. 38, No.1, (Spring 1992), 279–83 and 'Mr Bennett and Mrs Brown' (1924), *The Essays of Virginia Woolf*, Vol. 3, ed. Andrew McNeillie (New York: Harcourt Brace Jovanovich, 1988), pp. 384–9.

24 'Now, most writers are merely passive; in fact, they aim only at representing life, as they say, with the consequence that their readers for the most part become even more passive, even more spectatorial, and we have a world of Peeping Toms with fewer and fewer Lady Godivas to ride by. What I am trying to say is that a new attitude to life on the part of writers would first see life different and then make it different'. Katherine Mansfield in conversation with Orage reproduced in A. R. Orage, 'Talks with Katherine Mansfield at Fontainebleau', *The Century Magazine*, Vol. 109 (November 1924). www.gurdjieff-bibliography.com/Current/ KM_07_2006_02_ORAGE_Talks_with_KM.pdf. Accessed 11/01/2011.

25 Woolf, citing Samuel Butler's *The Way of All Flesh* (1903) and the plays of George Bernard Shaw as literary articulations of a seismic cultural shift, proposes that 'human character' changed (she offers the 'arbitrary' date of December 1910) as a response to the fact that during the opening decade of the Twentieth Century 'all human relations changed – those between masters and servants, husbands and wives, parents and children. And when human relations change there is at the same time a change in religion, conduct, politics, and literature'. Virginia Woolf, 'Mr Bennett and Mrs Brown' (1924) in Woolf (1988), p. 385.

26 Willa Muir, *Belonging* (London: Hogarth Press, 1968), p. 69.

27 See James Young, 'The Psychology of Dreams', *TNA*, Vol. 25, No. 27 (30/10/1919), pp. 438–40 and 'Elements of Practical Psycho-Analysis', *TNA*, Vol. 28, No. 25 (21/04/1921), pp. 294–5.

28 H. L. Mencken, 'Introduction', *We Moderns* (1920), pp. 18–20.

29 Edward Moore, 'We Moderns', *TNA*, Vol.21, No. 8 (21/06/1917), pp. 182–3, p. 183.

Primitivism in the Writing of
D. H. Lawrence and Neil M. Gunn

ANDREW J. SNEDDON

Neil M. Gunn was a leading figure in the movement that came to be known in its own time as the Scottish Literary Renaissance, and he became one of the most influential and widely read Scottish writers of the twentieth century as well as a significant spokesperson for Scottish political nationalism. The idea that Neil M. Gunn's aesthetic is in some way indebted to that of D. H. Lawrence, or that his writing can stand fruitful comparison with Lawrence's, has been a recurring feature in Gunn scholarship for almost forty years. However, despite this, no critic has engaged with the question in any depth. Gunn himself wrote relatively few essays on his fictional craft or influences, but approving references to D. H. Lawrence are to be found throughout his autobiographical *The Atom of Delight* (1956), and there is a more concentrated consideration in his earlier essay 'Nationalism in Writing I: Tradition and Magic in the Work of Grassic Gibbon' (1938).

Critics who have attempted to read Gunn through Lawrence divide loosely into two camps: those who see Gunn's writing as anti-Lawrentian (or even pre-Lawrentian) and those who perceive some similarity of method, or sympathy of sentiment. Francis Hart, for example, discusses Gunn's attempts to rescue valid experience from misguided primitivism, and positions Gunn as an 'anti-Lawrence', quoting in support of this view from Gunn's novel *The Shadow* where the character Nan denies that she is 'going all D. H. Lawrence [...] Blood and myth and stuff'. Where Hart sees a praiseworthy anti-primitive turn, Tom Scott saw both *Morning Tide* and *The Lost Glen* as suffering from a 'painfully pre-Lawrentian' lack on account of Gunn's own 'Victorian [...] buttoned-upness' and his resulting lacklustre writing on sexuality. On the other hand, the critic J. B. Caird saw a pleasing reflection of Lawrence's work in Gunn's evocation of the primitive and the unconscious mind and that, like Lawrence, Gunn was 'greatly concerned with the primitive, with what links us to our remote ancestors'.[1]

Richard Aldington's introduction to Lawrence's *Etruscan Places* (1932) emphasises the perceived plight of a lost people who have more than a little in common with Gunn's Picts:

> The Etruscans are one of the 'mystery people' of antiquity, perhaps less
> mysterious now than they were fifty or sixty years ago, thanks to archae-
> ological research, a lost civilisation belonging to a shadowy epoch
> of proto-history which in Italy precedes the Romans. So much that
> might have survived has perished through Vandalism, ignorance and
> the fanaticism of mankind. [Gradually, the Etruscans] were destroyed
> by the Romans, those Prussians of the ancient world. What is left of
> Etruscan art, especially the early tomb-paintings, shows a people who
> enjoyed life, and hence were called 'immoral' by the Romans who stole
> their country. [. . .] Their language is still not understood, and they left
> no literature; or if they did it was destroyed.[2]

The Etruscans are thus a people once believed 'lost' who *appear* to be on the
verge of being rediscovered through scholarly endeavours, and through creative
writing informed by such research. It is interesting to note that at exactly the
moment when Scottish writers (whether scholarly or not) are investing the
word 'Pict' with what Alfred P. Smyth would later call 'an elaborate superstructure of argument and meaning,'[3] Lawrence is exercising himself on the
Etruscans in the same manner. The intellectual circumstances of Lawrence's
enquiry again exactly mirror those of Scottish enquiry into the question of
the Picts: a lost language that cannot be translated; a culture known only
through material artefacts that are little understood and require active interpretation; a historical narrative of defeat at the hands of a stronger and more
brutal adversary; a symbolic discourse of Empire and power politics in which
the Etruscans / Picts are cast as the oppressed and conquered. Gunn's novel
Sun Circle (1933) provides a dramatic historical narrative within which this
very shift is played out as the lands of the Pictish Raven tribe are ravaged by
the boat-borne Northmen. Though it is considered an artistic failure by most
critics, the novel retained a unique significance to Gunn to the extent that he
continued to raise its importance in his own assessment of his work.

What I aim to show in the following discussion is that the symbolic
meanings constructed by Lawrence and Gunn are also startlingly similar,
although, as we shall see, they diverge in one key respect. Lawrence's primitivism begins with assumptions about ancient culture:

> They were, we must feel, of an old, primitive Mediterranean and
> Asiatic or Aegean stock. The twilight of the beginning of our history

was the nightfall of some previous history, which will never be written. Pelasgian is but a shadow-world. But Hittite and Minoan, Lydian,
Carian, Etruscan, these words emerge from a shadow, and perhaps
from one and the same great shadow come the peoples to whom the
names belong.[4]

Lawrence argues, although he offers no evidence for it, that the Etruscans
were a people closer to the root stock of the now diverse Indo-European
peoples. Ancient cultures from Syria, Crete, Turkey and Italy become conflated
in an argument predicated upon a notion of aboriginality. Indeed, later in the
same passage Lawrence makes this case explicit by reference to the Etruscan
language which he speculates was 'probably to a great extent the language of
the old aboriginals of Etruria, just as the religion is in all probability basically
aboriginal, belonging to some vast old religion of the prehistoric world.'[5] Here,
Lawrence is really in the notional realm of the *Ur*-European to whom he now
looks back as a notional ancestor. In Gunn's writing this claim to descent and
lineage is made much more explicitly and without ambiguity. For example, in
the opening scenes of *Highland River* the young hero Kenn is positively quick-
ened by the connections his mind makes between his hunting of a salmon,
those 'wild forays and epic stories' of his kinship group and the experiences
of his 'hunting ancestors of the Caledonian forest' which form an unbroken
thread of history that 'made the blood within him tingle to a dance.'[6]

From the point of view of the aesthetic, what is important in Lawrence's
writing is the way the visual clue of race is deployed to invest certain people
with primitive qualities. Looking at the painted walls in Etruscan tombs he
sees that: 'The men are dark and ruddy, and naked to the waist.'[7] This observation underpins subsequent descriptions of contemporary inhabitants of
modern Italy, so that a man who has the 'glint of ridicule in his black eyes',
or 'the black hair and sallow face and black bat's eyes of a certain type of
this district' or a group of men who all 'seemed to have queer, bright black
eyes, with a glint on them such as a mouse's have' stand as direct blood or
gene descendents of those dark figures on the tomb walls. In similar vein in
Gunn's *Highland River*, Kenn's 'dark hair [. . .] flattened to rat tails' and his
'brown eyes [. . .] black against the excited pallor of his face' betray his Pictish
ancestry as clearly as his flaming 'intolerant fighting spirit' does. It seems that
Kenn and the Pictish champion Bronach of *Sun Circle* are connected rather
than separated by the millennium or more of history between them:

His bearded face was lined, and his black eyes were piercing. There was a sinewy quality about him rather than brute strength, and though this was typical of them all, Bronach had the quality to a quickness that was explosive.[8]

Lawrence's Etruscans and Gunn's Pictish 'small dark people' are contrasted with, for example, the Italian guide Marco, who by comparison was 'quiet and determined-seeming – a brownish blond, not one of the queer *black natives* with the queer round soft contours', on the contrary he was of a 'much higher type'.[9] The italicised emphasis of *black natives* is mine and I have used it to signal two things. Firstly, and most importantly, it is necessary to draw attention to the radical slippage in language that has occurred. Lawrence is describing a group of people who are by any sensible definition Caucasians, yet the visual clues lead the white European reader inexorably towards the position that these Etruscans are not quite white and that they are indeed one of the 'primitive' races. The second point, and the other reason that I have emphasised the phrase in question, is to signal just how close this language is to Gunn's own use of language in *Sun Circle* and elsewhere when his Pictish types are described in similar terms. As the Northmen gain the upper hand over the struggling Picts in battle, the druidic apprentice Aniel runs away driven by the certainty that 'they are superior beings, that we are black brainless savages', which appears to be an internalisation of the Northmen's own complementary conclusion that the Picts are mere 'black painted savages'.[10]

Any notion of the primitive is clearly predicated upon a fundamental perception of difference, and requires, first and foremost, a conceptual framework that constitutes a notion of the civilised from which the primitive may be differentiated. This binary relationship is explored in Lawrence's playfully thought-provoking essay 'Pan in America' in which Pan is a seductively 'outlaw' figure, an emblem of the potentiality of a full life beyond modernity's pale: 'A sort of fugitive, hidden among the leaves, and laughing with the uncanny derision of one who feels himself defeated by something lesser than himself.'[11] Lawrence's modern-day Etruscans have this satiric, Pan-like quality:

Into the cavern swaggers a spurred shepherd wearing goatskin trousers with the long, rusty brown goat's hair hanging shaggy from his legs. He grins and drinks wine, and immediately one sees the shaggy-legged faun. His face is a faun-face, not deadened by morals. [...] They can't survive, the faun-faced men, with their pure outlines and their strange non-moral calm. Only the deflowered faces survive.[12]

In Lawrence's thinking, the primitive has a kind of power but this potential can only be realised outside of modernity, thus allowing it to stand on the margins as a cynical outsider, as a wise fool or satyr. The primitive's sly, knowing smile, and its dark, glittering-eyed defiance, are the source and visual clue to its strength.

Gunn, too, makes extensive use of this outsider status for his modern Picto-Scots and this symbolism is often related (though not always successfully) to sexual matters. Ewan McLeod, the antihero of the *Lost Glen* (1932), has the now familiar dark flashing eyes of the Pict / Etruscan, and something of his pagan, goatish potency. His desire for the blonde-haired and blue-eyed Clare Marlow causes him to smile a rueful grin that 'spread to a silent satyr laugh.' That Clare also understands the potent threat that Ewan poses is made explicit too: 'Her woman's intuition knew all at once that he was considering her. She felt it in a slight burning all over her body. Something forceful and black, and, perhaps, brutal.' In this particular example, Ewan's Pictish, Pan-like quality becomes merged with contemporary anxieties about sexuality and black ethnicity. Ewan for a brief moment resembles the mythical and diabolical hyper-sexed black male of white-cultural anxiety. Later, when Ewan regrets his own uninvited touch and physical advances towards Clare, he muses that he 'had not been a pagan, he had merely been an ill-mannered fool.'[13] By associating this primitive urge and the resulting breach of etiquette with that which is outside modern, polite society Gunn's writing displays marked sympathies with Lawrence's own thinking, although Gunn's use of this association in *The Lost Glen* encounter between Ewan and Clare does not have Lawrence's redemptive or liberating qualities.

Nevertheless, the importance of the primitive, in both Gunn's and Lawrence's writing, is that the primitive does not *yet* live inside the hermetically sealed box that modernity is alleged to supply. For, Lawrence this conclusion results only in the ache of loss, for 'we cannot return to the primitive life, to live in tepees and hunt with bows and arrow. Yet live we must.'[14] What Lawrence seems to be trying to communicate is the importance of the attempt to see the world through the eyes of the primitive and the attempt to seek value in the primitive on its own terms:

You've got to de-bunk the Indian, as you've got to de-bunk the
Cowboy. When you've de-bunked the Cowboy there's not much left.
But the Indian bunk is not the Indian's invention. It is ours [. . .] The
Indian is not in line with us. He's not coming our way. His whole
being is a different way from ours. And the minute you set eyes on him
you know it [. . .] To know the Indian conception of entertainment,
we have to destroy our own conception.[15]

What Lawrence's argument snakes its way towards is a construction of
precisely this 'de-bunked' Indian and the different operation of the primitive
mind in a discussion of the Hopi snake dance, in which he sees:

the spirit of man soothing and seeking and making interchange with
the spirits of the snakes. For the snakes are more rudimentary, nearer
to the great convulsive powers. [. . .] The snakes lie nearer to the source
of potency, the dark lurking, intense sun at the centre of the earth.[16]

This passage is almost wilfully opaque, so much so that the reader must
strain to follow the path of Lawrence's convolutions. Snakes are said to be
more rudimentary than humans, and Indians more rudimentary, by implication, than moderns because they seek communion with snakes. But in this
context the adjective rudimentary is presented as a positive virtue; that which
is rudimentary is argued to be closer to the pristine source. This is snake-as-
totem, rather than snake-as-animal. In this totemic sense they, and Indians
too by means of interchange, become more than they seem to be from the
perspective of a modern.

Interestingly, one of the examples that Lawrence uses as a way of
approaching the Hopi Snake Dance and making clear how its practice differs
from modern entertainments is traditional Gaelic song:

Or the wild fishermen of the Outer Hebrides will sing in their intense,
concentrated way, by the fire. And again, usually, the songs have words.
Yet sometimes not. Sometimes the song has merely sounds, and a marvellous melody. It is the seal drifting in to the shore on the wave, or the
seal-woman, singing low and secret, departing back from the shores of
men, through the surf, back to the realm of the outer beasts that rock
on the waters and stare through glistening, vivid, mindless eyes.

This is approaching the Indian song. But even this is pictorial, conceptual far beyond the Indian point. The Hebridean still sees himself human, and *outside*, the great naturalistic influences, which are the dramatic circumstances of his life.[17]

In Lawrence's logic what separates the Hebridean mind from the modern appears to be its affinity with the rhythms and sounds of the natural world. It is sympathetic to the primitive but not evidence of a truly primitive mindset. For Lawrence, what separates the Hebridean mind from the genuinely primitive is that Hebridean song is fundamentally 'pictorial' or idea-based. In Hebridean song the natural world is presented as being experienced one step removed; nature provides the backdrop to human experience and is evidence of the pathetic fallacy in operation. The song is not, of itself, evidence of a being's immersion in all-that-there-is in the way Hopi song and dance is:

> But the real Indian song is non-individual, and without melody. Strange, clapping, crowing, gurgling sounds, in an unseizable subtle rhythm, the rhythm of the heart in her throes: from a parted entranced mouth, from a chest powerful and free, from an abdomen where the great blood-stream surges in the dark, and surges in its own generic experiences. [...] Whatever the spirit of man may be, the blood is basic.[18]

The interesting point here is the alleged absence of the melodic and pictorial, its lack of what we might think of as an artistic narrative or logic. This is not an expression of something in the traditional sense, as Lawrence believes Hebridean song is. What Lawrence sees is that it provides the means of breaking out of consciousness with the individual reduced to nothing and in the process becoming more. One of the most interesting features of this position is Lawrence's use of Gunn's own favourite term for a kind of consciousness-negating, infinite expansion: 'delight'. It is not simply that Gunn and Lawrence use the same term, rather it is inescapable that they use the same term in the same way.

Gunn's own assessment of the meaning of 'native' song and what it can achieve or express is to be found in several of his novels. In the early novels, which are certainly the ones which show the greatest convergence with Lawrence's method, Gunn uses the figure of the traditional singer or musician extensively. In *The Lost Glen* the bagpipe-player Colin McKinnon actually experiences moments that appear very close to what Lawrence argues for in the Hopi dance. The title of the novel plays ambiguously with the notion of the community in question being dispossessed of their own inheritance, while it is also the title of a tune that Colin has composed following a mystical enchantment with the landscape from which he understands he derives. While playing the tune, Colin somehow is taken outside of himself:

> [...] so that the darkness becomes an ache and the glen extends to a universe set with stars. That emotion of space, how impersonal and how quivering sweet! The first shudder before art; man's shudder before God's art. And no man may know God, any more than he may know art, until he is alone.
>
> Was not that the place that his race had come out of? And was it not the spirit that his race had forever been concerned with? Not matter, not grubbing, not success, not 'getting on', but the play and the sparkle of the spirit in music and fun and work in the open and – poverty? No, not poverty, any more than Christ's poverty, or Socrates'.[19]

Colin's bagpipe playing, according to Gunn's narrator at least, is not expressive or artistic in the way complained of by Lawrence. It is not a call to maudlin sympathies, it has no narrative logic and it has no 'meaning' that is easily communicable. It is, in fact, primitive in exactly the way that interests Lawrence. The effect of this music is mystical, revelatory and transcendent. For the antihero of the piece, however, the disaffected malcontent Ewan, such piping means nothing positive. In a conversation with Colin, he describes the playing as:

> Laments and warlike strains and that sort of tribal stuff – we're away back in the delightful tribal stage. We have never evolved beyond that. We're living on a dead past like ravens on a dead sheep. When the sheep is completely rotten we too shall pass. Did you never get the smell, Colin, on the hill wind?[20]

Although he is of the native type, Ewan's problem is a sort of ennui and shame deriving from his own notion that he is a failure and a feeling that he is at odds with the servility and decay he sees around him on his return to the village. Because the disaffection and *ennui* arising from his colonised subject status lead him to believe his own people are backward, he cannot see anything of value in their 'tribal' culture, and is unable to obtain the kind of release and spiritual refreshment that Colin can. Yet what saves Ewan, spiritually at least, is another kind of ritualised music. The gifted singer Mary McKinnon, whose natural, native abilities are emphasised throughout the text, is able to 'cure' him of his paralysing indecision and spiritual sickness:

> It was in the case of Mary MacKinnon that this matter of race and environment got its point, its most barbed and poisonous point. Her singing voice had touched things in him forgotten for a thousand years. They went back together, side by side, every flicker of instinct or mind, every silence or listening, every thrill or despair, known most subtly each to each in a way dreadful and inescapable and ageless.[21]

Given the distinctly dark and distopian turn of this particular novel, Ewan's newly found spiritual charge and vitality can only end badly: he eventually resolves to murder the imperialistic bully Colonel Hicks and sails away to an ambiguous fate in an ending that signifies either permanent exile or death. What Lawrence would recognise, and perhaps applaud, is that Ewan's reintegration into the primitive allows him to resolve the passivity and despair of his modern existence.

Gunn's autobiography, *The Atom of Delight*, also makes frequent reference to the power of 'native' song, demonstrating that such preoccupations continued well into his later writing period unaltered:

> Folk music has this kind of extra-musical magic, which sometimes works quite involuntarily, as when out of a mood of weariness or depression the mouth on its own hums or whistles some snatch of it and in a strangeness of familiar surprise transformation takes place, the subtle change from the dreariness of woe to the honey of woe and then, with luck and a little effort, to the recognition of an ancient strength.

The passage cited argues, or imagines, that the singular ancient quality of the songs, 'winnowed' by 'countless generations' is one source of their strength and power, just as a natural, rhythmic, elemental quality is the other.[22] Gunn makes the connection between the two facets explicit as the supplement to his insistence of direct descent from the primitive:

> As has earlier been suggested, those brought up within the region of a distinctive and still active folk music are sometimes susceptible to qualities in it that seem extra-musical, as though the simple traditional tune carried racial characteristics, was archetypal in the Jungian sense. What can actually happen – did actually happen – is something like this. The time is the dusk of evening and the place a Highland sea loch; across the water comes the music of a traditional lament. The theme is stated – that awful terrible familiarity of the theme – until the head bows before it, as before what can hardly be borne, and the theme repeats itself with the inexorability that has in its simplicity, its final cleansing, all that can be said forever, and the body doubles over like another boulder on the shore, egoless and faceless, and bears the wind of time from all of the race who have gone before.[23]

Whether Gunn meant the half-apologetic 'as though [. . .] the tune carried racial characteristics' to sound defensive is not clear. But the argued-for effect of the music bringing the 'susceptible' listener, 'brought up' to be sensitive, is that it puts the listener back into primitive contact with the spirit of place and race. In *Butcher's Broom* (1934) exactly such a moment occurs, and indeed traditional music and song plays a pivotal thematic role in establishing the redeeming features of the otherwise spartan life enjoyed by the community depicted in the novel prior to the Clearance. As the community begins to sense its own doom, Elie sings:

> Here was the girl in the song comforting this unreason with humanity's final logic, tragedy. Elie knew all about that girl and gave her the dignity due so ultimate a role. Her voice could not be shamed by any sound between earth and heaven. And no personal stress or sentiment flawed its nameless power. Yet it went deeper than that. For she sang in a tongue and a rhythm that were not merely countless centuries old, but had been born out of the earth on which they starved and feasted and against which their feet pressed now, so that all the millions of influences and refinements that had shaped themselves to make the incommunicable understood were from the very first note altogether at her service.[24]

What has not traditionally been recognised in Gunn scholarship is the extent to which, like Lawrence, he is using the visual clues of race, discursively constructed through physical features such as skin, eye and hair colour, to construct an argument that positions 'the folk' as the primitive. In Lawrence's case the darkness of the primitive is always illustrative of a mysterious life-giving potential that modernity has lost. It is, for Lawrence, an exercise in constructing a metaphysical argument about ultimate value which he claims can only exist before and outside the mechanising-cash nexus of the modern, civilised, white, European world, and back towards which moderns must strive. For Lawrence, primitives do not yet have their wrists and ankles in the shackles that modernity unavoidably supplies. Yet, Lawrence tends, also, to see what he describes as moderns and primitives, lights and darks, as races apart. There is never a claim to a direct blood relationship between moderns and primitives because Lawrence perceives the real primitive only in prehistory or the margins of the new world, for example. For Gunn, on the other hand, and as we see in *Highland River*, and throughout the novels, the primitive is in a direct bloodline with contemporary moderns. Some moderns, indeed, by virtue of that line of descent, remain capable of being in touch with the primitive and in the right circumstances (which always involves a geographical and temporal distance from the metropolis) can do what Lawrence denies is possible and 'return to the primitive'. Kenn Sutherland's journey home in *Highland River* is completed geographically and spiritually at exactly the moment he returns to look upon the structure of a cairn or Pict's House: 'Its dumbness was eloquent of the continuity of the folk. It solved for him in a flash the interminable debate about the identity of the Pict. I am the Pict! he thought.'[25]

As I have argued, both Lawrence and Gunn deploy a symbolic discourse in which primitive bodies are painted black. These surfaces have been written on by blood and are said to carry associated primitive values. Today, we might argue that such a discourse is itself racist, predicated as it is upon colonial notions of essential difference. However, it ought not to be forgotten that both writers look at these primitive bodies and believe they 'contain' a positive potential that modern whites have lost. To Lawrence these beings remain remote and strange, though he invariably sides with this potential and even yearns for it for himself. For Gunn the primitive is much less exotic, more domestic, and much less 'Other'. When Gunn looks at his dark Picts he sees his own people and perhaps even himself. Gunn's Picto-Scots are more in tune with Lawrence aesthetically than is usually appreciated, but, unlike in Lawrence, they are a people who can sometimes survive or even prosper in modernity, just as Kenn Sutherland does, precisely because of their difference and their unique inheritance.

Notes

1   Francis R. Hart, 'The Hunter and the Circle: Neil Gunn's Fiction of Violence', *Studies in Scottish Literature*, 1.1 (1963), 65–82; Tom Scott, 'Neil M. Gunn: Scottish Novelist', in *Pembroke Magazine*, 10 (1978), 101–9 (109); J. B. Caird, 'Neil M. Gunn: Novelist of the North', *Essays on Neil Gunn*, ed. by David Morrison (Thurso: Caithness Books, 1971), pp. 41–51.

2   Richard Aldington, Introduction to D. H. Lawrence, *Etruscan Places* [1932], ed. by Richard Aldington, (Harmondsworth: Penguin Books Ltd., 1950), pp. 9–10.

3   Alfred P. Smyth, *Warlords and Holy Men: Scotland AD 80–1000*, (Edinburgh: Edinburgh University Press, 1995), p. 49.

4   Lawrence, *Etruscan Places*, pp. 37–8.

5   Ibid, p. 39.

6   Neil M. Gunn, *Highland River*, (London: Faber and Faber, 1937), p. 8.

7   Lawrence, *Etruscan Places*, p. 65.

8   Gunn, *Highland River*, p.16 and *Sun Circle* (1933: London: Souvenir Press, 1983), p. 60.

9   Gunn, *Sun Circle*, p. 80; Lawrence, *Etruscan Places*, pp. 121, 139, 134–5.

10 Gunn, *Sun Circle*, pp. 252, 180.

11 D. H. Lawrence, 'Pan in America' in *Phoenix*, pp. 22–31, 23.

12 Lawrence, *Etruscan Places*, pp. 16–17.

13 Gunn, *The Lost Glen*, pp. 204, 202, 242.

14 Lawrence, 'Pan in America', p. 31.

15 D. H. Lawrence, *Mornings in Mexico* (London: Martin Secker, 1930), pp. 100–3.

16 Ibid, p. 147.

17 Ibid, pp. 103–4.

18 Ibid, p. 105

19 Gunn, *The Lost Glen*, p. 47.

20 ibid, p. 107. Here the raven bird has a totemic quality that is not made explicit in his Raven tribe of *Sun Circle*, though the same argument is perhaps implicit.

21 Ibid, p. 341.

22 Gunn, *The Atom of Delight*, pp. 167–8

23 Ibid, p. 190.

24 Neil M. Gunn, *Butcher's Broom* (1934: London: Souvenir Press, 1977), pp. 292–3.

25 Gunn, *Highland River*, p. 241.

W. B. Yeats and Hugh MacDiarmid: Kingly Cousins

ALAN RIACH

They are two of the greatest poets of the twentieth century, figures of daunting magnitude, deep contradiction, wild humour and real political significance. They met only once, in Dublin on a Friday night in August 1928. Their lives and work overlap and share dynamics of commitment, responsibility and concern, in terms of the Celtic identities in Ireland and Scotland, the ruins of the nineteenth century and the structures of new visions of modernity, the actions of public personae in civic life and in writing for a self-consciously national readership, for readers universally, and in the legacy they deliver to the century we now inhabit.

Mainly Biographical

Their lives overlap significantly: Yeats, 1865–1939 and MacDiarmid, 1892–1978. Yeats was twenty-seven when MacDiarmid was born. When they met in 1928, Yeats was sixty-three and MacDiarmid thirty-six. When Yeats died, MacDiarmid was forty-seven, and lived on well into his eighties. Let us imagine them together in Dublin, the sixty-three-year-old Irishman and the thirty-six-year-old Scot. The famous story of Joyce meeting Yeats and turning away, saying that the poet was too old for the young novelist to teach him anything is inappropriate here.[1] MacDiarmid held Yeats in high regard and treasured the opportunity to meet him. How did they come to be together?

MacDiarmid had been invited to Ireland to attend the (nationalist) Tailltean Games in August 1928, as the guest of the Irish Free State, presumably because of his work in the foundation of the National Party of Scotland (NPS), whose formation had been agreed at a meeting in Glasgow on 10 May, earlier that same year. MacDiarmid, Compton Mackenzie and the Honourable Ruaraidh Erskine of Mar had all been invited (all had been founder-members of the NPS) though Mackenzie said it was impossible for him to go.[2] MacDiarmid wrote about the fortnight he spent in Ireland as one of the best experiences of his life.[3] He met De Valera and the Minister of Defence in the Cosgrave government. He was the guest of Oliver St John Gogarty, who took him flying in an Avro-Anson five-cylinder plane, drove him all around Ireland by car, covering, he said, about 1,000 miles, and they visited as many of the Dublin bars as they could, Gogarty talking of his friendship with Joyce. MacDiarmid met the writers F. R. Higgins, Walter Starkie, Eoin MacNeill, Seamus O'Sullivan (founding editor of the *Dublin Magazine* and dedicatee of the poem MacDiarmid called his finest love-lyric, 'Milk-Wort and Bog Cotton'), and AE (George Russell), who later met MacDiarmid in Liverpool and was to contribute an introduction and a portrait of MacDiarmid as a frontispiece to the *First Hymn to Lenin* volume in 1931. On Friday nights, Yeats visited Russell's home and MacDiarmid was invited to join a small gathering where, he observed, Yeats and Russell, both highly opinionated and given to rhetorical exposition rather than the cut-and-thrust of informed conversation, held forth extensively and eloquently. MacDiarmid was sorry that only lemonade was available. When Yeats asked him to explain the intricacies of Major Douglas's Social Credit banking scheme, then widely discussed, MacDiarmid said that he found his peer attentive and curious to learn, but that his efforts to expound the system met with incomprehension as Yeats seemed to have no understanding of how *any* banking system worked. At 1 a.m. he left with Yeats and they walked the night-time Dublin streets together, pausing only when W. B. asked to be excused, explaining, 'I must urinate.' MacDiarmid joined him: 'I crossed swords with him and we became very friendly after that.'[4]

The anecdote is cheerful in its absurd mix of aristocratic behaviour, formal gesture, rhetorical flamboyance, and the intrusion of impudent boyishness. The whole episode feels a little ghostly, as if Joyce were hovering nearby, and in MacDiarmid's account there is the suggestion that there was more to Gogarty than is implied by the bluff portrait Joyce drew of him as Buck Mulligan. But there is no reason to doubt MacDiarmid's sense of the affection between Yeats and himself. In a letter to MacDiarmid of 4 March 1934, Yeats wrote, 'you have done lovely and passionate things' – high terms of praise for him.[5] Yeats included four of MacDiarmid's poems two years later in *The Oxford Book of Modern Verse* (1936): 'Cattle Show', 'Parley of Beasts', 'The Skeleton of the Future' and 'O Wha's the Bride' from *A Drunk Man Looks at the Thistle* (which apparently Yeats memorised, he found it so haunting). When Sorley MacLean pointed out that a more representative selection from his work could have been made, MacDiarmid defended Yeats's choice as enhancing the book's purpose in opposing and offending certain Anglocentric critics and reviewers.[6]

How did Yeats read MacDiarmid? 'O Wha's the Bride' would have appealed as its ballad form and metre are haunting, mesmerising, but sharp with unanswerable questions, delivering senses of loss, horror, mystery and also consolation and physicality, acknowledgements of sexual appetite and domestic warmth. It is a dialogue, with dramatic tension and unspoken narrative implied behind it. If one were to offer a series of close readings comparing a selection of poems by MacDiarmid and Yeats, one might think of Yeats's 'No Second Troy' or 'Reconciliation' or 'Words' in these terms. Or one might propose that MacDiarmid's 'The Watergaw' be read alongside Yeats's 'The Fisherman' or 'The Eemis Stane' alongside 'Leda and the Swan'. There are certainly qualities of understanding time, ageing, sympathy, history and the imagination that could bear close analysis. Or one might listen to the traditional musical setting of 'Down by the Salley Gardens' and then the composer F. G. Scott's setting of MacDiarmid's 'First Love': the similarities of poise, delicacy and vulnerability, the contrasts of formalities and depths of perception, are considerable. In another of the poems Yeats included in the Oxford anthology, 'Parley of Beasts', there is evidently an engagement with the circus pageantry of Noah's Ark and the value of the quarrel with one's self that would have appealed immediately. This list could be extended but the attitude of opposition to the Anglocentric Establishment MacDiarmid emphasised to Sorley MacLean is notable. How did this come about? How closely was it shared by Yeats?

Both came out of the nineteenth century literally, and if Yeats was more deeply grounded in it, his roots in the Celtic west of Ireland and the rural people were matched by an urban sophistication and wiliness. He was, after all, the editor of the Oxford anthology as noted, in which MacDiarmid was pleased to be included. The duality of his stance is perhaps most evident in the way he brings together the city-dweller's longing for the country with the pastoral vision of rural life the urban drudge might most likely long for, in his widely anthologised, richest chestnut, 'The Lake Isle of Innisfree'. At a higher level of achievement entirely, it is evident in the way he brings together the countryman's sense of neighbourliness, friendliness and comradeship, with an urban sense of dislocation, disturbance and alienation in 'Easter 1916'. Both poets engaged with radical political change in their writing and as active men in society at large, as political candidates, representatives and delegates. The sexual revolution that was to change forever the representation of women in literature, both as subjects of male artists and writers and as practitioners, developing means of articulating their own experience in art, was something both male poets had to come to terms with in their private and personal lives as well as in their professional and public experience. Both came from and drew on related but different resources of Celtic identity.

Yeats's childhood was spent mainly in three locations: Sligo in the west of Ireland, Dublin and London. A cosmopolitan or metropolitan sensibility was interlinked, rather than meshed, with that of the Celtic sunset coast. He developed those complex counterpoints in everything he did. His brother, the great artist, Jack, was more profoundly earthed in the west, while professionally confident in the international art world, and W. B. was fluent in the Anglo-Irish Ascendancy world of urbane Dublin and the imperial centre of London. He developed a manner that demonstrated he was not to be condescended to: after all, London was a gateway to Europe and Byzantium was a capital city no-one west of the Bosphorus could treat with disdain. If Yeats had to correct the prevailing image of the stage Irishman as buffoon, MacDiarmid had to do something similar not only to the image of the comic, but also the dolorous, Scot. He had to engage both austere seriousness and common sympathy.

MacDiarmid came from the Scottish Borders, born about twelve miles from England. He grew up there, and after the First World War, set about stirring up the tornadoes of the 1920s in Scotland's literary, cultural and political world. He declared the 'propaganda of ideas' he was expounding should be known as the 'Scottish Literary Renaissance' and that it must pick up where the Irish Revival left off.[7] He produced hundreds of columns of literary and political polemical journalism, making many enemies. By the 1930s he was in poverty, physical and spiritual breakdown, estranged from his first wife and children, in isolation in the Shetland archipelago with his second wife and their young son. I will come back to his later work, a remarkable story of regeneration that could not have been predicted. But I would like to emphasise a key point which both Yeats and MacDiarmid reacted to strongly: the Easter Rising of 1916. Yeats was not in Ireland at the time of the rising but the significance of his poetic response, the poem 'Easter 1916' printed privately in 1916 but not published till 1920 in the *New Statesman*, is an essential testament.[8] He was hesitant, then decided. In a late interview, MacDiarmid declared that like thousands of other young men, he had volunteered to join the British army for the First World War, thinking that the end of the world was coming, and he might as well be there to see it. He went to Europe as a soldier in the Royal Army Medical Corps. He was twenty-four years old when news of the Easter Rising in Ireland came through, and he said that although he was in British army uniform, if it had been possible at all, he would have deserted the British army and joined the Irish fighting British imperialism.[9] He also said that the execution of James Connolly, one of the leaders of the rising who had been born in Edinburgh, and who had been wounded in the fighting and carried out strapped in a chair to his execution, was an image that remained with him forever. [10]

Declan Kiberd begins his essay 'W. B. Yeats – Building Amid Ruins' with this sentence: 'The greatness of Yeats lay in his constant capacity to adjust to ever-changing conditions.'[11] He says that Yeats began by writing poems of octogenarian sensibility and ended with passionate celebrations of the human body. There is also an essay by Seamus Heaney on Yeats which takes its title from Auden but adds a question mark: 'Yeats as an Example?' Heaney reminds us that:

> When Joyce rebelled, he left by the Holyhead boat and created his drama by making a fictitious character called Stephen Dedalus point up and respect the terms of his revolt. When Yeats rebelled, he remained – and Joyce scorned such 'a treacherous instinct for adaptability' – but he (Yeats) still made a W. B. Yeats (that is, he recreated himself) to tread the streets and stage of Dublin, a character (self-generated) who was as much a work of the imagination as Stephen Dedalus.[12]

What for Kiberd is the key to Yeats's greatness, an adaptability, was for Joyce a kind of instinctive treachery: unprincipled, flexible to the point of unreliable. Both Kiberd's and Heaney's essays offer points of connection between Yeats and MacDiarmid: building among ruins was a commitment they shared. Yet Heaney's description of Joyce's denouncement of Yeats's adjustments as treachery is indicative. MacDiarmid, too, made his 'adaptations', and like Yeats, unlike Joyce, when the time came for him to rebel, MacDiarmid came back to Scotland and stayed there. While most of the great modernists were making a beeline for Paris, he went to the small east-coast seaside town of Montrose, became a town councillor, newspaper reporter, socialist Justice of the Peace, and wrote his greatest early lyrics and *A Drunk Man Looks at the Thistle*. So from this key moment, the affinity appears to be more with Yeats than Joyce: with residence, rather than exile, with commitment to practical, day-to-day politics, rather than a position distanced from the locality, or more comprehensively from the nation that was to be so central in so much of his work. But the position is more complex than that, of course.

Drawing from the Celtic World

The Celtic twilight was Yeats's world in his earliest works, and his first planned book, *The Wanderings of Oisin* (1889) is a long narrative deriving from Celtic legend and evidently arising from the eighteenth-century Ossianic stories of James Macpherson. In the nineteenth century, Matthew Arnold identified the Celt as the soft, feminine and childish character aspect of British identity, where the Anglo-Saxon provided the hard-headed rational adult aspect. The Celtic component in British imperial identity was a significant aspect of *fin-de-siècle* literary culture and Yeats drew on its lore and ethos, but he pressed further back than many of his contemporaries and predecessors might have imagined possible, and moved further forward in practical application in the real political world than anyone might have deemed possible at the beginning of the twentieth century. He pushed further back by imagining a world of primitivism and orality, the ur-sources of western culture, in which an aristocracy of warriors and lovers, principles of nobility and honour in action, inhabited and inspired a Celtic world before recorded time. This world came forward into the Christian era. Stories of the Celtic gods, then the cycle of stories of kings, queens, heroes and lovers, of Conchobhar, Cuchulain, Deirdre and Naoise, then following that, stories of Finn MacCoul and the Fianna, roving warriors, the last remnants of a society that had gone: these stories formed a hinterland from which he drew freely, unsystematically, in his early poems. Yet he also carried figures and images from these stories forward into a modern political context, most powerfully in the ambiguous question at the heart of the poem 'The Statues' (written 9 April 1938), from *Last Poems* (1936–1939):

> When Pearse summoned Cuchulain to his side,
> What stalked through the Post Office?[13]

By bringing the Celtic warrior into the year and moment of 1916, in a poem written twenty-two years after that moment, Yeats was sheering away all traces of a softening twilight atmosphere and insisting on the brutal clarity of imaginative presence. The quality of commitment evoked here is deadly: both murderous and sacrificial, commemorating the actions of men who would die with and kill for their beliefs. The myth becomes presence. Fiction falls away.

Yet the ambiguities keep us at a distance, asking questions: In what sense did the historical man, Pearse, summon the mythical warrior? What are we to imagine stalking in the Post Office in Dublin in 1916? What or who was being stalked? Are we to think of Pearse and Cuchulain embodying a spirit of resistance against an oppression enforced by imperial power? Or is this a spirit of violence, incarnate in the men who killed and died? The poet is absent from the event and his readers follow the questioning, fumbling towards the difficult acknowledgement of the human fact of violence and the merciful distance we keep from it, with a deeper understanding of the human need to resist oppression.

Yeats's use of the English language in these poems is essential to their hard authority and imperious power. The monosyllables are insistent, staccato weight in a juggernaut syntax, in the second line quoted. He had read the myths and legends of ancient Ireland in Lady Gregory's wonderful versions, written in a poised and postured English affectionately – or derisively – known as 'Kiltartanese'.[14] She had drawn from Macpherson also, in her use of a language redolent with artifice and gesture, deliberately unnatural yet urgent in its narrative pace, episodic clashes and conflicts, vivid characters and confrontations. Yeats took the stern forms of poetry and a more essential vocabulary, entering the English language as an international idiom and riddling it with distinctively Celtic mythic identities. Cruelty is part of the human story, from time immemorial to now. Yeats puts that into the poems. When Cuchulain fights with his son and kills the boy, there is no apology, no sorrowing, but a rage at the violence he then turns to further violence, impossible war on the unturnable tide: he walks into the sea to fight with the waves.[15]

MacDiarmid's reconfiguration of the Celtic world in modernity was different, but not unrelated. He had no respect for the fabrication and sublimation involved in the Celtic twilight. He was unpersuaded, resolutely unseduced. Everywhere he insists on the value of contemporary work relating to contemporary experience. Nostalgia was anathema. In 'Good-bye Twilight' he contrasts the composers Delius and Sibelius, the former (English), standing for 'doped, drugged, besotted' morbid delusion, the latter (Finnish) for 'fine / Acute Northern wits', as in the 'gaunt El-Greco-emaciated ecstatic' Fourth Symphony: 'A long spell of Delius/Is enervating and relaxing like a muggy winter day in London,/ While Sibelius charges his hearer with nervous energy' and brings us 'Out of the Celtic Twilight and into the Gaelic sun!'.[16]

There is sleight-of-hand here, of course, having Delius stand for the ethos of the Celtic Twilight and Sibelius stand for distinctively Scottish clarity of vision and visceral understanding of nature, but the argument is effective and there is truth in it. For MacDiarmid, the Celtic twilight was a distraction of attention exemplified by William Sharp, writing as the feminine Fiona MacLeod, books with titles like *The Winged Destiny: Studies in the Spiritual History of the Gael* (1904). MacDiarmid wanted material altogether more contemporary, documentary, realistically responsible to Scotland's twentieth-century economic and social realities, yet not entirely shorn of a sense of mystery. In the 1920s, he edited a series of anthologies, *Northern Numbers*, in which poems of fondness for a Scotland glowing with golden affection are in contrast with poems literally describing the lives of unemployed city-people, prostitutes, outcasts in the wake of World War One. MacDiarmid's political effort might seem crude in comparison with Yeats, but his poetic achievement in the 1920s was equally convincing through his regeneration of a different language, a different linguistic idiom, from Yeats's English. MacDiarmid's early poems are in the language we call Scots, but a Scots from which clichés of facile humour and theatrical eccentricity have been surgically removed. If Scots has a vernacular appeal as speech drawing on a common idiom, it also has an austere strangeness on the page.

The Scottish and Irish components of the Celtic Twilight were entwined, in the late nineteenth century. While the ancient Celtic stories and songs of Cuchulain and the Red Branch cycle and Finn and Ossian and the Fenian cycle were recognised by both Yeats and MacDiarmid, Yeats inhabited and made use of them as a native of their time, whereas MacDiarmid was keen to see contemporary Scottish Gaelic poetry make a distinctive appearance, a major intervention in the Scottish literary scene, in the 1930s and 1940s. By the 1930s, he had travelled extensively in the Hebridean islands, had read the work of Daniel Corkery and Douglas Hyde, and after his visit to Ireland in 1928, had asserted a faith in Celtic identity that throws an imaginative bridge back to an Ireland which seemed to have been standing too long alone, without the support of sister nations. George Campbell Hay and Sorley MacLean began writing through these decades. When MacLean began corresponding with MacDiarmid in the 1930s and visited him, and then produced his first major book of poems in 1943, MacDiarmid's welcome of it was jubilant.[17] MacLean's poetry came out of the experience of contemporary reality – world war, alienation, dispossession, socialist commitment – while it was deeply passionate and intensely personal, capable of reference not only to Celtic and Greek myth, but also to the perennial fact of human bloodshed as he had experienced it in war.

In a very different linguistic and political context from Yeats, MacDiarmid was bringing together new poetry in Scots, Gaelic and English, pushing forward from complicity in British imperialism towards a national identity in which difference might be prized and uniformity rejected. At the same time, MacDiarmid recognises and offers salutation to Yeats, insisting on the connection between Scotland and Ireland as nations in which the Celtic identity of the ancient past persists in the present and occupies the imagination with a sense of unrealised potential. In *To Circumjack Cencrastus* (1930), MacDiarmid writes that the immediate condition of Scotland is debased, as if wit has turned to ignorance, laughter to the joke, humanity to swine:

> I blink at Yeats as micht a man whom some
> Foul sorcery had changed into a pig,
> At Yeats, my kingly cousin, and mind hoo
> He prophesied that Eire 'ud hae nae Burns
> (Tho' it has tried to mair than aince) but haud
> Its genius heich and lanely – and think o' Burns,
> That Langfellow in a' but leid, and hoo
> Scots since has tint his maikless vir but hains
> His cheap emotions, puir ideas, and
> Imperfect sense o' beauty.[18]

In other words, MacDiarmid approves the solitary height Yeats occupies and recognises the liability, as well as the privilege, of the more common factor exemplified in Burns: a poet whose work and language were much more 'of the people' in a social sense, but whose distinctiveness as a poet was therefore susceptible to exaggeration, sentimentalisation and unsubtle degradation. A little later, MacDiarmid has a two-line poem entitled 'The Weapon':

> Scots steel tempered wi' Irish fire
> Is the weapon that I desire.[19]

Yeats and MacDiarmid offer new visions of Ireland and Scotland. Both were hypersensitive to the political cusp of their times: Scotland and Ireland in relation to the British Empire, from the era of the late nineteenth century (Scotland as North Britain, Ireland as subject nation) to the rising of 1916, the international example of the Soviet revolution in 1917, the catastrophe of

World War One, and the regeneration of the small Celtic nation as a state: the birth of nationalist politics to resist the destructiveness of empire, economically, but more, culturally, linguistically, as valid ground, the earth from which the poetry arises.

Ruins and Structures

After his visit to Ireland in 1928, MacDiarmid wrote two essays describing the experience and offering an assessment of Ireland in its current political state. After the international acclaim of the Irish literary movement that had arisen in the 1890s and continued to develop, especially in poetry and drama, and after the bloodshed and horrific martyrdom following the Easter Rising in 1916, the establishment of the Irish Free State in 1922 and the annexation of Ulster led directly to Civil War. MacDiarmid's comments from September 1928 are therefore of particular interest:

> Yeats expressed the opinion that the Saorstat Eireann is at present in the trough of the wave. The impetus that led to its establishment, and to the Irish revival has spent itself. The objective has for the most part been attained. What remains to be done is less inspiring than what has been accomplished. The abnormal efflorescence of Irish genius could not be maintained: the immediate future must be relatively mediocre. What are needed now are not poets and fiery propagandists and rebel leaders, but administrators, economists, and practical experts. [...] There is an uneasy feeling in the minds of many intelligent Irishmen that autonomy is a delusion as long as there remains financial over-control by a junta of international financiers. This leads a certain type of mind to depreciate what has been achieved; it leads another to assert that the Irish movement has been short-circuited and that it ought to have been carried out of the ambit of English control or influence altogether. There was a considerable measure of enthusiasm for the revival of Gaelic prior to the Treaty, but the Gaelic encouraging policy of the Government has practically killed that enthusiasm. It could only thrive in an atmosphere of opposition. [...] A straw shows the way the wind blows: the future of the Irish literary movement undoubtedly lies along the line of Gaelic integralism: the most important Irish poet since Yeats is F. R. Higgins, an out-and-out Republican, whose work owes much of its strength to its resumption of old bardic

technique. But, politically, in the meantime, the brains are emphatically with the Government, and the immediate need of the country is for just that patient, thorough, unspectacular work which its able young ministers are doing [. . .].[20]

In MacDiarmid's assessment there is an astute balance between recognition of *realpolitik* and the status and achievement of literature and the arts. In his attentiveness to the status of Gaelic, there is a sensitivity to the way language works as a property of literary artists and simultaneously as a property of people generally: as literary artifice in writing, and in common speech. In this, his experience was not only of Gaelic and English but also of his native Scots language. His interest in the development of a new Ireland, he said, was reciprocated: 'I found eager interest in the new Nationalist developments in Scotland and in Wales, and the feeling that through these might lie a solution of some of Ireland's most subtle difficulties.' The subsequent article, 'What Irishmen Think of Ireland: a visit to the Free State', concludes: 'I certainly found innumerable reasons [. . .] to rejoice that the destiny of Ireland was again in the hands of Irish people, and to envy them their opportunities in the light of what they had already achieved.' The political development of Ireland was an example he wished to follow, but the revolution in poetic form, in the transition from the nineteenth to the twentieth centuries, in the emergence of the literary movement still known as modernism, was equally something he wanted to learn from. Yeats served as a key example here.

The politics of a new Ireland, a new Scotland, preoccupied the public lives of both men. The heart of their artistic work was the reinvention of poetry in the twentieth century for their respective nations. And the poems are not shy of major historical events: Yeats, in 'Easter 1916', in 'The Second Coming' and in 'Nineteen Hundred and Nineteen', writing about Irish and international revolutionary politics. MacDiarmid, in *A Drunk Man Looks at the Thistle* (1926), writing 'The Ballad of the General Strike' and appropriating Yeats's *A Vision* (1925) to the ending of that poem to introduce the idea of cosmic change, universal revolution, viewed with a youthful hope.[21] For Yeats, the persistence of youth was a key, especially in the later poems. Yet it is always held in balance with a respect for the quality of greatness. There is a monumental sense of value in the friends of past days commemorated in 'The Municipal Gallery Revisited' or in the commitment to deliberating statesmanship which the 'sixty-year-old smiling public man' of 'Among

School Children' adheres to, or in the invocation to Irish poets who should learn their trade, scorning 'the sort now growing up / All out of shape from toe to top [. . .] Base-born products of base beds.' Yet even in such pontifications, the irrepressible humour is always proximate. Yeats might approve 'the indomitable Irishry' with all pomp and fixity, but when it comes to politics of any kind, he is still more tempted by 'that girl standing there': 'O that I were young again' indeed.[22] This is one of the qualities that draws us back to his poetry, another kind of humility, another kind of admission of vulnerability, a kind of humour he allows to give himself away. The quickness and the monumentality are both there, the ruins of great houses, old worlds, the shining structures of new political states, a world that was changing.

Yeats was considerably less familiar with working-class experience. He hardly ever entered a pub in his life.[23] Yet austere loneliness of a Yeatsian kind is a central proposition in the crucial poem of MacDiarmid's career, 'On a Raised Beach'. This is located in the Shetland archipelago, where he was living in the 1930s, in conditions of extreme poverty, spiritual and physical crisis and breakdown. The poem is a philosophical enquiry into the value of human life, measured against the geological scale of material reality, in the context of revolutionary struggles to bring about a better world – but at what cost? It begins with the poet alone, lying down on the stones of the raised beach, contemplating an island world empty of trees, flowing rivers, fecundity of any kind, populated only by bare stones. Yet the title of the volume in which this poem was first published, *Stony Limits*, comes from a line in Shakespeare's *Romeo and Juliet*: 'For stony limits cannot hold love out' (Act II, Scene ii, line 67). Just so, MacDiarmid's victory in the poem is to move from a solitary, first person singular, to a first person plural and a sense of the shared life of humanity, the attempt to make life worthwhile. His task was to embody both the commitments of residence and adaptation Yeats exemplified, but also to demonstrate the objective view of Joycean exile. And in his later, book-length poems in which Yeats and Joyce are both referred to and praised directly, the triumph hard-won in 'On a Raised Beach' yields a marvellously farraginous outpouring and celebration of different languages, arts, sciences and information of all sorts. Both Yeats and MacDiarmid were imaginatively engaged in writing into poetry the interpenetration of particular historical moments and universal revolutionary aspiration, responsible to all the people of their respective nations engaged in the former, and to the position of austere loneliness from which the latter might be confirmed.

Notes

This essay is based on a paper delivered at the 49th Yeats International Summer School at Sligo, Ireland, on 7 August 2008. I am grateful to the organisers for the invitation and opportunity, and to my colleagues, students, and the people of Sligo I talked with during that sojourn.

1   See R.F. Foster, *W. B. Yeats: A Life. I. The Apprentice Mage* (Oxford and New York: Oxford University Press, 1998), p. 276.
2   See Hugh MacDiarmid, *The Company I've Kept: Essays in Autobiography* (London: Hutchinson, 1966), pp. 192–4.
3   'What Irishmen Think of Ireland: Some Prominent Literary Men' and 'What Irishmen think of Ireland: A Visit to the Free State', in Hugh MacDiarmid, *The Raucle Tongue: Hitherto Uncollected Prose, Volume II*, eds Angus Calder, Glen Murray and Alan Riach (Manchester: Carcanet, 1997), pp. 193–5.
4   See Alan Bold, MacDiarmid: *Christopher Murray Grieve: A Critical Biography* (London: John Murray, 1988), pp. 233–4. See also 'Valedictory' [1977 BBC radio interview with Tom Vernon] in Hugh MacDiarmid, *The Thistle Rises: An Anthology of Poetry and Prose*, ed. Alan Bold (London: Hamish Hamilton, 1984), pp. 286–94 (p. 291).
5   W. B. Yeats, letter to Hugh MacDiarmid dated 4 March 1934 (Edinburgh University Library), in *My Dear Grieve: Letters to Hugh MacDiarmid (C. M. Grieve)*, ed. John Manson (forthcoming, Kennedy & Boyd, 2011).
6   See Hugh MacDiarmid, *New Selected Letters*, eds Dorian Grieve, Owen Dudley Edwards and Alan Riach (Manchester: Carcanet, 2001), pp. 128–9.
7   See, for example, 'C. M. Grieve, from Dunfermline Press, 5 August 1922, in Margery Palmer McCulloch (ed.), *Modernism and Nationalism: Literature and Society in Scotland 1918–1939. Source Documents for the Scottish Renaissance* (Glasgow: Association for Scottish Literary Studies, 2004), p. 23. See also, Margery Palmer McCulloch, *Scottish Modernism and its Contexts 1918–1959: Literature, National Identity and Cultural Exchange* (Edinburgh: Edinburgh University Press, 2009), pp. 17–18, 95. And also, 'Arne Garborg, Mr Joyce and Mr M'Diarmid' [by 'J. G. Utterstone Buglass', September 1924], in *Hugh MacDiarmid, The Raucle Tongue: Hitherto Uncollected Prose*, eds Angus Calder, Glen Murray and Alan Riach (Manchester: Carcanet 1996), Vol. 1, pp. 233–8.
8   See R. F. Foster, *W. B. Yeats: A Life. II. The Arch-Poet* (Oxford and New York: Oxford University Press, 2005), especially pp. 44–66.
9   See 'Valedictory' [1977 BBC radio interview with Tom Vernon], in Hugh MacDiarmid, *The Thistle Rises: An Anthology of Poetry and Prose*, ed. Alan Bold (London: Hamish Hamilton, 1984), pp. 286–94 (p. 289).
10 Hugh MacDiarmid, *The Revolutionary Art of the Future: Rediscovered Poems*, eds John Manson, Dorian Grieve and Alan Riach (Manchester: Carcanet, 2003), p. xv.
11 Declan Kiberd, 'W. B. Yeats – Building Amid Ruins', in *Irish Classics* (London: Granta Books, 2001), pp. 440–62 (p. 440).
12 Seamus Heaney, 'Yeats as Example?', in *Preoccupations: Selected Prose 1968–1978* (London: Faber and Faber, 1984), pp. 98–114.
13 Yeats, 'The Statues', in *The Poems*, ed. Daniel Albright (London: Everyman / J. M. Dent, 1994), pp. 384–5.

14 Lady Gregory, *Cuchulain of Muirthemne: The Story of the Men of the Red Branch of Ulster* (1902: Gerrards Cross: Colin Smythe, 1976) and *Gods and Fighting Men: The Story of the Tuatha de Danaan and of the Fianna of Ireland* (1904: Gerrards Cross: Colin Smythe, 1976). The term 'Kiltartanese' comes from Kiltartan, an area near Coole Park, where Lady Gregory lived and which Yeats visited.

15 Yeats, 'Cuchulain's Fight with the Sea', in *The Poems*, pp. 54–7.

16 MacDiarmid, 'Good-bye Twilight', *Collected Poems*, volume II, eds Grieve and Aitken (1978: Machester: Carcanet, 1994), pp. 1124–6.

17 MacDiarmid, 'Scottish Arts and Letters: the Present Position and Post-War Prospects (1942)', in Hugh MacDiarmid, *Selected Prose*, ed. Alan Riach (Manchester: Carcanet, 1992), pp. 152–70. See also Hugh MacDiarmid, *Lucky Poet: A Self-Study in Literature and Political Ideas*, ed. Alan Riach (1943: Manchester: Carcanet, 1994), pp. 354–5 and pp. 358–9.

18 MacDiarmid, *Complete Poems*, volume I, p. 185.

19 Ibid, p. 263.

20 MacDiarmid, *The Rauchle Tongue*, volume II, pp. 193–5.

21 MacDiarmid, *A Drunk Man Looks at the Thistle* (1926), annotated edition ed. by Kenneth Buthlay (Edinburgh: Scottish Academic Press, 1987), pp. 172–7.

22 Yeats, *The Poems*, 'The Municipal Gallery Revisited', pp. 366–8; 'Among School Children', pp. 261–3; 'Under Ben Bulben', pp. 373–6 ; 'Politics' p. 395.

23 See [unattributed] *Irish Literary Portraits: W. B. Yeats, James Joyce, George Moore, George Bernard Shaw, Oliver St John Gogarty, F. R. Higgins, AE: W. R. Rogers's broadcast conversations with those who knew them* (London: British Broadcasting Corporation, 1972), pp. 3–4.

On Cosmopolitanism and Late Style:
Lewis Grassic Gibbon and James Joyce

SCOTT LYALL

Edna Longley's wise reminder that 'comparative criticism, surely the *sine Qua non*, is harder work than trading in superficial parallels or imposing prepared templates' should give pause to the student of Irish-Scottish Studies.[1] It is tempting to unite the State without a complete historical nation with the nation without a fully independent State in a hyphenated critical amalgam.[2] Longley, however, calls attention to important asymmetries between Irish and Scottish cultural experience. She points in particular to the disputed place of Northern Ireland and calls for us to beware of aligning Ireland and Scotland too easily in some imagined Celtic fraternity of anti-metropolitan marginality.

Comparison of the work of Lewis Grassic Gibbon with that of James Joyce certainly requires us to bear Longley's counsel in mind. Gibbon and Joyce both occupy ostensibly anti-nationalist political positions. Yet each writer reveals stereotypical national (or perhaps, more accurately, denominational) prejudices when looking in opposite directions across the Irish Sea. Gibbon has splenetic moments of anti-Irishness, such as this from 'Glasgow' (1934): 'The South Irish of the middle class were never pleasant persons: since they obtained their Free State the belch of their pride in the accents of their unhygienic patois has given the unfortunate Irish Channel the seeming of a cess-pool.'[3] Equally, as Willy Maley points out, Joyce's 'references to Scotland are infrequent and generally uncomplimentary, and come back time and again to the question of Scotland's alleged or apparent complicity with England in the plantation of Ulster and the pursuit of empire'.[4]

In terms of any grounding in biography the relationship between Gibbon and Joyce is non-existent. Joyce never mentions Gibbon in any letters or criticism, and Gibbon mentions Joyce but briefly, most pertinently in his essay 'Literary Lights' from the 1934 book that Gibbon co-authored with Hugh MacDiarmid, *Scottish Scene*. Indeed, it was MacDiarmid who sought most firmly to ally his literary manifesto for the Scottish Renaissance movement with Joyce's avant-garde aims and credentials. MacDiarmid's first published collection of poems in Scots was *Sangschaw* from 1925, but his turn to the Vernacular, or the Doric, was justified theoretically two years previously in his *Scottish Chapbook* where, writing as C. M. Grieve, he draws comparison between John Jamieson's *Etymological Dictionary of the Scottish Language* (1808–9) and Joyce's *Ulysses*. The 'moral resemblance' discerned by Grieve between Jamieson's *Dictionary* and *Ulysses* indicates his far-sighted comprehension of the links between language, repression and the state of the body politic.[5] Grieve hopes that the deployment of a previously buried vernacular will produce a similar moral disturbance in Scotland as that caused by Joyce's censored masterpiece in Ireland; like the psychoanalysed who undertake a talking cure for repression, he wants the national cultural unconscious to find liberation in a 'tremendous outpouring' of words.[6] *A Drunk Man Looks at the Thistle*, MacDiarmid's 1926 odyssey of spiritual emancipation, is his Scots *Ulysses*; his later, more obscure attempt at the ultimate Joycean outpouring, *In Memoriam James Joyce* (1955), his own misunderstood and ill-received 'Work in Progress'. In spite of MacDiarmid's best efforts to position himself in the provocative role of Scotland's Joycean modernist pioneer, in 'Literary Lights' Gibbon alludes to the possibility, the desirability, yet the dearth of 'contemporary experimentation' in modern Scottish literature and the absence of what he calls a 'Scots James Joyce'.[7] Referring to his own work in the same essay, Gibbon wonders if his 'peculiar style' of adapting literary English to the spoken rhythms of Mearns-Scots in the yet to be completed trilogy *A Scots Quair* is fit to meet the demands of writing about urban experience, or whether his prose 'may not become either intolerably mannered or degenerate, in the fashion of Joyce'.[8]

Perhaps consciously covering his tracks, Gibbon's negative assessment of Joyce's late style masks the extent to which he attempted in certain regards to be that missing Scots Joyce he remarks upon in 'Literary Lights'. The two writers have more in common than has been commented on previously, particularly if the co-ordinates of comparison focus on nationalism and cosmopolitanism in relation to their respective late styles. Robert Crawford has argued in *Devolving English Literature* for a provincial modernism and while his book contains, for the present author certainly, a liberating central argument, I wish to dispute his terminology.[9] Provincial in location, perhaps – although cultural geography, of all things, is surely relative; but in values, ideas and artistry: no. To devolve still implies a subsidiary position to a controlling metropolitan power, and whilst it is almost unquestionably not Crawford's intention, 'provincial' remains a derogatory term, an inferior(ist) intellectual position and cultural location to inhabit. While the 'new cosmopolitans'[10] of contemporary academia and theory have sought to claim what they regard to be the anti-essentialist ethical upper hand in positioning themselves as anti-nationalist, the so-called provincial should not shy away from the ethical reclamation of cosmopolitanism. In what follows I will argue that Gibbon and Joyce are cosmopolitan modernists, but cosmopolitan modernists distinctly un-metropolitan in cohering to the pressured cultural specificities of their respective nations. In the work of Gibbon and Joyce we witness the attempted *cosmopolitanation* of modern Scottish and Irish cultural experience.

Exile

> 'Even today, the flight of the wild geese continues.'[11]

Joyce and Gibbon, like many modernist artists, both experienced exile from their respective native lands. Joyce first went to Paris in 1902, after graduating from University College, Dublin. He came back to Dublin the following year because his mother was dying (after her death he returned to Ireland twice, in 1909 and 1912, to seek a publisher for *Dubliners*, which appeared finally in 1914). 1904 saw his return to Continental Europe, this time with Nora Barnacle. The couple lived briefly in Pola, but Trieste, Zurich and Paris, the famous cosmopolitan signature cities of *Ulysses*, were Joyce's main homes from the outbreak of World War One until his death in 1941.

It is a commonplace of Joyce criticism that the author had a somewhat ambivalent attitude to Dublin and Ireland. This, according to Colin MacCabe, was exacerbated by the conservatism of William Cosgrave's 1922 Free State – 'the most reactionary in Europe'.[12] (Cosgrave was to be founder of the Irish fascist Blue Shirts, but it should be noted also that in 1922 Mussolini came to power in Italy.) In his influential *James Joyce and the Revolution of the Word*, first published in 1978 and 'written under the enormous impact of Barthes' *S/Z*', MacCabe argues that Joyce was forced to leave Ireland because there was no readership for his challenging and progressive work in a provincial and nationalist, morally purist State.[13] MacCabe claims that, 'deprived of an audience that would allow his texts to function politically, Joyce's writing becomes a more and more desperate attempt to deconstruct those forms of identification which had allowed the triumph of the national revolution to mean the very opposite of a liberation of Ireland.'[14] For Declan Kiberd, in contrast, Joyce has actually been deprived of a mass audience, most significantly for *Ulysses*, by the loss of a common culture. Kiberd's *Ulysses and Us* attempts, in some measure, to do for Joyce what Alain de Botton's *How Proust Can Change Your Life: Not a Novel* (1997) did for Proust: canonical modernist literature, usually seen as elitist, as self-help for the masses. Kiberd argues that *Ulysses* has been divorced from its intended ordinary readership through the increasingly transnational professionalisation of literary studies. Serious literature is now exiled in university departments where it is cut off from the public and dissected by academic specialists, many of whom 'reject the notion of a national culture'.[15] Unlike such critics, according to Kiberd, Joyce 'knew that national epics give people their ideas of what sorts of persons they should be'.[16]

In a lecture delivered in Trieste on 27 April 1907 called 'Ireland, Island of Saints and Sages', Joyce in exile gives his clearest critical account of what sort of nation he believes Ireland is and should be. Ireland may be a 'colonial country', but Joyce claims that 'nations have their ego, just like individuals', and he argues that the current revival of Irish culture, particularly the renaissance of Gaelic, demonstrates 'the demand of a very old nation to renew under new forms the glories of a past civilization'.[17] His talk is notable, however, for its emphasis on the impure, mixed nature of Irish racial ancestry and civilisation. 'Our [Irish] civilization is a vast fabric, in which the most diverse elements are mingled' and this means that 'it is useless to look for a thread that may have remained pure and virgin without having undergone the influence of a neighbouring thread.'[18] Miscegenation, for Joyce, is not a multicultural, cosmopolitan aim; it is a fact of national life.

Many critics have seen modernist exile, in general and in Joyce, as an aesthetic necessity in the rush from the philistine provinces to the centres of bona fide artistic action. For Malcolm Bradbury, for instance:

> Modernism is a metropolitan art, which is to say it is a group art, a specialist art, an intellectual art, an art for one's aesthetic peers; it recalls, with whatever ironies and paradoxes, the imperium of civilization. Not simply metropolitan, but cosmopolitan: one city leads to another in the distinctive aesthetic voyage into the metamorphosis of form. The writer may hold on to locality, as Joyce did on to Dublin [...]; but he perceives from the distance of an expatriate perspective of aesthetic internationalism.[19]

In this critical view it is as if modernist creators formed an elite transnational guild, based on the most scrupulous aesthetic standards, from which any embarrassing taint of provincial vulgarity must be barred. This generalising thematic emphasis on periodicity simplifies the complex biographical and socio-political relation of individual writers such as Joyce and Gibbon to their countries of origin. Joyce recognises that for the Irish artist 'the economic and intellectual conditions that prevail in his own country do not permit the development of individuality'.[20] In the Ireland of Joyce's era this stultification of individual and cultural development was a side-effect of the nation's political position as a British satellite. For Richard Rowan, in Joyce's play *Exiles*, set in Ireland, this necessitates a choice: 'If Ireland is to become a new Ireland she must first become European. [. . .] Some day we shall have to choose between England and Europe.'[21] In *Stephen Hero*, likewise, Ireland is described as 'an afterthought of Europe'.[22] In another Trieste lecture, this in 1910, Joyce perceives that Ireland 'has abandoned her own language almost entirely and accepted the language of the conqueror without being able to assimilate the culture or adapt herself to the mentality of which this language is the vehicle'; situated as such, Ireland 'has hounded her spiritual creators into exile'.[23] Provincialised in relation to the British centre, exile for the Irish writer is not simply a seeking after the aesthetic conditions conducive to the rarefied cosmopolitan artist, but a very real circumstance of nationality.

While Joyce came from a colonised nation, the position of Gibbon's Scotland was (and remains) less clear-cut. Born in 1901 as James Leslie Mitchell into a crofting family at Auchterless in Aberdeenshire, Gibbon, unlike Joyce, did not go to university, but left school to become a journalist, determined to escape farming life. He writes in 'The Land' (1934) of 'the hatreds of my youth' and of once having 'had a very bitter detestation for all this life of the land and the folk upon it'.[24] So when journalism in Aberdeen and Glasgow failed to work out for Gibbon the army provided the only route out of going back home to become a crofter. Joining the Royal Army Service Corps took Gibbon to the Near and Middle East – Egypt, Mesopotamia (now Iraq) and Palestine – in a period of travel and experience that was immensely influential for his fiction and beliefs. When Gibbon did come back to Britain after his military discharge he settled his family in Welwyn Garden City, southeast England. Aside from visits home, he did not live in Scotland again.

Gibbon, at least as the exiled novelist J. Leslie Mitchell, would arguably have approved of Stephen Dedalus's comment to his friend Davin in Joyce's

A Portrait of the Artist as a Young Man (1916): 'When the soul of a man is born in this country there are nets flung at it to hold it back from flight. You talk to me of nationality, language, religion. I shall try to fly by those nets.'[25] Gibbon's early fiction shares with Joyce's *Stephen Hero* and *Portrait* a certain ironical, callow pomposity of style and characterisation that is yet somehow suited to the parodic vivisection of modern life that each novelist undertakes. Both were to move from the individualism of their youthful *Bildungsroman* (or *Künstlerroman*, in the case of Joyce's *Stephen Hero* and *Portrait*) to the communalism of their national epics *Ulysses* and *A Scots Quair*. While Joyce's creative coruscation never loses sight of Ireland or Dublin, Gibbon's early work as Mitchell, such as his first novel *Stained Radiance* (1930), and the even more heavily autobiographical *The Thirteenth Disciple* (1931), ranges from Aberdeenshire to London to Central America. Without a settled location for the action Gibbon's style remains in flux between conventional narrative and rivulets of modernist interiority. Early Gibbon, like early Joyce, exteriorises ideas, not yet wholly assimilating these ideas in a fully matured style.

This stylistic externalisation of ideas is most obvious in Gibbon's diffusionism. Gibbon, an ardent Egyptologist, had been interested in prehistory and the beginnings of civilisation since his boyhood passion for archaeology. But his spell in the Middle East, and long reading sessions in the British Museum, drew him to the diffusionist theory. Diffusionism as imagined by Gibbon is the belief that primitives had lived in a Golden Age free from the purportedly constraining influences of civilisation. The Golden Age was a time of peace and freedom for its inhabitants who survived as hunter gatherers in an epoch of 'ultimate cosmopolitanism'.[26] However, the accidental flooding of the Nile basin produced agriculture and, with the adoption of agricultural practices, humans were tied to a particular community in which the restricting and divisive systems of civilisation began to develop. After this secular fall, we have all lived in exile. The Golden Age primitives created by Gibbon resemble the Noble Savage, a concept popularly attributed to Rousseau.[27] Like Rousseau, Gibbon thought human nature in its origins to be intrinsically good, but that a malign civilisation acted on the human personality as a distorting influence. This is contra to the Calvinist belief in original sin held by Gibbon's family, represented most strictly by his father, James. One speculates if, first and foremost, his adaptation of a utopian diffusionist theory was not so much a revolt against the powers-that-be of civilisation, but rather an unconscious act of rebellion by Gibbon against his father's patriarchal control and the narrow beginnings of his life at Bloomfield. From the grim limitations of provincial life emerged the fantasy freedoms of ultimate cosmopolitanism. Whatever its expressly psychological genesis may have been, for Gibbon, who was also an early convert to communism, diffusionism became a kind of replacement religion that he adapted for literary use in virtually all of his writings, even, in rather more sublimated form, in *A Scots Quair*. As the son of farm labourers Gibbon was proud of his peasant roots, yet it is an intriguing mark of the divisions of his own life that, as an author who fled so vigorously from the dreaded prospect of working the land, he advanced a theory which regarded agriculture as the source of the evils of modern civilisation.

Diffusionism had for Gibbon explicit political implications and he made himself diffusionism's propagandist. If humans had once been free then they could be so again. The diffusion, the migration of culture undermines the idea of distinct or pure national cultures. And diffusionism in Gibbon's hands also challenges the evolutionary and the imperialist concept of history as a timeline of progress into the future, a great chain of being led by the metropolitan nations of the West. As Ester, in *Image and Superscription* (1933), says of the 'fool lie' that humans are innately barbarous, 'We've been reared up on lies like that [. . .] Darwin began it, Haeckel – all those folk with Man the raving primordial beast 'n' his slow climb up to – *this!*'[28]

Joyce and Gibbon, in common with many modernists, conceived of History as a failed project. If the *Odyssey* is the published modern product of an ancient oral tradition then *Ulysses* is a modernist aural epic. Joyce tells us that Oscar Wilde called the Irish 'the greatest talkers since the Greeks', and *Ulysses*, like *A Scots Quair*, is certainly meant to be read aloud and heard.[29] Stephen Dedalus is trying to awake from the nightmare of history, and the narrative scaffold of the mock-epic *Ulysses* is famously provided by Homer's tale: the greatest story of western civilisation, and the cultural base of traditional western narrative history. Gibbon takes us back in his diffusionist imagination to an Arcadian pre-history to start civilisation again. Some of the ideological framework of Gibbon's *Sunset Song* has been freely adapted from the ancient sources mined by diffusionist W. J. Perry's *The Children of the Sun*, a 1923 study concerning the migrations and settlements of the pre-civilisation Indo-Egyptians. In Gibbon's view of modern civilisation, we are in the capitalist hell of pre-history: revolutionary history is yet to be achieved. In both *Ulysses* and *A Scots Quair* we find the movement through history from ancient to modern involves a loss of the sense of communal wholeness, a loss each author recognises as inevitable but is ambivalent about. A linear world history has given way to a circular view of history reflected in style and plot: Leopold Bloom walks unknowingly in Odysseus's tracks; Chris Guthrie, haunted by primitive ghosts, ends where she started in life, every chapter a time-loop back to the future. Each writer's refusal of History (as idea) stems from their respective nation's problematic history (as national narrative).

Revival/Renaissance

The national revivals in Ireland and Scotland in the early decades of the twentieth century were not parallel cultural experiences, but both can now be broadly seen as reactions to the centralising impulse of metropolitan British culture and, in the case of Ireland, colonialism. The case of Ireland must come with provisos, however, the most obvious being that the Anglo-Irish Literary Revival headed by W. B. Yeats was a largely Protestant programme of cultural recuperation. It can be argued that, somewhat in the manner of the current devolutionary political arrangements in the United Kingdom, the Yeatsian cultural revival was a bid by a ruling class, or caste even, to hold on to its waning political power – by giving a little, we keep more. If this argument has some purchase, and I believe it does, then Joyce's resistance to the Anglo-Irish Revival can be seen in a different, perhaps more nativist light than the standard interpretation often allows. This standard interpretation – let us call it the canonical Anglo-American liberal humanist interpretation – smoothly assimilates Joycean cosmopolitanism into the metropolitan canon on the basis, in part at least, of Joyce's resistance to the devolutionary nationalism of the Anglo-Irish Revival.[30] For this liberal critical line the Anglo-Irish Revival is the only palatable historical alternative to British imperialism; Joyce's much-touted pacifism, his objection to the physical force tradition in Ireland, would seem to condemn Republican national independence as extremist.

This view of the liberals is backed up by a passage from *Stephen Hero*:

> They wanted no foreign filth. Mr Daedalus might read what authors he liked, of course, but the Irish people had their own glorious literature where they could always find fresh ideals to spur them on to new patriotic endeavours. Mr Daedalus was himself a renegade from the Nationalist ranks: he professed cosmopolitanism. But a man that

was of all countries was of no country – you must have a nation before you could have art. Mr Daedalus might do as he pleased, kneel at the shrine of Art (with a capital A), and rave about obscure authors. In spite of any hypocritical use of the name of a great doctor of the Church [Aquinas] Ireland would be on her guard against the insidious theory that art can be separated from morality. If they were to have an art let it be a moral art, art that elevated, above all, national art,

> Kindly Irish of the Irish
> Neither Saxon nor Italian.[31]

The speaker here, Mr Hughes, is responding to a paper entitled 'Art and Life' that Stephen has delivered to the college debating society. Stephen's essay centres on his controversial reappraisal of Aquinas on art; it also mentions Ibsen and Maeterlinck, described by the president of the Jesuit Clonliffe College as 'these theistic writers'.[32] Mr Hughes, a law student and poet, is Joyce's name for Patrick Pearse: teacher, poet and one of the executed leaders of the 1916 Easter Rising.[33] Joyce, who skits the Celtic Twilight as the 'cultic twalette' in *Finnegans Wake*, nonetheless took classes in Irish with Pearse for two years and, significantly, in *Stephen Hero* the weekly Irish class held by Hughes takes place in O'Connell Street, named after the Liberator in the cause of Catholic emancipation, Daniel O'Connell.[34] Although he was put off by Pearse's negative attitude to English, Joyce appears to have been much more interested in the language than his hero Stephen, and so his resistance to Yeats's cultural programme cannot simply be ascribed to progressive Joycean cosmopolitanism opposing conservative Yeatsian cultural nationalism – the advance of a younger generation superseding the reaction of an older. Actually, according to Kiberd, Joyce was suspicious of 'the English substratum in the Irish revival'.[35] Stephen Dedalus, in *Portrait*, wants to 'forge' the 'uncreated conscience' of his 'race', and while the concept of race may make some contemporary readers understandably apprehensive, Deleuze and Guattari's oppositional definition of race is arguably pertinent here:

> The race-tribe exists only at the level of an oppressed race, and in the name of the oppression it suffers: there is no race but inferior, minoritarian; there is no dominant race; a race is defined not by its purity but rather by the impurity conferred upon it by a system of domination. Bastard and mixed-blood are the true names of race.[36]

Further, Stephen's 'soul frets in the shadow' of the English dean's language, and even though he wishes to awake from the nightmare of history in *Ulysses*, his comment, spoken by an Irish Catholic and so inevitably commended as anti-nationalist, is addressed significantly to the Unionist schoolmaster Mr Deasy, whose own reading of history is highly suspect.[37]

Gibbon's attitude to the Scottish Renaissance movement powered by MacDiarmid was as ambivalent, nuanced and easily misinterpreted as Joyce's position on the Yeatsian Anglo-Irish Literary Revival. Most of Gibbon's early writing, as well as more accomplished work such as *Spartacus* (1933), was published under his birth name and written in English. Gibbon as Mitchell was deeply influenced by H. G. Wells and his dream of Cosmopolis and a World Language, but ultimately renounced Wells for what he discerned as the elitism of Wells's social progressivism, his 'liberal fascism'.[38] While *The Time Machine* (1895), for instance, can be interpreted in Marxist terms, with Eloi and Morlocks representing capitalists and workers, superstructure and base in an unequal society, really the novel is a stark warning to the upper class to keep its house in order lest it be consumed by the barbarous proletariat. Significantly, a communist navvy spits with 'contempt' at the sight of a photograph of Wells in Mitchell's *Stained Radiance*.[39] Mitchell's good-natured, peaceable primitives in *his* science fiction, *Three Go Back* (1932) and *Gay Hunter* (1934), demonstrate the hope that a more egalitarian vision will triumph. The works Mitchell wrote under his pen-name are *Sunset Song* (1932), *Cloud Howe* (1933) and *Grey Granite* (1934), united as *A Scots Quair*; the short stories 'Greenden', 'Smeddum', 'Forsaken', 'Sim' and 'Clay', first published in *Scottish Scene*; and *Niger*, a biography of the Scottish explorer Mungo Park first published in 1934 by Edinburgh's Porpoise Press. The doubleness in the Gibbon/Mitchell oeuvre – 'English' Mitchell, 'Scottish' Gibbon – might constitute multi-vocal modernism *a la* Fernando Pessoa. Yet it is also reflective, I would argue, of the polarisation there has been, and continues to be, in Scottish experience between love of nation and leaving nation in emigration and exile. Indeed, David Craig finds the roots of the 'plangent emotion' of *A Scots Quair* in the exiled Gibbon's 'nostalgia for the countryside of his birth'.[40] In *Sunset Song* Will Guthrie, Chris's brother, leaves for the Argentine while Chris stays at home – as much a symptom of gender as national conditions. Gibbon, however, writes a duality into Chris's female experience that is an insightful and poignant expression of the over-determined association of nation and class in a provincialised environment.

So that was Chris and her reading and schooling, two Chrisses there were that fought for her heart and tormented her. You hated the land and the coarse speak of the folk and learning was brave and fine one day; and the next you'd waken with the peewits crying across the hills, deep and deep, crying in the heart of you and the smell of the earth in your face, almost you'd cry for that, the beauty of it and the sweetness of the Scottish land and skies. You saw their faces in firelight, father's and mother's and the neighbours', before the lamps lit up, tired and kind, faces dear and close to you, you wanted the words they'd known and used, forgotten in the far-off youngness of their lives, Scots words to tell to your heart how they wrung it and held it, the toil of their days and unendingly their fight. And the next minute that passed from you, you were English, back to the English words so sharp and clean and true – for a while, for a while, till they slid so smooth from your throat you knew they could never say anything that was worth the saying at all.[41]

English is not placed within inverted commas in Gibbon's text when Chris says 'you were English', yet clearly she has not literally become English: English, here, equals educated, denationalised middle-class Scots. Gibbon claims in the opening note to *Sunset Song* that his prose adapts what he calls 'the great English tongue' – elsewhere he calls English 'that lovely and flexible instrument' – but, equally, his novel characterises how English and its adoption alter and strain the Scottish subject.[42] English is talking fine, talking above your station. And while *A Scots Quair* is not straightforwardly Marxist it is a brilliant study of class in general and how class manifests in language registers in particular. This central theme is achieved through Gibbon's innovative modernist style cleaving to localism.

Having for much of his short but full writing career written in English, he declared in 1934, in 'Literary Lights', that the Scots cannot write English: 'The prose – or verse – is impeccably correct, the vocabulary is rich and adequate, the English is severe, serene ... But unfortunately it is not English. The English reader is haunted by a sense of something foreign stumbling and hesitating behind this smooth façade of adequate technique: it is as though the writer did not *write* himself, but *translated* himself.'[43] The 'essential foreignness' of Scots writing in English identified by Gibbon is reminiscent of Joyce's late style.[44] Gibbon does not define what constitutes that essential foreignness for him, but his own early Mitchell novels give a clue in their formality and stiffness of technique, their rather forced hyper-self-consciousness – although this might be explained as much by literary immaturity as through some sort of cultural incompatibility with English. Like the provincial social climbers of *Sunset Song* and *Cloud Howe* who attempt to talk proper English but make a hash of it, an excessively correct English prose style can seem unnatural – revealingly so. Gibbon may have questioned the literary sanity of Joyce's late style, yet, for all the stylistic experimentation of *Ulysses* and *Finnegans Wake*, and however difficult to pin down in *its* essential foreignness, Joyce's style is no provincial's mistranslation of Standard English. It is, rather, a translation, not only of different genres, periods and styles of writing into modernist parody, as in the 'Oxen of the Sun' chapter of *Ulysses*, but a translation also of an imperial language not entirely his own into a postcolonial English belonging to everyone and no-one.

Joyce said that *Ulysses* was about the last of the great talkers, which implies both loss and valediction.[45] *A Scots Quair* is also one long gossip where, like *Ulysses*, inverted commas are discarded and speech and storyline become one: narrative as blether. Like *Ulysses*, particularly in the figure of Bloom, only the most sympathetically portrayed, and, often, the most politically progressive characters of the *Quair*, such as, for instance, Chris, young Ewan, Chae Strachan and Long Rob, are exempt from the charge of gossiping. Gossip bonds, but it also destroys; it is universal, yet necessarily local: one must know the gossiper and the gossiped about for the bonding and invective of gossip to be effective. Fittingly enough for novels that valorise the ordinary, gossip stands as a symbol of the equivocal modernist response of *Ulysses* and *A Scots Quair* to the relationship between the local and the universal, the national and the cosmopolitan.

D. P. Moran's 1900 essay 'The Battle of Two Civilizations' has Ireland as a cultural and political battleground between the Anglo-Irish and their literary revival and the Gaelic nationalism of Irish Ireland. Joyce could not belong to either camp; rather, his wish that *Ulysses* should Hellenise his country seeks the *cosmopolitanation* of Ireland.[46] In *A Scots Quair* the essential battle to be waged is not between two supposedly incompatible cultures, Scots on the one hand and Anglo-Scots or English on the other, but is in fact the class war. Gibbon says in 'Glasgow' that the poverty of many of the people of the city during the Depression gives him the motive he had previously lacked to attack nationalism:

Small Nations. What a curse to the earth are small nations! Latvia, Lithuania, Poland, Finland, San Salvador, Luxembourg, Manchukuo, the Irish Free State. There are many more: there is an appalling number of disgusting little stretches of the globe claimed, occupied and infected by groupings of babbling little morons – babbling militant on the subjects (unendingly) of their *exclusive* cultures, their *exclusive* languages, their *national* souls, their *national* genius.[47]

Scotland is not mentioned here, but Gibbon's implication, particularly in relation to the Scottish Renaissance movement, is made aggressively clear. He does believe, however, that 'Braid Scots may yet give lovely lights and shadows not only to English but to the perfected speech of Cosmopolitan Man', and that the desperate economic conditions of Glasgow and Scotland may prompt the social revolution which will finally bring 'cosmopolitan freedom'.[48]

Ulysses, set on one day, but holding the national past and future within it, and *A Scots Quair* register the painful movement of their respective national cultures through the advance of capitalism into modernity, a movement eroding distinct national characteristics. But if novels narrate the nation then both *Ulysses* and *A Scots Quair* are distinctly national epics, for all their respective authors' complex ambivalence over national*ism*. Yet they are also examples of modernist cosmopolitanism, arguably in a truer sense than that of the assured metropolitan cosmopolitanism of modernist work by such as the early Eliot, Woolf and Proust – truer in that the *cosmopolitanation* of Joyce and Gibbon, performed in their unique adaptation of English to their own national narrative, apprehends the essential relatedness of cultures. In *Ulysses* the Irish-Jew Bloom – a character rooted in Dublin, yet archetypal of his wandering, exilic race – answers the Citizen's comment of 'We want no more strangers in our house' by saying that 'A nation is the same people living in the same place'.[49] This is a response the cosmopolitan Scot Lewis Grassic Gibbon would surely have agreed with.

Notes

1   Edna Longley, 'The Whereabouts of Literature', in Gerard Carruthers, David Goldie and Alistair Renfrew (eds), *Beyond Scotland: New Contexts for Twentieth-Century Scottish Literature* (Amsterdam and New York: Rodopi, 2004), p. 163.

2   On this point see Ray Ryan, *Ireland and Scotland: Literature and Culture, State and Nation, 1966–2000* (Oxford: Oxford University Press, 2002), in particular his Introduction, 'The Republic of Ireland and Scotland: What Difference Does it Make?', pp. 1–34.

3   Lewis Grassic Gibbon, 'Glasgow', in Lewis Grassic Gibbon and Hugh MacDiarmid, *Scottish Scene or The Intelligent Man's Guide to Albyn* (London: Jarrolds, 1934); reprinted in Valentina Bold (ed.), *Smeddum: A Lewis Grassic Gibbon Anthology* (Edinburgh: Canongate, 2001), pp. 106–7.

4   Willy Maley, '"Kilt by kelt shell kithagain with kinagain": Joyce and Scotland', in Derek Attridge and Marjorie Howes (eds), *Semicolonial Joyce* (Cambridge: Cambridge University Press, 2000), p. 210

5   C. M. Grieve, 'Causerie: A Theory of Scots Letters', *Scottish Chapbook*, 1:7 (1923); reprinted in Margery Palmer McCulloch (ed.), *Modernism and Nationalism: Literature and Society in Scotland 1918–1939: Source Documents for the Scottish Renaissance* (Glasgow: Association for Scottish Literary Studies, 2004), p. 27.

6   Ibid.

7   Gibbon, 'Literary Lights', in *Scottish Scene*; reprinted in *Smeddum*, p. 127.

8   Ibid., p. 135. Margery Palmer McCulloch is likely correct in her assessment that Gibbon is here referring to 'Work in Progress', published in 1939 as *Finnegans Wake*, although certain sections of *Ulysses* may have also prompted Gibbon's critical displeasure; see Palmer McCulloch, *Scottish Modernism and its Contexts 1918–1959: Literature, National Identity and Cultural Exchange* (Edinburgh, 2009), p. 152 (fn. 7).

9   Robert Crawford, 'Modernism as Provincialism', *Devolving English Literature* (1992: Edinburgh: Edinburgh University Press, 2000), pp. 216–70.

10   For an example of 'new cosmopolitanism' see, for instance, Berthold Schoene, *The Cosmopolitan Novel* (Edinburgh: Edinburgh University Press, 2009).

11   James Joyce, 'Ireland, Island of Saints and Sages' (lecture: 27 April 1907, Trieste); reprinted in Ellsworth Mason and Richard Ellmann (eds), *The Critical Writings of James Joyce* (London: Faber and Faber, 1959), p. 172.

12   Colin MacCabe, *James Joyce and the Revolution of the Word* (1978: Basingstoke: Palgrave Macmillan, 2003), p. 169.

13   Ibid., p. xxviii.

14   Ibid., pp. 169–70.

15   Declan Kiberd, *Ulysses and Us: The Art of Everyday Living* (London: Faber and Faber, 2009), p. 8.

16   Ibid., p. 14.

17   Mason and Ellmann (eds), *The Critical Writings of James Joyce*, pp. 163, 154, 157.

18   Ibid., p. 165.

19   Malcolm Bradbury, 'The Cities of Modernism', in Malcolm Bradbury and James McFarlane (eds), *Modernism: A Guide to European Literature 1890–1930* (1976: Harmondsworth: Penguin, 1991), p. 101.

20   Mason and Ellmann (eds), *The Critical Writings of James Joyce*, p. 171.

21   James Joyce, *Exiles: A Play in Three Acts* (1921: London: Paladin, 1991), p. 57.

22   James Joyce, *Stephen Hero*, ed. Theodore Spencer, foreword by John J. Slocum and Herbert Cahoon (London: Jonathon Cape, 1960), p. 58.

23   James Joyce, 'The Home Rule Comet' (lecture: 22 December 1910, Trieste); reprinted in Mason and Ellmann (eds), *The Critical Writings of James Joyce*, pp. 212–3.

24   Gibbon, 'The Land', in *Scottish Scene*; reprinted in Bold (ed.), *Smeddum*, p. 83.

25   James Joyce, *A Portrait of the Artist as a Young Man* (1916: London: Paladin, 1990), p. 207.

26 Gibbon, 'Glasgow', in *Scottish Scene*; reprinted in Bold (ed.), *Smeddum*, p. 108. See Scott Lyall, '"East is West and West is East": Lewis Grassic Gibbon's Quest for Ultimate Cosmopolitanism', in Michael Gardiner, Graeme Macdonald and Niall O'Gallagher (eds), *Scottish Literature and Postcolonial Literature: Comparative Texts and Critical Perspectives* (Edinburgh: Edinburgh University Press, 2011).

27 Ter Ellinngson, in *The Myth of the Noble Savage* (Berkeley, Los Angeles, London: University of California Press, 2001), argues that Rousseau neither invented nor endorsed the idea of the Noble Savage.

28 J. Leslie Mitchell, *Image and Superscription: A Novel* (London: Jarrolds, 1933), p. 225.

29 Joyce, 'Ireland, Island of Saints and Sages', in *The Critical Writings of James Joyce*, p. 174.

30 I am indebted to Emer Nolan's *James Joyce and Nationalism* (London and New York: Routledge, 1995) for enabling me to develop this point.

31 Joyce, *Stephen Hero*, pp. 107–8.

32 Ibid., p. 96.

33 Nolan, *James Joyce and Nationalism*, p. 44.

34 James Joyce, *Finnegans Wake* (1939: Harmondsworth: Penguin, 1976), p. 344.

35 Kiberd, *Ulysses and Us*, p. 46.

36 Joyce, *A Portrait of the Artist as a Young Man*, p. 257; Gilles Deleuze and Félix Guattari, *A Thousand Plateaus: Capitalism and Schizophrenia*, trans. Brian Massumi (1980: London: The Athlone Press, 1988), p. 379.

37 Joyce, *A Portrait of the Artist as a Young Man*, p. 194.

38 For the genealogy of this phrase see Philip Coupland, 'H. G. Wells's "Liberal Fascism"', *Journal of Contemporary History*, 35:4 (2000), pp. 541–58; and Jonah Goldberg, *Liberal Fascism: The Secret History of the American Left, from Mussolini to the Politics of Meaning* (London: Penguin, 2009), p. 21.

39 J. Leslie Mitchell, *Stained Radiance: A Fictionalist's Prelude*, intro. Ian Campbell (1930: Edinburgh: Polygon, 2000), p. 28.

40 David Craig, *Scottish Literature and the Scottish People, 1680–1830* (London: Chatto & Windus, 1961), p. 292.

41 Lewis Grassic Gibbon, *Sunset Song* (1932), in *A Scots Quair*, ed. and intro. Tom Crawford (1946: Edinburgh: Canongate, 1995), p. 32.

42 Ibid., xiii; 'Glasgow', in *Smeddum*, p. 107.

43 Gibbon, 'Literary Lights', in *Smeddum*, p. 125.

44 Ibid.

45 Nolan, *James Joyce and Nationalism*, p. 35.

46 James Joyce, *Letters, vol. II*, ed. Richard Ellmann (London: Faber and Faber, 1966), p. 109.

47 Gibbon, 'Glasgow', in *Smeddum*, p. 106.

48 Ibid., pp. 108, 109.

49 James Joyce, *Ulysses*, Annotated Students' Edition, intro. and notes Declan Kiberd (1922: Harmondsworth: Penguin, 1992), pp. 420, 430.

'That cry alone will last': Scottish and European Perspectives in Sorley MacLean's *An Cuilithionn / The Cuillin*

EMMA DYMOCK

While Sorley MacLean's long poem, *An Cuilithionn*, is often regarded as his most political poem, it could also be judged as one of his most experimental works. It is reasonable that MacLean's *Dàin do Eimhir*[1] can be viewed as a perfect example of a modernist text, complete with illustrations by William Crosbie to accompany its first publication, but *An Cuilithionn* nevertheless deserves to be placed alongside it as the epic poem in contrast to MacLean's shorter lyrics. This essay will take two approaches in order to provide different perspectives of the place of MacLean's poem within a modernist context. Its 'public' reception among his Scottish literary circle of friends will be studied, and *An Cuilithionn's* content will also be assessed in order to align it with some of the main characteristics of literary modernism, drawing on some of the writings of T. S. Eliot and Edwin Muir in the process. The Gaelic perspective played an important role within Scottish literary modernism and, to some extent, the Gaelic influence and the part it played in Scotland has only recently been fully acknowledged in significant ways.[2]

An Cuilithionn was composed in 1939 in seven parts and MacLean's commitment to communism and hatred of fascism is evident throughout. *An Cuilithionn's* content became something of an embarrassment to the poet in later years – his belief in Stalin as a hero during the composition of the poem meant that when more knowledge of Soviet atrocities became apparent MacLean tended to view *An Cuilithionn* as out-of-date. He appears to apologise for the poem in *O Choille gu Bearradh/ From Wood To Ridge: Collected Poems* when he writes: 'the behaviour of the Russian Government to the Polish insurrection in 1944 made me poetically as well as aesthetically disgusted with most of [*An Cuilithionn*].'[3] There is also a case for MacLean being too close to the subject matter at what was a very volatile period of European history. He goes on to write that 'I reprint here what I think tolerable of it'[4] adding to the assumption that it is an incomplete poem. Christopher Whyte has devoted a great amount of study to the manuscript versions of *An Cuilithionn* and his work has been invaluable in illustrating more fully the extent to which the poem has been altered, with lines and whole sections excised. He argues that two *An Cuilithionns* exist – the 1939 manuscript version and what is published of it to date in *Chapman* and *O Choille gu Bearradh.*⁵ However, despite these issues, *An Cuilithionn* still deserves attention as a late modernist 'epic'. Young men in MacLean's circle of friends were questioning the nature of heroism and assessing their principles regarding action and pacifism as well as exploring their literary stances and beliefs. *An Cuilithionn* can be viewed as a general meditation on human nature and a cathartic journey by MacLean into his own Gaelic history.

An Cuilithionn begins with a short introduction in which MacLean dedicates his poem to the eighteenth-century Gaelic poet Alexander MacDonald (Alastair mac Mhaighstir Alastair) and Hugh MacDiarmid, whom MacLean greatly admired and with whom he developed a close friendship in the late 1930s. This short dedication is actually very effective as a statement of intent in which MacLean is acknowledging both his own Gaelic tradition (as symbolised by an older Gaelic poet, albeit an innovative one) and modernism (as symbolised by MacDiarmid). In Part I the main voice in the poem ascends the Cuillin and ghosts of the Skye oppressors from history rise up and celebrate the exploitation, exile, and clearance.

Perhaps as an antidote to the despairing ending of Part I, Part II begins with the poet reaffirming that the Cuillin is with him in spite of life's horrors. His initiation with the Cuillin continues and the mountain takes on the characteristics of a primal mother figure and/or lover.

> a' cheud la phòg mi do ghruaidh
> b' e choimeas fiamh an Tuile Ruaidh;
> a' cheud la phòg mi do bhial
> dh'fhosgail Iutharn a dhà ghiall;
> a' cheud la laigh mi air d' uchd-sa
> ar leam gum faca mi an luchdadh
> aig na speuran troma, falbhaidh

> *The first day I kissed your cheek,*
> *its likeness was the face of the Great Flood;*
> *the first day I kissed your mouth*

hell opened its two jaws;
the first day I lay on your breast
I thought I saw the loading
of the heavy swift skies.[6]

There is a definite case for viewing this section from a psychoana-
lytical perspective and MacLean's friend, the Classical scholar and Scottish
Renaissance figure, Douglas Young, also notes the possibilities inherent in
this part of the poem. Writing to MacLean on 26 June 1940 he states that:

> These passages gave me very strongly the sensations of physical and
> psychological effort in climbing steep mountains, and contribute to
> the intensity of the whole poem by a stimulation of the sub-conscious.
> Mountaineering has been said in the usual jargon to be a sublimation
> of the urge to copulation. You have, perhaps unknowingly, worked on
> that at a few places.[7]

There is a clear difference between this sort of passage and traditional
Gaelic poetry of the past. Eighteenth-century poems such as Duncan Bàn
MacIntyre's 'Moladh Beinn Dobhrain' showed an awareness of nature and
landscape,[8] while the concept of the sublime is prevalent in Gaelic nature
poetry of the nineteenth century,[9] but MacLean's psychological 'coupling'
with the mountain is a far more modern device.

In Part III the morass (which has previously been mentioned in Part II of
the poem as an actual landscape feature below the Cuillin ridge) takes on a
greater symbolic significance as a world-wide bog which swallows everything
in its path. In this section of the poem the Skye Stallion is mentioned for the
first time. Like the morass of Mararabhlainn, the 'Stallion' is also a real landscape feature; the sea-cliff at Waternish. MacLean wishes that he had been
in the Stallion's saddle in order to catch up with the brilliance of the poetry
of Hugh MacDiarmid and Alexander MacDonald, showing a perhaps typically twentieth-century self-consciousness regarding his poetry. He describes
the mountain as the place where contradictions and polar opposites can exist
together and he uses Christ and Lenin to illustrate this point. For a self-
proclaimed communist who had been brought up on the island of Raasay
where he had been well versed in the beliefs of the Free Presbyterian Church,
the religious and political figures of Christ and Lenin respectively were

understandably obvious personal signifiers for him, but there are also shades of G. Gregory Smith's and MacDiarmid's 'Caledonian Antisyzygy' in these contrary figures, placed as they are within his local and poetic landscape.

Part IV further highlights the poet's despair. The morass makes his ascent up the mountain more difficult and a personal struggle ensues. He writes:

Cus dhen bhoglaich na mo spioraid,
cus dhen mhòintich na mo chridhe,
cus dhen ruaimle na mo bhuadhan:
ghabh mo mhisneachd an tuar ghlas.

Too much of the morass in my spirit,
too much of the bog in my heart,
too much of the scum in my talents
my courage has taken the grey hue.[10]

If the bog symbolises all that he sees is wrong with the world including capitalism and the bourgeois, it is interesting that he turns this hopelessness in on himself as well. He is not simply an onlooker in this modern landscape of despair but in fact, an active victim and participant in the struggle. As a positive answer to the depths of the poet's misery, Part V is the point in which hope begins to take hold with the arrival of the Skye Stallion – the symbol of the rising power of socialism. It is the turning point and 'lyrical peak' of the poem with the energetic, surging spirit of the Stallion stamping the oppressors of the masses into the bog. As the Stallion leaps from peak to peak the Cuillin also becomes charged with energy. To underline this point, Part V ends with a Gaelic translation of MacDiarmid's poem, 'If there are bounds to any man'.[11]

In Part VI new voices from the past begin to encroach into the poem and MacLean's voice gives way to a female perspective. The girl from Gesto describes her hardships and her longing for Skye after she has been forcibly taken into slavery to work in America. The voice of Clio, Muse of history, takes over and she recounts the fate of mankind through the ages, beginning with Skye and the Highlands and moving further afield to encompass Europe and the rest of the world. It is in this sixth part of the poem that the modernist trait of multiple narrative points of view and overlapping voices is at its strongest. The Gesto girl, taken from Gaelic oral tradition,[12] appears to be the voice of a past golden age of Highland history:

agus a chaoidh cha ruig mi fàire
om faic mi Loch Harport 's taigh mo mhàthar
far an robh cridhealas is gàire
aig luaidhean ri linn mo chàirdean;

and never may I reach a horizon
to see Loch Harport and my mother's house
where there was warmth and laughter
at waulkings in the time of my people.[13]

Clio, on the other hand, is not rooted in the past but is all around, a timeless presence transcending linear time:

'S mise Clio an t-saoghail:
tha mo shiubhal sìorruidh, aognaidh,

I am Clio of the world:
my wandering is eternal and chill with death.[14]

There is actually nothing new in employing the female voice in traditional Gaelic poetry – the tradition is full of the women's voices in what MacLean describes as the 'old songs' and it could be surmised that he is employing this traditional device here.[15] However, what makes this inherently modern is the way in which the voices mingle – the timeline is disjointed and the Gesto girl's local narrative informs the meta-narrative of human development, oppression and heroism as described by Clio.

In Part VII MacLean's vision has turned from the past to the more timeless and limitless space of the eternal in which all heroes become as one in the quest for justice and the end of suffering through self-sacrifice. Like many modernist texts, the Classical allusions are overt. Prometheus becomes one of the central figures and fulfils the role of individual hero for mankind against the established gods. MacLean uses these Classical myths to inform his very modern frustrations and disillusionment, acknowledging in the process other poets, such as Shelley, who have used Prometheus as their inspiration. In surrealist fashion the mountain becomes the site of events which the poet sees as significant, irrespective of place and time. Thus it becomes a 'world mountain' with the rebels of the Easter Rising and the Glasgow funeral procession of

John Maclean winding up the 'streets' of the mountain while the chains of Tatu Ho swing between the mountain peaks. However, the last section of Part VII focuses on the poet's personal identity and experience – he glimpses a spirit, the naked ghost of the heart and brain who journeys a little in front of him and whom he cannot catch up with or fully comprehend. He writes:

Có seo, có seo oidhche chinne?
Chan eil ach samhla an spioraid,
anam leis fhéin a' falbh air sléibhtean,
ag iargain a' Chuilithinn 's e 'g éirigh.

Who is this, who is this in the night of mankind?
It is only the ghost of the spirit,
a soul alone going on the mountains
longing for the Cuillin that is rising.[16]

While MacLean is clear that he has rejected the Free Church belief system,[17] there is nevertheless a clear revelation of hope for mankind with this vision of 'am falbhan/the journeying one' at the end of the poem operating on a personal level. Like many modernist writers MacLean was scrutinising the traditional authorities of God and religion but this did not stop him from yearning for a personal spiritual experience.

MacLean gained a First Class degree in English at Edinburgh University in 1934 and it was during these years that he familiarised himself with, and deepened his understanding of, poets such as W. B. Yeats, T. S. Eliot, Ezra Pound and Hugh MacDiarmid as well as movements in literature such as Romanticism and modernism. MacLean was constantly reshaping his ideas and stances regarding his own work and his sense of Gaelic heritage or 'dùthchas'. While there is obvious Gaelic historical and literary content woven throughout *An Cuilithionn*, there can be no doubt that its structure and outlook was a departure for Gaelic poetry. The multitude of voices which take over from the poet's singular voice later in the poem hint at a decentring of the subject, and the style and rhythm, often mimicking old Gaelic metres, was another way of introducing various 'voices' in the poem.[18] It is not too difficult to imagine the image of a land ravaged by the Clearances as a 'Gaelic' version of T. S. Eliot's wasteland. However, it is the Cuillin itself as multi-faceted symbol ranging from the embodiment of hope and heroism, the meeting place of mind, body, and spirit, the mother breasts of the world, and at the same time of thrusting, antlered power[19] that best sums up the parallels between *An Cuilithionn* and MacDiarmid's constantly changing thistle in 'A Drunk Man Looks at the Thistle'. This is not to say that the two poems necessarily share the same purpose but the same visionary scope and energy is present in both poems. In a letter to Douglas Young, dated 7 September 1941 MacLean admits to Young:

> I think you exaggerate Grieve's influence on my style. He has very little and it is very superficial but he constantly stirs me emotionally and intellectually. I am not one of Hugh's sons in poetry. In fact I think the vast gulf of difference between his mental set up and mine makes that impossible.[20]

MacLean is clearly aware of their differences but in this letter MacLean also pinpoints MacDiarmid's emotional and intellectual impact on him and, if this point is followed to its logical conclusion, it may be that MacDiarmid's impact on MacLean was largely driven by the spirit of modernism itself. Discussing the lyrics of *Sangschaw* and *Penny Wheep* with Young in the same letter as above, MacLean writes: 'I regarded them in much the same way as I regarded the greatest things of Blake's, things completely new and unbelievable.'[21] This statement encapsulates the modernist philosophy of 'making things new'. MacLean also set out to achieve something new for his own language and culture with *An Cuilithionn*. In his essay, 'My Relationship with the Muse' he elaborates on how his long poem came into being:

> It was in Mull in 1938 that I conceived the idea of writing a very long poem, 10,000 words or so, on the human condition, radiating from the history of Skye and the West Highlands to Europe and what I knew of the rest of the world. Its symbolism was to be, mostly, native symbolism [...] The idea came from *The Drunk Man* [...] The long poem was always to me a *faute de mieux* as compared with the lyric but I have come to regard it as a necessity if poetry is to deal adequately with much of the human condition.[22]

In many ways *An Cuilithionn* is a product of modernism but with the added ingredient of politics – the Russian Revolution was the catalyst to fuse political radicalism and utopianism with a more political stance and MacLean's Marxism is evidently the driving force in the poem in contrast to Hugh MacDiarmid's nationalism. MacLean's hopes lie in a radical change of political and social organisation.

While MacLean shares the sense of frustration and need for change with many of his fellow poets of the 1930s, he is likewise very aware of his own tradition and his influences. *An Cuilithionn* is a very self-conscious poem and MacLean constantly looks back to his own tradition throughout the poem. One of the instances when this is most noticeable is in Part III in his mention of Màiri Mhór, the great Skye poet of the nineteenth century. In this section he appears to be embarrassed that his generation does not possess the greatness of the past:

> Ach chan fhaca mi a' mhórachd
> 's feumar stad far am fóghainn,
> Sgitheanach ri taobh Màiri Móire.
> Ach chan inns mi dh' a spiorad làidir
> nach tàinig tilleadh air an tràigh ud;
> seachnaidh mi clàr treun a h-aodainn
> 's mo sgeul air buaidh ar n-Eilein traoighte.

> *But I did not see the greatness*
> *and I must stay where it suffices,*
> *a Skyeman by the side of the great Mary.*
> *But I will not tell her strong spirit*
> *that no turning has come on that ebb-tide;*
> *I will avoid her brave forehead,*
> *as my tale is of the ethos of the island ebbed.*[23]

For MacLean, Màiri Mhór is not just a distant memory – her presence is very much alive in *An Cuilithionn*. While the Highland Clearances and the subsequent Land Agitation can be classed as one episode within Highland history, MacLean's admiration for Màiri Mhór is not based upon a fascination with 'dead' voices – Màiri Mhór's poetry, with its strong call for social justice is as pertinent in MacLean's time as it was in the nineteenth century and a vibrant Gaelic oral culture enables the past to become more immediate. MacLean channels these voices from oral tradition and, in the process, his own voice recedes in the face of the eternal sufferings of mankind. It is perhaps not difficult to compare what MacLean is doing here with T. S. Eliot's stance in his 1919 essay 'Tradition and the Individual Talent'. Eliot writes:

> The progress of an artist is a continual self-sacrifice, a continual extinction of personality. [. . .] And the poet cannot reach this impersonality without surrendering himself wholly to the work to be done. And he is not likely to know what is to be done unless he lives in what is not merely the present, but the present moment of the past, unless he is conscious, not of what is dead, but of what is already living.[24]

In some ways, it is perhaps natural for MacLean to do this, with his perception of the Gaelic oral tradition and clan mindset in which the individual often gives way to a more collective outlook. However, MacLean's sense of tradition and the individual was not solely directed by his Gaelic background. This would be to simplify the situation and also deny MacLean's poetry its internationalist scope. MacLean begins in his own land and culture in Part I and II of *An Cuilithionn* but as the poem progresses he moves out from his own locality to encompass Europe and the whole world. MacLean was as horrified about events such as the Spanish Civil War as he was about the Clearances and other Highland events. This is because the plight of humanity as a whole is what is at the root of MacLean's vision – this can be linked to his socialism but equally it can be connected to the influence of modernism. In 1918 Edwin Muir wrote about modernism and other movements connected to it:

> It is not sufficient that movements should be new – if they are ever new; the question is, to what end are they? If they are movements in the direction of emancipation, 'the elevation of the type Man', then they are modern. [. . .] If modernism be a vital thing it must needs have roots in the past and be an essential expression of humanity to be traced, therefore, in the history of humanity: in short, it can only be a tradition. The true modern is a continuator of tradition.[25]

MacLean writes in Part VII of *An Cuilithionn*:

Latha dhomh sa' Chuilithionn chreagach
chuala mi phìob mhór 'ga spreigeadh,
nuallan cinne-daonna freagairt,
an eanchainn 's an cridhe leagte.

I was one day in the rocky Cuillin,
I heard the great pipes incited,
the roar of mankind in answer,
brain and heart in harmony.[26]

His hope is that if brain and heart can be in harmony then mankind will be able to reject the old order of capitalism and reach its true potential. In *An Cuilithionn* he is calling for a rising up of the masses across the world, not just a reinvigoration of his own Gaelic culture. His vision is as all-encompassing and groundbreaking as the modernist movement itself but the effectiveness of *An Cuilithionn* lies in MacLean's intimacy and knowledge of the local first and foremost, rather than the universal. His originality comes from the fact that he uses his tradition as a foundation for his philosophical ideas, and thus develops modern Gaelic concepts and meanings of locality and identity in the process.

If modernism is all about progression, the capacity for mankind to move forward and achieve 'the heights', then *An Cuilithionn* certainly fits the definition of a modernist poem, with MacLean's ascent of the Cuillin acting as a fitting metaphor for reaching new literary 'heights'. It is clear that MacLean's peers believed this to be true also. Hugh MacDiarmid wrote to MacLean that receiving *An Cuilithionn* had been 'a tremendous event' in his life[27] but it is perhaps the letters between Douglas Young and MacLean that give us the most insight into the impact of *An Cuilithionn* on the Scottish intelligentsia. On the 26 June 1940 Young wrote:

> This is very great poetry.
>
>   In literature, apart from Aeschylus' Prometheus, Sophokles' Oidipous at Kolonos, and one or two passages of Dante and Goethe, I cannot think of any sustained flight on a similar scale which keeps on a plane of such intensity and ardour. But the comparison is rather with music, with one of the great symphonies or quartets of Beethoven. I

refer to the recapitulation in different forms [. . .] and the way in which you have used different metres to give the effect a musician attains by modulation into different keys.[28]

The musical reference is interesting. In 1940 George Davie was keen for MacLean to meet the composer F. G. Scott who had been given a copy of *An Cuilithionn*. However, while Scott had set some of MacDiarmid's poetry to music, his potential treatment of MacLean's work may have been more difficult. In an example of tradition and innovation in opposition, Davie hints that Scott viewed Gaelic traditional metres as outdated and in need of an injection of modern styles.[29] It may be that a non-Gaelic speaker such as F. G. Scott failed to fully appreciate the very modern way MacLean was incorporating traditional styles with freer forms in his poetry and a proper study of metre and musicality in modern Gaelic poetry in context with more widespread stylistic and musical progressions would be a welcome addition to this field. Musical compositions aside, it is clear that *An Cuilithionn* created something of a stir among those with Scotland's modern literary interests at heart. Douglas Young writes on the subject of *An Cuilithionn*:

> I don't know if you would want to challenge comparison with Grieve's rants, or Blake or Nietzsche. But I should put it above any of them on the ground of more thorough [. . .] intensity of passion, and I think more skill in exposition. However my judgement may be biased here by the facts that I know you personally, (though not so well as I hope to yet), and I am naturally attracted by this theme, and have long been looking for a really great poem in Gaelic of interest to modern men everywhere.[30]

This last sentence especially is reminiscent of MacDiarmid's Gaelic Idea of the 1930s – the modern answer to the destruction of Gaelic culture in Scotland. MacDiarmid hoped to build Scotland back up, firstly with the use of Scots and then as time went on, he viewed Gaelic as the real answer, the 'Ur' language of Scotland which was, in his mind, of an older tradition and more firmly established than Scots.[31] Young, also a nationalist like MacDiarmid, was perhaps alluding to this hope that Gaelic would become great in a truly modern sense – it is understandable that a long poem like *An Cuilithionn* would provide him with this hope. It may be that *An Cuilithionn*, with its epic scope, was the type of literature which MacDiarmid longs for in a long poem such as *To Circumjack Cencrastus*. George Davie also wrote to MacLean that 'without question, your poem is the most important event in Scots literature since the advent of Grieve in the Scottish Chapbook.'[32] In their minds, MacLean was giving an authentic Gaelic voice to their Gaelic Idea. Young told MacLean on 29 July 1940 that he had shown *An Cuilithionn* to

> my much respected friend Prof. R. M. Henry, the old Ulsterman, who is some judge, having been reading the best things in half a dozen languages for fifty years, having been acquainted with the leading literary figures in the Irish revival for over forty years, and having a reading knowledge of Irish Gaelic.[33]

The fact that he did so shows that Douglas Young was not only aware of the Scottish Renaissance, but also its precursor, the Irish Renaissance, and he viewed MacLean as having a place within this tradition. It is also noticeable that Young compared *An Cuilithionn* with Classical and Renaissance literature[34] and, while this may simply be due to Young being very well read and enthusiastic about other languages and cultures as well as being a Classical scholar himself, Edwin Muir's words about modernism come to mind in instances such as this:

> Meantime, for this tradition may be claimed with confidence such events as Greek Tragedy, the most of the Renaissance and the emancipators of last century.[35]

Young writes to MacLean on 29 July 1940 regarding *An Cuilithionn*:

> What comes home very intimately to the heart is the pervasive generality of the theme; it is not a study of someone's private disaster [. . .] I should say what gives it, for me, most of its power is that it is the best expression of the voice of the people.[36]

This idea of the 'voice of the people', a collective voice overriding the individual personality, is reminiscent of the belief held by writers such as T.S. Eliot that modern literature calls for the self-sacrifice of the poet's identity in order for the tradition to continue. However, it is also very 'Gaelic' in essence since the role of the poet or bard was as the voice of the people. Therefore it could be argued that the supposedly contrasting notions of tradition and innovation sit well with a Gaelic poet like MacLean in particular, whose awareness of himself as a modern-day bard as well as a poet conversant with his place within the modernist movement means that he stands as a significant figure in twentieth-century Scottish literature, bridging the gap between the past and the present.

In conclusion, *An Cuilithionn* provides a valuable contribution to the study of Scottish modernism, not only because of its content and general themes, but also because of the role it assumed in the minds of Scottish writers of the period, who viewed it as an important progression within Scottish literature. It was duly scrutinised by those who were themselves very conscious of Scotland's position within a greater European tradition. While *An Cuilithionn* was delayed in its publication, affecting its reception from a wider readership, its background and history within the Scottish literary circle of the 1940s provides a snapshot of a specific time and mindset and provides a Gaelic response to the modern Scottish literary situation as well as to the political situation in Europe and beyond. *An Cuilithionn* proves that tradition and innovation can exist side by side but that in spite of these 'higher' literary concerns of the intelligentsia who were debating the *zeitgeist* of the nation, there is also a place within modernism for the more immediate sociopolitical concerns of the people. With the current interest in interdisciplinary study and cross-cultural links, the field of Gaelic studies is starting to more fully realise the potential of its literature in the wider world. However, in many ways, figures of the Scottish Renaissance such as Hugh MacDiarmid, Sorley MacLean and Douglas Young were already exploring these avenues, which is the main reason why their poetry and ideas are still of such importance long after their own current political and literary realities have altered and progressed.

Notes

1   Sorley MacLean, *Dàin do Eimhir agus Dàin Eile/ Poems to Eimhir and Other Poems* (Glasgow: William Maclellan, 1943).

2   See for example Margery Palmer McCulloch's *Scottish Modernism and its Contexts 1918–1959* (Edinburgh: Edinburgh University Press, 2009) for a discussion of Hugh MacDiarmid's fascination with the Highlands and Gaelic culture and the place of Gaelic within his vision for modern Scotland. Susan Wilson's recently published *The Correspondence Between Hugh MacDiarmid and Sorley MacLean: An Annotated Edition* (Edinburgh: Edinburgh

University Press, 2010) explores the relationship between Gaelic, Scottish Modernism and the Scottish Renaissance through the letters of MacDiarmid and MacLean. The contribution of epistolarity in the study of the Scottish literati is invaluable in assessing their attitudes, ideas and philosophical beliefs within a modernist context and I am currently editing the correspondence between Sorley MacLean and Douglas Young in order to add another facet to this period of literary and cultural resurgence.

3 Sorley MacLean, *O Choille gu Bearradh/ From Wood to Ridge: Collected Poems* (Edinburgh: Carcanet/ Birlinn, 1999), p. 63.

4 MacLean, *O Choille gu Bearradh*, p. 63.

5 For the instalments of 'An Cuilithionn' see *Chapman*, 50–51 (Summer 1987), 158–63; 52 (Spring 1988), 36–49; 53 (Summer 1988), 68–74; 54 (Autumn 1988), 58–69; 55–6 (Spring 1989), 152–63; and 57 (Summer 1989), 30–9. Also, MacLean, *O Choille gu Bearradh*, pp. 63–131. Christopher Whyte's edition of the 1939 *An Cuilithionn* was published in 2011 by the ASLS and has allowed the poet's original vision and thought processes in relation to the genesis of *An Cuilithionn* to be seen properly for the first time. For the purpose of this essay, I will be referring to *An Cuilithionn* as it appeared in *O Choille gu Bearradh*.

6 MacLean, *O Choille gu Bearradh*, pp. 76–7. This translation is by Sorley MacLean, as are all subsequent translations from the original Gaelic into English throughout this chapter. Page numbers refer to the Gaelic original and the English translation.

7 MS 29540, f.15, Letters from Douglas Young to Sorley MacLean, National Library of Scotland. I would like to thank the Trustees of the National Library of Scotland for their permission to publish extracts from the Sorley MacLean–Douglas Young Correspondence.

8 See William Gillies, 'The Poem in Praise of Ben Dobhrain', *Lines Review* 63 (1977), pp. 42–8 for a more detailed commentary of the poem and its themes in relation to nature and mankind.

9 See Donald Meek, '"Nuair Chuimhnicheam an Cuilithionn": Àite Samhlachail na Tìre is Cruth na Tìre ann am Bàrdachd Ghàidhlig na Naoidheamh Linn Deug' in Wilson McLeod and Máire Ní Annracháin (eds.), *Cruth na Tíre*. (Dublin: Johnswood Press, 2003), pp. 1–38. Donald Meek's research on nineteenth-century Gaelic landscape poetry and the sublime shows how Gaelic poetry developed alongside Romanticism and thus it is not difficult to see how this influence from the 'outside' can similarly be applied to twentieth-century Gaelic poetry and modernism.

10 MacLean, *O Choille gu Bearradh*, pp. 94–5.

11 MacLean, *O Choille gu Bearradh*, pp. 104–05. 'If there are bounds to any man' is taken from Hugh MacDiarmid's *Second Hymn to Lenin and Other Poems* (London: S. Nott, 1935); *Complete Poems 1920–1976* ed. by Michael Grieve and W. R. Aitken (London: Martin Brian & O'Keeffe, 1976), p. 555.

12 On 19 August 1940 MacLean wrote to Douglas Young that 'The emigrant girl passage is quite original based only on the story that such a girl, kidnapped from Gesto shore, was responsible for the rhymed list of Skye placenames of which I have two lines in the Cuillin'. Acc 6419 Box 38b, National Library of Scotland. Douglas Sealy writes 'The girl who was kidnapped in Gesto [and sold into slavery in America] is said to have been met by a Highlander in the King's army in America who asked her the time. She could not understand his English or his French, but when he spoke in Gaelic she replied: "am crodhadh chaorach mu dhà thaobh Beinn Dubhagraich" (It is the time one folds the sheep on the slopes of Beinn Duagraich).' Douglas Sealy, 'Out from Skye to the World: Literature, History and the Poet' in Raymond J. Ross and Joy Hendry (eds) *Sorley MacLean: Critical Essays* (Edinburgh: Scottish Academic Press, 1986), pp. 53–79 (pp. 59–60).

13 MacLean, *O Choille gu Bearradh*, pp. 106–07.

14 MacLean, *O Choille gu Bearradh*, pp. 116–17.

15 For a full article on MacLean's admiration for the 'old songs' of Gaelic tradition and how they influence his own work see 'Old Songs and New Poetry' in William Gillies (ed.) *Ris a' Bhruthaich: The Criticism and Prose Writings of Sorley MacLean* (Stornoway: Acair, 1985), pp. 106–19.

16 MacLean, *O Choille gu Bearradh*, pp. 128–31.

17 In a letter dated 7 September 1941, MacLean wrote to Douglas Young 'At the age of twelve I began to get over my Secederism. I was never properly reconciled to it even as a child … since only about 2 or 3 per cent, even of Seceders, were to be saved (judging by communion table statistics) it was impossible that any more than one or two of the people I loved most would be "saved". Salvation without them was a desolate prospect.' Acc 6419, Box 38b, National Library of Scotland.

18 For example, in Part VI of 'An Cuilithionn', directly after the Gesto girl section, the praise lyric for Skye is in simple strophic form (MacLean, *O Choille gu Bearradh*, pp. 108–09), very much in the style of seventeenth-century poets such as Iain Lom and Mary MacLeod, thus echoing the 'voices' of these poets. Sealy, p. 60.

19 For a lengthier article on the multi-faceted symbol of the mountain in MacLean's 'An Cuilithionn' see Emma Dymock, 'Interpreting the symbol of the Cuillin: The relationship between Sorley MacLean's "An Cuilithionn" and his "Cuillin praise poem"' in Colm Ó Baoill and Nancy R. McGuire (eds.), *Scottish Gaelic Studies*, Vol. XXV (Aberdeen: University of Aberdeen, 2009) pp. 143–80.

20 Acc 6419, Box 38b, National Library of Scotland.

21 Acc 6419, Box 38b, National Library of Scotland.

22 Sorley MacLean, 'My Relationship with the Muse' in William Gillies (ed.) *Ris a' Bhruthaich: The Criticism and Prose Writings of Sorley MacLean*, pp. 6–14.

23 MacLean, *O Choille gu Bearradh*, pp. 90–91.

24 T. S. Eliot, 'Tradition and the Individual Talent' in *Selected Essays by T. S. Eliot* (London: Faber and Faber, 1951), pp. 13–22 (pp. 17, 22).

25 Edward Moore [Edwin Muir], 'We Moderns: Enigmas and Guesses' (1918) quoted in Margery Palmer McCulloch (ed.) *Modernism and Nationalism: Literature and Society in Scotland 1918–1939* (ASLS: Glasgow, 2004), p. 168.

26 MacLean, *O Choille gu Bearradh*, pp. 124–25.

27 MS 29533, f. 28, Letter from C.M. Grieve to Sorley MacLean on 5 June 1940, National Library of Scotland.

28 MS 29540, f. 14, Letters from Douglas Young to Sorley MacLean, National Library of Scotland.

29 MS 29501, f. 11–12, Letter from George Davie to Sorley MacLean on 1 February 1940, National Library of Scotland.

30 MS 29540, f. 18, Letters from Douglas Young to Sorley MacLean, National Library of Scotland.

31 C.M. Grieve, 'The Caledonain Antisyzygy and the Gaelic Idea' (1931), in Duncan Glen (ed.) *Selected Essays of Hugh MacDiarmid* (London: Cape, 1969), pp. 56–74.

32 MS 29501, f. 8, Letter from George Davie to Sorley MacLean on 25 December 1939, National Library of Scotland.

33 MS 29540, f. 19, Letters from Douglas Young to Sorley MacLean, National Library of Scotland.

34 For a more detailed discussion of Douglas Young's opinions on the impact of 'An Cuilithionn' see Emma Dymock, 'Sorley MacLean's "Overture": A Study of Douglas Young's introduction to "An Cuilithionn"', *Aiste* 2 (Department of Celtic: University of Glasgow, 2008), pp. 30–42.

35 Edward Moore [Edwin Muir], 'We Moderns', *Modernism and Nationalism*, p. 168.

36 MS 29540, f. 19, Letters from Douglas Young to Sorley MacLean, National Library of Scotland.

Willa Muir, Modernism and Gender

AILEEN CHRISTIANSON

Gender is central to everything that Muir wrote; in *Belonging*, her memoir of Edwin Muir, she comments that 'I had been too often roused to resentment in my youth by the bland assumption around me that men were superior to women in all ways, especially where intelligence was needed', and that she had felt surrounded by a 'fog of ignorant prejudice about women [. . .] thick around me when I was growing up'.[1] The short chapter twelve of the memoir is mainly concerned with Edwin's character, his 'true self', a 'rare phenomenon, a wonder to me, and a mystery', as she describes him in paragraph two. But the chapter begins with Muir's view of the 'militant patriarchy' of Britain and ends with a long passage on the position of women: 'Male dominance had been my mother's creed and as a child I met it like a toad meeting the teeth of a harrow' (*B*, pp. 136, 140). The chapter itself is called 'Basic Underlay' which might well refer to Edwin's character and his role in Willa Muir's adult life but certainly also applies to her absolute assumption of the centrality of gender to society and her own life. The position of Muir's work in relation to modernism is less clear cut. In this chapter I concentrate on teasing out some aspects of modernism and how Muir's works might relate to them. But I assume that gender is the 'basic underlay' to all of her work, published and unpublished.

Modernism is a complicated concept. If it is confined to 'high modernists' such as T. S. Eliot, James Joyce, Ezra Pound and Virginia Woolf (all representing what Joseph Allen Boone calls 'high modernist bravado'[2]), it means that too many cultures, writers and artists are excluded. The early use of the term was for architecture and painting, not for writing, the *Oxford English Dictionary* listing the earliest use of 'modernism' in 1929 in relation to a city's architecture. The 1932 publication, *Oxford Companion to English Literature*, edited by Sir Paul Harvey, contains no definition for modernism; it does have entries for Albert Einstein, J. G. Frazer (with a separate entry for *The Golden Bough*), Sigmund Freud, Eliot and Woolf, but not for Pound. Indeed, an entry for modernism does not appear in any of Harvey's subsequent three editions (1937, 1946 or 1967); an extensive entry finally appeared in Margaret

Drabble's fifth edition of 1985. But the characteristics of modernism exist separately from its naming. Michael Levenson, in the *Cambridge Companion to Modernism* (1999), writes of the twentieth century discovering early that it 'would be the epoch of crisis':

> The catastrophe of the First World War, and before that, the labor struggles, the emergence of feminism, the race for empire, these ines-capable forces of turbulent social modernization were not simply looming on the outside as the destabilizing context of cultural Modernism; they penetrated the interior of artistic invention. They gave subjects to writers and painters, and they also gave forms, forms suggested by industrial machinery, or by the chuffing of cars, or even, most horribly, the bodies broken by war.[3]

This provides a succinct expression of many of the characteristics of modernism with the breakdown of supposed Victorian certainties and the representation of twentieth-century uncertainties shown in a fragmentation of stylistic conventions whether in art or literature.

But if particular kinds of writing were defined as being more 'modernist' than other kinds, does this mean that more 'peripheral' writing of the same period might be dismissed as 'parochial' or 'old-fashioned'? This is something that Houston Baker, the African-American scholar, describes as having been applied to writers of the Harlem Renaissance (generally dated as happening in the 1920s and 1930s, although Baker places what he terms '"renaissancism" in Afro-American expressive culture' as early as 1895.[4] Are those more 'conven-tional' novelists and poets, not working in streams of consciousness or the fractured styles for which Eliot, Joyce, or Woolf are noted, somehow sidelined culturally, perhaps seen as too akin to the despised Edwardian novelists that Woolf was so scathing about in her 'Modern Fiction' in 1925? Nan Shepherd satirises the fractured style of the high modernists in her last novel *A Pass in the Grampians* (1933):

> Like a manuscript that came in last month.[. . .] I couldn't make head nor tail of what it meant. The words were all in the wrong places. But the author thanked me for the beautiful typing, so I suppose he meant them like that.[5]

Shepherd writes in her second novel, *The Weatherhouse* (1930), one of the great modernist novels, about the effect of the war on a rural community in Kincardineshire, and early in that novel a passage clearly references those ideas of change in which modernism was rooted:

> The world and its modes passed by and [Ellen] ignored them. [...] She saw – as who could have helped seeing – the external changes that marked life during the thirty years she had lived at the Weatherhouse: motor cars, the shortening skirt, the vacuum cleaner; but of the profounder revolutions, the change in temper of a generation, the altered point of balance of the world's knowledge, the press of passions other than individual and domestic, she was completely unaware.[6]

This passage shows clearly the interaction of the traditions and the changes of the early years of the twentieth century, showing the way that less obviously 'modernist' writers were equally attuned to the temper of the times.

Willa Muir's two published novels, *Imagined Corners* (1931), taking place pre-World War One, and *Mrs Ritchie* (1933), running from late nineteenth century to immediately post-World War One, are also rooted in the north east of Scotland; they are both more conventional stylistically than Shepherd's *The Weatherhouse*. Muir uses the same idea as Woolf's 'looking within' advocated in 'Modern Fiction',[7] moving the narrative concern in *Imagined Corners* in particular from character to character, their preoccupations and the roots of their psychologies laid out for the reader's attention, through their thoughts and dreams as well as the anthropological narrator's analyses of them. It gives the interlocking stories of two clearly differentiated family groups, the Shand family: John and Mabel, Elise (Lizzie in her youth), Hector and Elizabeth, and Aunt Janet; and the Murray family: William, the United Free Church minister, Sarah, the unmarried, housekeeping sister, and their brother Ned, paranoid and unsettling, the failed University student. The Murray family, firmly within the post-Kailyard tradition, leans towards tragedy with no solutions other than death, madness or dependence on charity. The Shands, on the other hand, provide for possibilities of growth and change as well as an exploration of sexuality through Hector, Elizabeth and Elise, and of the socially constructed roles of women and men. A novel concentrating solely on the Murrays would have referred back only to the harsh anti-Kailyard world of George Douglas Brown's enraged novel *The House with the Green Shutters*

(1901). One dealing only with the more expansive Shand family would have allowed a modern exploration of gender and sexuality, linking it with Catherine Carswell's *Open the Door!* (1920) and D. H. Lawrence's novels, and showing a more obviously modernist approach.

If Baker's term 'renaissancism' is used as well as modernism, then the apparently more conventional writing of the women novelists (including Lorna Moon, Carswell and Nancy Brysson Morrison, as well as Shepherd and Muir) can be incorporated more easily into ideas of the modern in Scotland. The Scottish Renaissance, like Anglo-American modernism, the Irish renaissance and the Harlem renaissance, can be seen more broadly as a cultural movement, not just a literary one, with an agenda for change (of both culture and politics), partly pursued by rejecting its recent literary forebears while still invoking (as MacDiarmid did) the Scottish golden literary age of the first Renaissance of William Dunbar. And the Scottish women writers, representing that great change in the position of women after World War One, whether they directly or obliquely addressed this, are part of that cultural force. If Brown's *The House with the Green Shutters* is taken as the starting point of a Scottish literary revival, providing, in MacDiarmid's words, a 'very deep cleavage between us and all our predecessors', thus giving Brown an 'irreversible contribution to Scottish letters',[8] its publication in 1901 can be seen as marking an essential turning point in the desired rupture with the nineteenth century. And this allows the clearly anti-Kailyard strands in Muir's writing in both her published novels to be read as part of 'renaissancism' and modernism in Scotland.

Hugh MacDiarmid was later bitterly to reject Edwin Muir for the views on the Scots language that were expressed in *Scott and Scotland* (1936). MacDiarmid apparently independently disliked Willa Muir; he encouraged the publication of an unpleasant caricature of a huge Willa in a bathing costume, overshadowing Edwin as a tiny fawn, in *Voice of Scotland*, the new magazine he launched under his editorship in 1938.[9] It is clear that Muir had a prickly relationship with both MacDiarmid and his second wife Valda Grieve.[10] She describes MacDiarmid almost affectionately in *Belonging*, his 'yellow hair fizz[ing] up [. . .] radiant with sheer daftness', when he was on the spree in London intending to steal the Stone of Scone (*B*, p. 165). But during her time in St Andrews in the 1930s, Muir clearly felt enough scepticism about MacDiarmid and the Scottish renaissance to write the short story 'Clock-a-doodle-doo'. It appeared in June 1934 in *The Modern Scot*, the journal published in St Andrews between 1930 and 1936 that acted as a house journal of the revival movement. Essentially the tale pokes fun at modernism's perceived preference for illegibility and incomprehensibility. It concerns a group of clocks, 'of every conceivable size and shape' which cover the three walls of a room; the fourth wall is 'clear glass as if it were an enormous showcase', setting up the idea of an outside monitoring gaze. Both the rays of the sun and of the moon sweep the room. The only human being is 'a Woman' who comes in every day to wind up the clocks, a 'mere servant of the cogwheels', uninterested in the mechanisms of the clocks, puzzling the clocks by her indifference. An opposition between natural and clock time is established, then the story moves from an opposition between nature and the mechanical into a satire on modernism itself. For the 'Clever Clock', convinced that time runs according to the powerful, if erratic, 'super-clock' of the moon, the whole point of the unreadable numbers on the moon's face (with which the young clocks identify) is that they are 'illegible, because its meaning lies hidden in its private cog-wheels, because it is an intricate and baffling piece of mechanism, unlike your hum-drum, bourgeois sun'. This is modernist art, the more intricate and baffling, the more successful, precisely because of its incomprehensibility. The readable is humdrum and bourgeois (like the Victorian and Edwardian novel or pre-Cubist art).[11]

Muir mischievously satirises the young, too-clever-by-half, Clever Clock. She surely has in mind MacDiarmid, the passionate instigator of the Scottish Literary Renaissance for the previous ten years, intent on rejecting and casting off the cultural Fathers and Mothers of Victorian Scotland. Always something of an *enfant terrible*, politically both Marxist and nationalist, and swinging wildly between the two at times, MacDiarmid seems pointedly represented by the Clever Clock's joyful embracing of illegibility: 'I am I. I am my cogwheels. [...] We must free our terminology from the materialism of content, if we are to discover the laws of Pure Horological Thought'[12]. The Clever Clock might also represent metropolitan modernists such as Wyndham Lewis, both artist and writer, founder of the modernist journal *Blast*, and satirist in a particularly ageist way of Muir and her relationship to Edwin in *The Apes of God*.[13] Of course, Lewis (born 1882) was older than Muir, and MacDiarmid only two years younger, but it is the impulse of rebellious youth assumed by male modernists, rather than actual youth, that is satirised in 'Clock-a-doodle-doo'. The story ends with the Clever Clock, broken and carried from the room, proclaiming 'Now I am Really Unique. [...] Now I can swing from one extreme to the other as much as I like! There is no other clock like me in the whole universe. [...] This is—clackety-clack—this is the Horological Renaissance!'[14] This, Muir's only published piece of direct satire, cannot have endeared her to MacDiarmid who must have been able to interpret its obvious strokes against him and the revival movement he initiated.

Muir dashed off verses most of her life, with some published during her lifetime, others written into her 1940s journals and notebooks as well as in two handmade little books of poems ('Ephimeridae') on Scottish and other writers that she made for Edwin in the early 1950s. The oppositions between nature and intellect hinted at in 'Clock-a-doodle-doo' can be found in one of her later poems, 'Not for Me', which gives a retrospective critique of modernism with its supposed angularity of architecture and ideas, before concluding with her own preference for the curves of nature:

> Not the organ cactus
> categorical with its straight lines,
> prickly with refutations
> making too heady sap.
> Not the urban towers
> categorical with their ruthless right-angles,
> cutting the living air into sections of nothing,
> channelling its flow into false certainties.
>
> Not the intellectual-isms,
> categorical, sundering,
> splitting personalities,
> splitting hairs.
>
> For me the curves of an embracing arm,
> or the flowing contours of moving animals
> the joyous freakish shapes of moths and flowers
> on this well-rounded planet.[15]

The poem's juxtapositions / oppositions of man-made 'ruthless right-angles' with nature's 'flowing contours' and the interconnection of intellectuality, rigidity and modern city shapes with aridity seem backward looking as though, in the 1960s, Muir is still fighting her battles with the interwar renaissancists and modernists. Given Muir's connections with European intellectual life and her own intelligence and education, it always seems reductive that she should take such a conventional and pejorative attitude to intellectualism. But it is probably as much part of her gendered insecurity as well as of the attitudes of post-Second World War Britain where 'intellectual' was seen as an insult.

Willa Muir, Freud, Dreams and the Unconscious

There is no direct mention of Sigmund Freud in *Belonging*, despite Muir's work in child educational psychology, researching the 'problems raised by sex in education' [16], and her appointment as vice principal and lecturer in English, Psychology and Education at Gypsy Hill Teacher Training College, September 1918. This means that her relationship to Freud and the new discipline of psychoanalysis has to be traced more obliquely. Muir does make one reference to Carl Jung in *Belonging*, connecting him to her already existing fascination with the unconscious:

> For years I had been probing more or less ignorantly into the underworld of feeling, ever since I discovered Jane Ellen Harrison's *Prolegomena to Greek Religion,* which I had carried in my bosom during my first university summer, and I was now exploring Jung – after all I was lecturing on Psychology in my training college. (*B*, p. 13)

I only noticed this reference to Harrison's *Prolegomena* (1903) on a recent rereading of *Belonging*. Muir's first term at St Andrews was in 1907 so it was the first edition of Harrison's work that Muir treasured.[17] Jane Ellen Harrison (1850–1928) studied at Newnham College, Cambridge; she published on Greek religion and ritual from 1899 and acknowledged the importance of J. G. Frazer to her work in the introduction to *Prolegomena*: 'To all workers in the field of primitive religion Dr Frazer's writings have become so part and parcel of their mental furniture that special acknowledgment has become almost superfluous'.[18] She was also later impressed by Henri Bergson and by Freud's *Totem and Taboo*. Frazer's articles on 'Taboo' and 'Totemism' had appeared in the ninth edition of *Encyclopaedia Britannica* (1875–89) and his groundbreaking work, *The Golden Bough*, was published between 1890 and 1915, with Freud drawing on his ideas in *Totem and Taboo* (1912–13, trans. 1919). Muir's devoted reading of *Prolegomena* when she was a student, probably means that

Harrison's ideas became part of Muir's own 'mental furniture'[19], possibly as much as either Freud's or Frazer's.

Freud is named obliquely in one of Muir's slighting comments in *Belonging*. One of the few references to Muir's life during World War One is to a discussion group: 'In my club, too, the 1917 Club, there was constant discussion about the psychology of the unconscious. We all believed that a new liberal-minded era was about to dawn' (*B*, p. 17). In one other reference to this 1917 group, she mentions a 'fellow member [...] Barbara Low [...] a Freudian pyscho-analyst'. Edwin and Willa Muir shared the tenancy of their first married home in Guilford St., London, with her: 'we thought her an unhappy old woman' (Low was 42 in 1919, thirteen years older than Muir). She adds: 'D. H. Lawrence used to visit her occasionally; she boasted that he once threatened her with a bread-knife. Probably he did'. (*B*, p. 29). Muir has a tendency to be slighting about women who were not married, unable to see similarities to her own experiences. Barbara Low (1877–1955) was Anglo-Jewish, born in London, of Austro-Hungarian parents; university educated, she taught at both schools and a training college (not unlike Muir); she was indeed friendly with Lawrence, corresponding with him. She gave up teaching to pursue psychoanalysis, going to Berlin for her own analysis. In 1920, the year after the Muirs knew her, she published *Psycho-Analysis: A Brief Account of the Freudian Theory* (1920), an early work on Freudian practice. The first New York edition (also 1920) had an introduction by Ernest Jones.

I mention Muir's passing references to Harrison and Low as further illustration of the extent to which Frazer and Freud were important influences in early twentieth-century Britain. There is a handy summary of intellectual excitements in the first two decades of the twentieth century in Edwin Muir's *Autobiography* about his pre-Willa life in Glasgow:

> We [...] discussed everything under the sun: biology, anthropology, history, sex, comparative religion, even theology. [...] We followed the literary and intellectual development of the time, discovering such writers as Bergson, Sorel, Havelock Ellis, Galsworthy, Conrad, E. M. Forster, Joyce, and Lawrence, the last two being contributed by me, for I had seen them mentioned in *The New Age* by Ezra Pound.[20]

Later in his *Autobiography*, Edwin mentions the development of his own understanding of psychoanalytic ideas:

For some years *The New Age* had been publishing articles on psycho-analysis, in which Freud's and Jung's theories were discussed from every angle, philosophical, religious, and literary, as well as scientific. The conception of the unconscious seemed to throw new light on every human problem and change its terms, and [. . .] I [. . .] snatched at it as the revelation which was to transform the whole world of perception.[21]

Though Willa Muir implicitly connects Jung rather than Freud to her belief in the importance of the unconscious, it is impossible to believe that she had not read any Freud; these quotations from Edwin (with his close connections to Muir), the early influence of Harrison on Muir, and the existence of Low in their circles, provide some grounding for this view. Further evidence of the common presence of psychoanalytic knowledge can be traced in popular culture of the 1930s. A link can also be provided to Muir by taking Dorothy Sayers and Ngaio Marsh as representative of a particular kind of popular culture; Muir, a keen reader of women's detective fiction, owned many of their (and other women detective fiction writers') works.[22] In a selection of Marsh's fiction published between 1937 and 1941, alienists, psychiatrists, and 'hysteria' are terms casually used, often indicating scepticism about one character by another. But in Sayers, whose detective fiction clearly laid claims to greater seriousness and intellectual pretensions, knowledge of the unconscious and psychoanalytic terminology is assumed to be a necessary and normal part of the intellectual capacities of the two detectives Harriet Vane and Lord Peter Wimsey.[23]

Peter Gay, in his magisterial 2007 book *Modernism: the Lure of Heresy from Baudelaire to Beckett and Beyond*, notes that 'the impact of Freud's psychoanalytic theories on modern Western culture has not yet been fully mapped. Indirect as much of it was, it was certainly enormous, especially among educated bourgeois, whose tastes were also inextricably implicated in the origins and progress of modernism'.[24] Gay then writes in his introduction about the defining of any idea of modernism:

For there is something about certain prints, compositions, buildings, or dramas that we classify 'modernist' without hesitation or fear of contradiction. A poem by Arthur Rimbaud, a novel by Franz Kafka, a piano piece by Eric Satie, a play by Samuel Beckett, a painting—*any* painting—by Pablo Picasso, all offer trustworthy testimony to what we are attempting to identify. And over all these classics there broods the saturnine, trimly bearded face of Sigmund Freud. Each carries its own credentials. *That*, we say, *is modernism.* [25]

While not arguing that 'the saturnine, trimly bearded face of Sigmund Freud' broods over all of Muir's writing, the assumption that Muir was herself implicitly affected by Freud's belief in the effect of the unconscious on all our actions is valid. She writes of the idea of the collective unconscious: 'what *was* the Collective Unconscious, after all? An accumulation of human vibrations, perhaps, through many, many centuries, hanging in our air like invisible clouds and fogs, making climates of opinion and belief and tradition, which we breathed in daily and daily helped to form, usually without knowing it?' (*B*, p. 44). Freud was indubitably part of Muir's 'climates of opinion and belief' in the first decades of the twentieth century. The access point to the unconscious taken by psychoanalysts was through dreams, as Edwin himself found when he was being psychoanalysed by Maurice Nicoll in late 1919; he began to have vivid dreams and Willa 'had no misgivings about these, being a persistent dreamer' herself (B, p. 43). Laura Marcus, author of *Auto/biographical Discourses: Theory, Criticism, Practice* (1994) and editor of *Sigmund Freud's The Interpretation of Dreams : New Interdisciplinary Essays* (1999), and much more expert in this field than I, has suggested to me in conversation that Nicoll, as a Jungian psychoanalyst, would have encouraged Edwin to read more Jung, and Muir's reading of Jung mentioned above would also have been taking place at this time. Muir's own belief in the importance of dreams is shown in her novels *Imagined Corners* and *Mrs Ritchie* in the use she makes of her characters' dreams, which, she believed, represented a reality as strong as anything in the conscious world.[26]

What is interesting to touch on briefly here, though, are Muir's own dreams. These have a strong presence in her journals written in the late 1940s and early 1950s. I feel sure that it is the importance of dreams to Freudian and Jungian psychoanalysis which leads someone like Muir to analyse their more than surface importance. The long passage of August 1953 headed '*Why I am to be described as a mess*' is preceded by a 'vivid dream' in which Muir 'crossed the half-derelict, ruined piece of ground that recurs in my dreams. [. . .] It seems to be in England, not Scotland. It is on the side of a small hill; the landscape is undulating about it, not flat. I always cross it on my way to somewhere else'. She then includes her own analysis of the possible reason for this recurring dream: 'Does it represent the ruined piece of my *life* in Hampstead when Gavin was run over and his nervous system ruined?'[27] While Muir's references to sexuality are mainly oblique or metaphoric in her novels, in her journals she is direct and analytic. She records waking up with an orgasm after a dream about a train to St Andrews coming 'right into the station'.[28] In 1953, after having a dream when 'two children came rushing in & I *couldn't* get them to go out. [...] The tension was very great, and then I had an orgasm! and woke up', Muir briskly analyses the function of these orgasms:

> I suppose one manufactures excuses for tension in a dream. Is the tension the cause of the discharge? or the need for the discharge the cause of growing tension? An orgasm is probably the easiest & most direct discharge of tension, preventing hysterical or other morbid results?[29]

The Influence of Muir's Translation Work

Willa Muir and Edwin Muir were the first translators of Franz Kafka into English,[30] and therefore material in introducing knowledge of Kafka to the Anglophone world. This translating work also provides one of Muir's clearest links into modernism, Kafka's novels being (in Peter Gay's view) another of those immediately recognisable modernism signifiers. Muir does not comment in *Belonging* on the effect of translating Kafka on her psyche, but does exempt the work from being 'worse than breaking stones' or a 'subsistence farming' kind of translating, as she described much of their other translation work (*B*, pp. 149, 115). But there is an interesting footnote to her feelings about translating Kafka in Muir's unpublished novel, *Mrs Muttoe and the Top Storey*. Written in St Andrews, 1938–39, but closely based on the Muirs' life in Hampstead in 1932–35, its main character, Alison Muttoe, is a translator like Muir. It concludes with a nightmare when Alison Muttoe moves around a many-layered city world, looking in on a capitalist structure, industrialised and mechanised, and out at an apparent rural paradise (itself contained under a glass dome and therefore also a closed world with no escape). The nightmare is indicated as stemming from Alison's recent 'nightmarish' feelings about her work translating 'Garta' (clearly Kafka):

> It was true that Garta's work seemed to come straight out of the region which evoked dreams and nightmares. He showed an uncanny skill in

describing the twists and turns of frustrated feelings; merely to read him was like having an anxiety dream by proxy. And every incident in his stories, almost every phrase, carried so many implications that the translation had to be done slowly, with extreme care. Yes, Garta is making me fearful, decided Alison Muttoe, opening her jotter. [31]

Mrs Muttoe's nightmare resonates with a kind of Kafkaesque world from which there is no escape (other than waking up).

It is clear that the Austrian novelist Hermann Broch influenced both Muirs in their view of the developing political situation in mainland Europe in the 1930s, his pessimism eventually overriding any unfounded optimism they might have felt. Muir sees the 'real theme' of Broch's three-volume novel *The Sleepwalkers* (1933) as 'the inevitable break-up of civilization in contemporary Europe. [. . .] We spent nearly a whole year of our lives translating this trilogy, and so were bound to be influenced by its pessimism' (*B*, p. 152). In relation to their translation work, strong links to the presumed style of 'high modernism' can be seen in the Muirs' translations of Hermann Broch's *The Sleepwalkers* and of *The Unknown Quantity* (1935). Broch's style and its relationship to Joyce and Eliot are touched on by Muir in one of the few direct discussions of modern literature in *Belonging*:

> Broch, who admired Joyce's experiments with form and language (especially *Finnegan's Wake*) had experimented with the form of his own narrative in the third novel, breaking it up into disconnected pieces, set down side by side, much as Eliot in his poetry had set side by side disparate aspects of experience; perhaps Eliot, too, had fragmented his observations as an image of disintegration. [. . .] We did not agree that the unconscious should be despised as Broch despised 'the irrational', and the notion that it could and would overwhelm European civilization in a cataclysm like the break-up of an ice-floe gone rotten was entirely repugnant to us, even unthinkable'. (*B*, p. 152)

Edwin Muir's own response to *The Sleepwalkers* in 1959 was that 'difficulty itself became an essential quality of his prose; his attempt to show the almost inexpressible'.[32] The differing styles of Broch's three volumes with their attempts to express fragmentation and disintegration, made the task of translating Broch challenging, but it is *that* that links the Muirs' work on Broch into the fragmentation and disintegration existing in the styles and preoccupations of many modernist writers.[33]

The translation work of German, Czech and other European writers that both Muirs did to fund their travels and their lives in the 1920s and 1930s provides me with a concluding link to the Europeanism of modernism (for example, Ezra Pound, Gertrude Stein[34]) and 'renaissancism' (MacDiarmid's many 'borrowings' from Russian and other European poets for *A Drunk Man Looks at the Thistle* in particular). The Muirs with their peripatetic life in Europe in much of the 1920s are exemplars of John Carswell's 'literary freelance' world:

> The literary world of London attracted recruits from far afield, geographically and socially [. . .] all flow together in this 'literary underworld'. And then explode again over the surface of the earth. They are in constant movement from cottage to cottage, from country to country, from one side of the Channel to the other, in search of new places to sense their emancipation and cheap lodging to suit their short purses. [. . .] Most of them pioneered a new form of travel – the unladen, intellectual kind.[35]

Part of this intellectual circle, amongst those who had no access to private incomes, the Muirs had to fund their lives by writing for small reviews, by journalism, by teaching, by translating. This cross-border intellectual world is represented in Muir's character Elise in *Imagined Corners*; she had run away with the German teacher many years before and returns during the novel as the sophisticated Europeanised Elise who, through her early study of Saint-Simonianism and Enfantin, her relationship with Karl Mütze, the armchair anthropologist, and her talk of teleology, represents questioning, radical, intellectual traditions, coming home to lay the ghost of her earlier self.[36] And the heroine Elizabeth's departure with Elise to southern France at the end of the novel, shortly before the start of World War One, represents Muir's own solution to the repressions or difficulties of living in Scotland: flight into Europe. The overlapping of the cultural and literary worlds in Scotland, London and Europe in the Muirs' interwar lives and in Willa Muir's writing is clear. Baker's 'renaissancism' as a concept is perhaps more easily a fit for Muir's work than modernism, but her preoccupation with dreams, her explorations of sexuality (oblique or otherwise), the internalisation of much of her novels' narratives, and her constant preoccupation with gender and the injustices of the patriarchal world, all give her a central, if at times ambivalent, connection to modernism.

Notes

This chapter is based on parts of my study of Willa Muir, *Moving in Circles: Willa Muir's Writings*, with the addition of new material. As Willa Muir is the subject of this chapter, she is referred to throughout as Muir or Willa Muir. Edwin Muir, peripheral in the context of this chapter, is referred to as either Edwin or Edwin Muir.

1   Willa Muir, *Belonging* (London: Hogarth Press, 1968), p. 38. Page numbers for subsequent quotations will be given in parenthesis in the text, prefaced by *B*.

2   Joseph Allen Boone, *Libidinal Currents: Sexuality and the Shaping of Modernism* (Chicago: Chicago University Press, 1998), p. 5.

3   Michael Levenson (ed.), *The Cambridge Companion to Modernism* (Cambridge: Cambridge University Press, 1999), p. 4.

4   Houston A. Baker, *Modernism and the Harlem Renaissance* (Chicago: Chicago University Press, 1987), p. 8.

5   Nan Shepherd, *A Pass in the Grampians* (1933), reprinted in *The Grampian Quartet* (Edinburgh: Canongate, 1996), pp. 29–30.

6   Nan Shepherd, *The Weatherhouse* (1930), reprinted in *The Grampian Quartet* (Edinburgh: Canongate, 1996), pp. 10–11.

7   Virginia Woolf, 'Modern Fiction' (1925) in *Collected Essays* ed. Leonard Woolf (London: Hogarth Press, 1966), vol. 2, p. 106.

8   C. M. Grieve, 'Neil Munro', *Modern Scot* 1.4, Jan. 1931, 20–24 (p. 23)

9   Hugh MacDiarmid, *Voice of Scotland* vol.1, Sept.–Nov. 1938, p. 10.

10 For more on Willa Muir's relationship with Hugh MacDiarmid and Valda Grieve, see Aileen Christianson, *Moving in Circles: Willa Muir's Writings* (Edinburgh: Word Power Books, 2007), pp. 29–31.

11 Willa Muir, 'Clock-a-doodle-doo', *Modern Scot* 5, 1–2 (June 1934), 46–50 (pp.47, 46, 48, 46–7, 47).

12 Ibid, pp. 48–9.

13 See Wyndham Lewis, *The Apes of God* (1930: London: Grayson & Grayson, 1931), pp. 298–302.

14 *Modern Scot* 5, 1–2, p. 50.

15 W. J. A. Muir, *Laconics Jingles & other Verses* (London: Enitharmon Press, 1969); for discussion of Muir's poetry and further examples, see Christianson, *Moving in Circles*, pp. 161–6 and 218–25.

16 Muir's research was funded by the Carnegie Trust; see Carnegie Annual Report 1916, Appendix C.

17 Muir later owned another copy of Harrison's *Prolegomena* (New York, 1955), the third

edition; it is in St Andrews University Library with her marginal notes. For an interesting exploration of Harrison's life and work, see Mary Beard, *The Invention of Jane Harrison* (Cambridge, Mass.: Harvard University Press, 2002).

18 Jane Ellen Harrison, *Prolegomena to the Study of Greek Religion* (Cambridge: Cambridge University Press, 1903), p. xiv.

19 Ibid.

20 Edwin Muir, *An Autobiography* (1954: Edinburgh: Canongate, 1993), pp. 115–16.

21 Ibid, p. 150.

22 Willa Muir made a list of her books in 1963, marking those that were to be kept and those that were to be given to New Hall and Hughes Hall, women's colleges in Cambridge. Copies of many of the works of the prominent women detective fiction writers, Marjorie Allingham, Agatha Christie, Ngaio Marsh, Dorothy Sayers and Josephine Tey, were to be kept. The list is in St Andrews University Library (MS: 38466/6/17).

23 See, in particular, Ngaio Marsh, *Surfeit of Lampreys* (1941), and Dorothy Sayers, *Gaudy Night* (1935), both owned by Muir.

24 Peter Gay, *Modernism: The Lure of Heresy from Baudelaire to Beckett and Beyond* (London: Heinemann, 2007), p. xxi.

25 Ibid, p. 2.

26 Muir drew attention to this in her comments to Neil Gunn soon after *Imagined Corners'* publication: 'nobody [...] has seen that the dreams I give my characters are meant to be at least as important as their waking actions' (quoted by J. B. Pick in his introduction to the Edinburgh Canongate 1987 reprint of *Imagined Corners* (1931), pp. viii–ix). For discussion of Muir's use of dreams in her fiction, see the relevant chapters in Christianson.

27 Willa Muir, 19 August 1953, Journal 1951–3, University of St Andrews Library MS 38466/5/5/.

28 Muir, 14 Jan 1947; Journal Nov. 1946–June 1947; St Andrews MS 38466/5/2.

29 10 Aug. 1953; notebook; ca.1953; St Andrews MS38466/6/9.

30 Willa and Edwin Muir's main translations of the works of Franz Kafka were: *The Castle*, with introductory note by E. Muir v–xii (London: Martin Secker, 1930); *The Great Wall of China and Other Pieces* (London: Martin Secker, 1930); *The Trial*, with introductory note by E. Muir vii–xvi (London: Victor Gollancz, 1937); *America* (London: Routledge & Sons, 1938).

31 Willa Muir, *Mrs Muttoe and the Top Storey* (1938–40), typescript, St Andrews MS 38466/1/2, pp. 252–3.

32 Edwin Muir, 'Translating from the German', part I (part II by Willa Muir) in Reuben A. Bower (ed.), *On Translation* (Cambridge, Mass.: Harvard University Press, 1959), p. 94.

33 Broch was to translate poems by two of those most central to Anglo-American modernism, T. S. Eliot and James Joyce (see Huberman, 1989, p. 52).

34 Gertrude Stein, of course, was one of the central modernist Euro-American figures. One of Muir's poems combines a satire of Stein with a satire of the British Council administrative practices that she observed post-World War Two in Czechoslovakia:

> What is the matter, baby mine?
> Why do you burble like Gertrude Stein?
> I've been with the British Council, my dear,
> A year is a year is a year is a year,
> And so I have simply ceased to cohere.

Whatever I say goes up in a vapour,
and so I scribble on bits of paper,
with burnt-out matches instead of a pen,
numbering all from one to ten,
then spike them on files and do it again.

[10 May 1947; Journal, Nov. 1946–June 1947; MS: St Andrews 38466/5/2]

35 John Carswell, *Lives and Letters: of A. R. Orage, Beatrice Hastings, Katherine Mansfield, John Middleton Murray, S. S. Koteliansky: 1906–57* (London: Faber, 1978), pp. 272–3.

36 See Willa Muir, *Imagined Corners* (1931) in *Imagined Selves* (Edinburgh: Canongate, 1996), pp. 156, 231.

Testing the Boundaries in Life and Literature:
Catherine Carswell and Rebecca West

MARGERY PALMER McCULLOCH

Recent researches into modernist writing, including some of the essays in this collection, point to variations in modernist concerns and expressive practices within different national cultures and between writers even from the same cultural context. One notable variation relates to the lives and literary work of women in the early twentieth century. As Bonnie Kime Scott comments in the introduction to her anthology *The Gender of Modernism*:

> Modernism as we were taught it at midcentury was perhaps halfway to truth. It was unconsciously gendered masculine. The inscriptions of mothers and women, and more broadly of sexuality and gender, were not adequately decoded, if detected at all. [. . .] Typically, both the authors of original manifestos and the literary historians of modernism took as their norm a small set of its male participants, who were quoted, anthologized, taught and consecrated as geniuses. [. . .] Women writers were often deemed old- fashioned or of merely anecdotal interest.[1]

In contrast, as is now increasingly recognised, women writers contributed significantly to an understanding of modernity as it manifested itself in the early years of the twentieth century. This was especially so in relation to the ongoing revolution in the social roles of women through education and the aspiration to take up work outside the home; to have a vote and therefore an equal say in the political life of the nation. Yet what was equally important in women's lives and in their expression of these lives through their creative writing was the psychological revolution brought about by the researches of Freud and Jung which opened up exploration into related areas of sexuality and gender relationships. And from such explorations grew new forms of writing. As Virginia Woolf argued in her review 'Women Novelists', 'from the difference between the man's and the woman's view of what constitutes the importance of any subject [...] spring not only marked differences of plot and incident, but infinite differences in selection, method and style'. [2]

This chapter will focus on two women who tested boundaries in their personal lives and in their literary work, thus contributing to the remaking of the literature of their time: Catherine Carswell and Rebecca West. Carswell was born Catherine Macfarlane in Glasgow in 1879 to middle-class Scottish parents and spent her childhood and young adulthood in the city. Rebecca West, the pen-name of Cicely Fairfield, was, like Byron before her, born 'half a Scot', with a Scottish mother and English father, and spent much of her childhood in Edinburgh after her father deserted the family and her mother took her children from London north to her home city. Although never well-off, the children were well educated, with Cicely winning a bursary to the fee-paying George Watson's Ladies College, and her elder sister Letitia a Carnegie scholarship to train as a doctor at the Edinburgh Medical College for Women.[3] Cicely Fairfield was younger than Catherine Macfarlane, having been born in 1892 (the same year as C. M. Grieve /Hugh MacDiarmid), but for both women the determining years of their adult lives were around that 1910 period which Virginia Woolf suggested was the time when 'human character changed'.[4] This was also the time of the launch of Dora Marsden's *Freewoman* magazine, the first issue of which appeared on 23 November 1911. Its aim was to change the character of women, to transform them from what Marsden called 'Bondwomen' to 'Freewomen'. In Marsden's view, the social and psychological problem that women have to face is that they are not 'spiritual entities [...] are not individuals': 'By habit of thought, by form of activity, and largely by preference, they round off the personality of some other individual, rather than create or cultivate their own'. She believed that marriage and motherhood as traditionally entered into and socially structured have a principal role in maintaining a situation where 'all women are servants, and all the masters are men. [...] For man, woman has become a kind of human poultice'.[5]

This was the kind of revolutionary thinking which attracted the young, politically conscious Cicely Fairfield at the end of the first decade of the new century. At the age of fourteen, she had written a letter to the *Scotsman*, published in October 1907 under the heading 'Women's Electoral Claims'. In this she defended the split which had taken place between the National Women's Social and Political Union (NWSPU) and the Liberal Party, which had not brought forward the cause of female suffrage as had been hoped. She pointed to the 'sex degradation implied in manhood suffrage' and 'the profound national effects of the subjugation of women on the nation'. Four years later, having left Edinburgh for London, she began to write for Marsden's *Freewoman*, 'cutting away the dead things men tell us to revere'.[6] It was at this time that she chose the pen-name of 'Rebecca West', after the character of that name in Ibsen's *Rosmersholm*, and apparently in order not to embarrass her mother or her professionally qualified elder sister by her revolutionary writings. In a very short time she had become one of the best-known names in literary journalism in London, her articles and reviews described by Viola Hunt as making 'not so much a splash, as a hole in the world'. Jane Marcus, in her selection of West's early writings, characterises her as 'a propagandist of genius' in relation to her interrogation of society's need for change in social, sexual and political matters.[7]

Catherine Macfarlane's entry on to the public stage was less deliberate and dramatic but also had implications for social change in gender relations. She was educated at Park School for Girls, a recently established private Glasgow school with a good academic reputation, and when her father died unexpectedly in 1899, she used a small legacy from a relative to study piano at the Frankfurt Conservatoire from which she graduated in 1901. Her next venture was to enrol as a literature student at Queen Margaret College, the women's higher education college attached to Glasgow University, where she was promoted to the Honours class taken by Professor Walter Raleigh and won the Nicholl essay prize for the session 1902–03. She was active in student committees and in the debating society. She also would appear to have been the kind of young woman who had the potentiality to become one of Marsden's Freewomen.

Yet there is something of an enigma in accounts of Catherine's early adult life which appears less focused than that of Cicely Fairfield. Her talent as a pianist would appear to have been modest, and she was attracted to the School of Art where the 'Glasgow Style' was associated with its architect Charles Rennie Mackintosh, and where female painters and designers such as Margaret and Frances Macdonald, Jessie M. King, and Bessie McNicol (whose career was cut off by death in childbirth in 1904) were exhibiting their work in Vienna, Turin and other European cities, thus challenging the painters known as the 'Glasgow Boys'. The imagistic nature of her later writings show that she herself had an appreciative eye for painting and decorative work, and in her unfinished autobiography *Lying Awake* she speculates as to whether she should have chosen to go to Art School as a young woman instead of studying piano at Frankfurt. She concludes that she could not have borne to be a 'dilettante painter'.[8] Instead she opted to study literature, yet she did not matriculate for a degree course as it was open to her to do at that time, but merely took the literature classes at the university. She did not seem to know what she wanted to do with her life. And perhaps it is here that Marsden's arguments about women being conditioned into accepting that their role in life was to be a complementary one through marriage and a (subsidiary) relationship with a husband can be seen to be relevant to Catherine Macfarlane's unfocused restlessness. Whatever the cause, her future became determined when in the summer of 1904 she took up an invitation to visit Professor Raleigh's family at their Oxford home. There she met the brother of Raleigh's wife and married him on the basis of a few months' acquaintanceship. On their honeymoon on the continent she discovered that he suffered from delusions, and when he later produced a gun on discovering that she was pregnant (believing that he himself was infertile and so she must have been unfaithful to him) he was committed to a mental hospital. She returned to her mother's home in Glasgow where she gave birth to a daughter in 1905. She later wrote:

> Since I remember I have more than anything else wanted to be deeply loved. At first it was a blind, instinctive desire – to be entirely loved by an individual [...] I made what may truly be called a rash and foolish marriage to a man I scarcely knew. [...] The result was what may fitly be called in the appropriate connexion a disaster, and it did not take long to happen. [...] I was thrown up on the shore of a single life again, returned home to my mother and bore a girl child.[9]

Disastrous as it was, this event proved to be a positive turning point in her life as she found herself unwittingly in the situation that would be prescribed for Marsden's 'Freewoman' a few years later:

> If the Freewoman is not going to be the protected woman, but is to carve out an independence for herself, she must produce within herself strength sufficient to provide for herself and for those of whom Nature has made her the natural guardian, her children.[10]

This Catherine did by taking responsibility for herself and her child, contributing to their upkeep in her mother's house by literary journalism. Then in 1907 she took the momentous decision to put forward a legal case for the annulment of her marriage on the grounds of her husband's mental incapacity before the marriage – a fact known to Professor Raleigh and her husband's doctors but kept hidden from herself. The case was held in public in London between 20 and 22 May 1908 and fully reported in the London *Times,* with a strong argument against the annulment being that any such decision would mean that the child of the marriage would be illegitimate – not an acceptable status in early twentieth-century Britain. The decision, which made legal history, went in her favour, with an award of costs and the custody of her daughter. She was now once again a 'free woman'.

On the other hand, for both women, emotional independence was not so readily achieved. Catherine's achievement in fighting and winning the case for the annulment of her marriage was followed (and perhaps inspired) by her entering into a sexual relationship with the painter Maurice Greiffenhagen, who had come to Glasgow in 1906 as Head of the Life Class at Glasgow School of Art. Cicely/Rebecca followed a similar path when, having reviewed H. G. Wells's novel *Marriage* caustically in *The Freewoman* in September 1912 ('he is the old maid among novelists'[11]), she succumbed to the personal attentions of Wells himself – who already had a reputation for 'womanising' – and bore him a son, Anthony, in 1914. Both women seemed unable to detach themselves in their emotional lives from the men they had become involved with, continually hoping against all too real evidence that a permanent marriage relationship with their lovers might be possible. Having moved to London where Greiffenhagen had his family home, Catherine eventually ended her long-standing relationship with him and in 1916 married a friend from her Glasgow years, Donald Carswell, publishing her future literary work under the name of Carswell. Rebecca West finally parted from Wells in the later 1920s, marrying Henry Andrews in 1930.

On the other hand, what is of more lasting significance than the tangled web of these love stories is that as writers West and Carswell transformed and made use of their experiences in their future literary work in order to introduce new ways of writing about relations between the sexes, and to explore the contradictory relationship between male and female desire, as well as between conscious and unconscious being. Katherine Mansfield – another writer who tested the boundaries of female roles – pondered similar issues in her journal in 1920, turning Polonius's advice to his son Laertes in Shakespeare's *Hamlet* towards her own attempts to make a truer way forward for herself in her present life:

> True to oneself! Which self? Which of my many – well really, that's what it looks like coming to – hundreds of selves? For what with complexes and repressions and reactions and vibrations and reflections, there are moments when I feel I am nothing but the small clerk of some hotel without a proprietor, who has all his work cut out to enter the names and hand the keys to the wilful guests.'[12]

The 'old stable ego' of the character, as D. H. Lawrence called it, appeared no longer tenable, either in literature or life.[13]

Lawrence himself was of course central to contemporaneous explorations in literature about being 'true to oneself', especially in the matter of relations between the sexes, and he was also a player in the lives of both Carswell and West – although more tangentially in the case of West. Carswell had first come into contact with Lawrence's fiction when she reviewed *The White Peacock* for the *Glasgow Herald* on its publication in 1911, and had been 'deeply impressed' by it.[14] She reviewed *Sons and Lovers* positively in the *Herald* in July 1913 and she met Lawrence himself in the early summer of 1914 when he and Frieda came to tea with her and two friends in Hampstead. The visit resulted in a friendship and literary correspondence with Lawrence which lasted until his death in 1930. Catherine's daughter from her unfortunate marriage had died as a result of appendicitis in 1913. She says little about this period in her letters or other writings, but in *The Savage Pilgrimage*, the memoir of Lawrence she wrote in 1932, she comments that as she and her friends walked the Lawrences to their bus after tea:

> He and I walked in front; and as we passed the churchyard where my child was buried and I had paid for a grave for myself, I found that I was talking to him as if I had known him all my life. It was not that Lawrence encouraged confidences. He had none of the traits, still less of the tricks of what is usually understood to be the 'sympathetic' man. There were no 'intimacies', either physical or mental. But he gave an immediate sense of freedom, and his responses were so perfectly fresh, while they were puzzling, that it seemed a waste of time to talk about anything with him except one's real concerns.[15]

Later, in November 1915, Carswell was one of the few critics to review in an objective way Lawrence's *The Rainbow*, the subject of much vituperation in the press, and soon to be banned as an obscene book. She wrote in *The Savage Pilgrimage*:

> After *Sons and Lovers* it puzzled and disappointed me. I had been expecting a masterpiece of fiction, and this did not correspond to my notions of such a thing. Neither did I understand the book. But the processional beauty, the strangeness, the magnificence of the descriptive passages, which passed far beyond anything in the earlier novels, gave me much to admire and praise whole-heartedly. No other writer could have risen to such heights or plumbed such depths, and I said so as well as I could at considerable length. But I had no grasp, and I found it a hard review to write.

The consequences for Carswell of the writing of the review were also hard, as it lost her 'my reviewing of ten years' standing on the *Glasgow Herald*. Lawrence wrote from Cornwall: 'I am sorry about your reviewing because I believe you enjoyed the bit you had. And one *does not* want to be martyred.' [16]

By the time of her meeting with Lawrence, Carswell's love affair with Greiffenhagen would appear to have come to an end, and she was already attempting to explore in fiction the experiences of her own life as a young adult. Lawrence read what she had already written soon after their first meeting and wrote in response:

> I must tell you I am in the middle of reading your novel. You have very often a simply beastly style, indirect and roundabout and stiff-kneed and stupid. And your stuff is abominably muddled – you'll simply have to write it all again.

And then he added: 'But it is fascinatingly interesting. Nearly all of it is *marvellously* good.'[17] *Open the Door!*, as the book was finally called, took a number of years and many encouraging and scolding letters from Lawrence before it won the Melrose prize for fiction on its publication in 1920. Its successor *The Camomile*, also drawing to some extent on autobiographical material, but written in epistolary form and more distanced from the personal experiences and responses of its author's life, was published in 1922.

It is not surprising that Lawrence took an interest in these two books, for in them their author was exploring themes of female sexuality and relationships between men and women which were related to his own themes in novels such as *The Rainbow* and *Women in Love*. Lawrence had a wide range of female acquaintances and correspondents, several of them artists and/or writers, and it is probable, as has often been suggested, that it was important for him to talk with these women, and, as with Carswell, to deconstruct their fictional works in order to help him create viable female characters and scenarios of his own. Yet although novels such as *The Rainbow* and *Women in Love* have prominent and strong female characters such as the Brangwen sisters, and their sexual desires and relationships with the men they became involved with are talked out repeatedly and with differing perspectives throughout the narratives, it is perhaps truer to say – especially from *Women in Love* onwards – that it is masculine identity and male desire that most preoccupies Lawrence in his fiction and essays, together with the disruption of traditional power relationships between men and women which the concept of the new woman put forward in Marsden's *Freewoman* aimed to encourage. *Open the Door!* and *The Camomile* are different in that they are written out of a woman's search for an identity more true to herself, and out of experiences of female sexual desire and sexual relationships which are at first hand as opposed to being imagined by a male author. There is not in Carswell's depictions the female sexual violence found between Gudrun and Gerald in *Women in Love* and at times between Ursula and Skrebensky in the later stages of their relationship in *The Rainbow*. Lawrence wrote to Carswell in 1916 when she was still struggling to bring *Open the Door!* to a conclusion that he firmly believed in her novel. He continued:

> I think you are the only woman I have met, who is so intrinsically detached, so essentially separated and isolated, as to be a real writer or artist or recorder. Your relations with other people are only excursions from yourself. And to want children, and common human fulfilments, is rather a falsity for you, I think. You were never meant to 'meet and mingle', but to remain intact, *essentially*, whatever your experiences may be.

And he ended: 'Therefore I believe your book will be a real book, and a woman's book: one of the very few.'[18] Lawrence was right in thinking that

Carswell's book would be 'a real book' and 'a woman's book'. Yet he was not entirely right in his assessment of why this would be. For what makes *Open the Door!* (and *The Camomile*) 'a woman's book' is not the author's detachment from others, but her capacity to portray the tensions in a woman's life from the inside and yet with an objectivity derived from skilful writing, often in imagistic form: tensions in relation to sexual desire and its expression within a given social code system; between the recognition of talent and the social inhibitions which get in the way of its fulfilment (as in the desire of a woman to be a creative writer); the tug between instinct and rationality – not only in sexual matters but in various decision-making aspects of life. It is this dissonance that gives her fiction its authenticity. Nor, as Lawrence seems to suggest, did she put aside 'common human fulfilments', for in her marriage to Donald Carswell she had a son born in 1918. It was also this mixture of contrary qualities that enabled her to write with insight about the poet Robert Burns, when her novelistic biography (which dealt among other things with Burns as a sexual being) outraged the Scottish Burns Clubs. Similarly, her memoir of Lawrence was written out of friendship and affection for him, yet also out of understanding and wariness of his character. She wrote in *The Savage Pilgrimage*:

> From beginning to end I had for Lawrence, as he well knew, a special kind of love and admiration which I never had for any other human being. It was impossible not to pay him the profoundest tribute and at the same time to rejoice in his companionship in ordinary ways. But I also felt the need to save myself [. . .] For my age and experience I was still very immature. But there are wounds in life to which one does not twice expose oneself, and I had known such wounds.

And she adds: 'Lawrence had the capacities of giving, taking and demanding in a marvellous if terrifying degree. [. . .] I have a cowardly dread of a mess. It was necessary, I believe, for Lawrence to create a great deal of mess in his human contacts – necessary to his work.'[19]

Rebecca West had a much less personalised contact with Lawrence. She met him only once, in Italy in 1921, but like Carswell she immediately noted the simple, direct way in which he could draw people to him:

> He made friends as a child might do, by shyly handing me funny little boxes he had brought from some strange place he had recently visited;

> and he made friends too as if he were a wise old philosopher at the end
> of his days, by taking notice of one's personality, showing that he rec-
> ognised its quality, and giving it his blessing.[20]

The above quotation comes from her obituary essay 'Elegy' in the American
Bookman, which was later published in pamphlet form by Martin Secker.
She wrote: 'He laid sex and those base words for it on the salver of his art
and held them up before the consciousness of the world, which was his way
of approaching creation.'[21] Lawrence, of course, knew of West's literary and
political journalism, and had shortly before his death tried to encourage her
to take up an offer to write an article on his work. Although she had not
done this, she had often taken up arms against the kinds of ideas Lawrence
was battling with in his short essays as well as in his fiction: the biolog-
ical essentialism of 'Fantasia of the Unconscious', for example, where he
insisted:

> Sex – that is to say, maleness and femaleness – is present from the
> moment of birth, and in every act or deed of every child. [...] Women
> can never feel or know as men do. And in the reverse, men can never
> feel and know, dynamically, as women do. [...] Meanwhile women
> live for ever by feeling, and men live for ever from an inherent sense
> of *purpose*.[22]

This kind of argument is close to that put forward by Willa Muir in her
Hogarth essay *Women: An Inquiry*, published in 1925, where having started
out with the aim 'to find a conception of womanhood as something essentially different from manhood' and through this exploration 'to discover if
the division of the human race into men and women involves a division of
spiritual as well as of sexual functions, so that the creative work of women is
different in kind from the creative work of men', her conclusion is that since
'all women are potential mothers, and must have the necessary reserve of
energy for this function whether they intend to become mothers or not [...]
men have more energy at their conscious disposal'. Men's energies are therefore directed towards the creation of 'systems of philosophy or government',
while women's qualities are for 'creating individual human beings.'[23] Such
views were still widely held in the early years of the century, encouraged by
the research of biologists such as Patrick Geddes and J. Arthur Thomson into

male and female evolutionary development, popularised through their book *Sex*, published in 1914 in the Home University Library series.[24] There are also similarities here with the Lawrentian nature of Catherine Carswell's letter to her friend F. Marian McNeill in 1928 when she suggested that many 'thinking and educated women' of their time

> go against our natures by striving to *force* ourselves to deal first through the intellect, living too much with ideas and not sufficiently trusting to the truths that would come to us through the deeper and emotional channels. So we get confused, uncreative and 'pathological'.[25]

Carswell also seems to have had some sympathy with Lawrence's belief in a hierarchical power structure of the genders as in his comment in a letter to Katherine Mansfield in December 1918: 'I do think a woman must yield some sort of precedence to man, and he must take this precedence'.[26] She wrote in *Lying Awake*:

> Women writing anything have never set up as rivals to men writers. [...] even such original writers as Jane Austen, George Eliot, the Brontës, Christina Rossetti and others, whose work could not have been done except by women, never made any claims that I know of to exceeding, or even to equal excellence, with men writers.

And then she adds: 'Virginia Woolf is a possible exception, but there have been men writers also of overweening vanity'. She also wrote to a friend about Rebecca West: 'too much brass there & considerably too little precious metal.'[27]

This kind of thinking was entirely foreign to Rebecca West's ideas of what a woman could or could not be and do, and her 'brassiness' was an essential element in her high profile journalism, as was the kind of witty riposte she made to articles such as Lawrence's 'Matriarchy' and 'Cocksure Women and Hensure Men': 'There have been times when I wonder why we fought to get women the vote, instead of fighting to take it away from men', she wrote in her 'Reply to D. H. Lawrence's "Good-boy Husbands"' in 1929.[28] West's impact in her own time came principally through her literary journalism and her travel writing, which caught the rapidly changing climate of ideas in the period – what Edwin Muir called in *We Moderns* 'the whirlwind of modern thought'[29] – together with the inconsistencies and hypocrisies that so often accompanied public pronouncements and private lives. Her fiction is less well known, yet her novels and her later fictionalised biographical writings show the same concern with women's lives and with emotional and psychological conditioning as does her journalism. We see this in her second novel *The Judge* (1922), set in Edinburgh, which in its early chapters draws on its author's youthful experiences as a suffragette in the city. Yet its main theme is the psychological and emotional damage (which in this narrative lead to suicide and murder) done by broken relationships and illegitimacy, and their capacity to echo and repeat themselves over the generations.

As we have seen, Catherine Carswell and Rebecca West were very different in personal character and in the nature of their literary achievements. Carswell, although she spent most of her adult life in London, remained closely related to Scotland in her relationships and values. Her literary output was small, but made a substantial contribution to literary modernism in Scotland by bringing new topics and a fluid, impressionistic writing style into Scottish fiction. Her biography of Burns and her reviews of Scottish books assisted in the revaluation of Scottish culture being carried out in the interwar period. She was a friend not only of Lawrence but also of MacDiarmid and the Muirs, and was part of a network of female correspondents whose letters tell us much about the changing climate of ideas in their time. She was a good European, and travelled and made contacts in Europe throughout her life. In contrast, she did not appear to move in any of the more celebrated London literary and artistic circles. West, on the other hand, was both metropolitan and cosmopolitan in her reach. Although attempts have been made to claim her as a 'Scottish writer' on the basis of *The Judge* and her Scottish mother, she herself did not consider herself bound to Scotland or Scottish affairs, commenting that 'I could happily have discarded many of my relatives on the Scottish side'; happy also to have eradicated 'that delightful pinched Edinburgh accent' when she went to study at the Academy of Dramatic Art in London.[30] West, however, was appreciative of Carswell's writing, concluding her short memoir of Lawrence with the quotation of a letter about Lawrence by Carswell, published in *Time and Tide*, and describing her as 'an infrequent but gifted writer'.[31] Both women, in their distinctive ways, opened doors to a changing world and to our later understanding of that early twentieth century modernity.

Notes

1 Bonnie Kime Scott, Introduction, *The Gender of Modernism: A Critical Anthology* (Bloomington and Indianapolis: Indiana University Press, 1990), p. 2.

2 Virginia Woolf, 'Women Novelists' (1918), reprinted in David Bradshaw (ed.), *Virginia Woolf: Selected Essays* (Oxford: Oxford University Press, 2008), p. 131.

3 Victoria Glendinning, *Rebecca West: A Life* (London: Weidenfeld and Nicolson, 1987), pp. 28–9.

4 Virginia Woolf, 'Character in Fiction' (1924), Bradshaw, p. 38.

5 Dora Marsden, 'Bondwomen' in *Freewoman* 23 November 1911, pp. 1–2.

6 Cicily [sic] Isabel Fairfield, letter to *Scotsman* 16 October 1907, reprinted in Bonnie Kime Scott (ed.), *Selected Letters of Rebecca West* (New Haven and London: Harvard University Press, 2000), p. 5; Rebecca West, *The Freewoman* 7 March 1912, reprinted in Jane Marcus, *The Young Rebecca: Writings of Rebecca West 1911–17* (London: Macmillan, 1982), p. 23.

7 Glendinning, p. 38; Marcus, p. ix.

8 Catherine Carswell, *Lying Awake* ed. by John Carswell (1950: Edinburgh: Canongate Books, 1997), p. 120.

9 Ibid, pp. 131–2.

10 Marsden, *Freewoman* 30 November 1911, p. 22.

11 Rebecca West, '*Marriage* by H. G. Wells', *The Freewoman* 19 September 1912; reprinted in Marcus, *The Young Rebecca*, pp. 64–9 (p. 64).

12 Katherine Mansfield, 'The Flowering of the Self', *The Gender of Modernism*, p. 307.

13 D. H. Lawrence, letter to Edward Garnet 5 July 1914, *The Letters of D. H. Lawrence* ed. George J. Zytaruk and James T. Boulton, vol. 2 1913–16 (Cambridge: Cambridge University Press), p. 183.

14 Carswell, *Glasgow Herald*, 18 March, 1911, p. 12; *The Savage Pilgrimage*, p. 4.

15 Carswell, *The Savage Pilgrimage*, pp. 16–17.

16 Ibid, pp. 34, 41–2.

17 Lawrence, letter to Carswell 29 June 1914, *Letters* vol. 2, pp. 187–8.

18 Lawrence, letter of 16 April 1916, *Letters* vol. 2, p. 595.

19 Carswell, *The Savage Pilgrimage*, pp. 37–8.

20 Rebecca West, *D. H. Lawrence* (London: Secker, 1930), p. 23.

21 Ibid., p. 40.

22 D. H. Lawrence, *Fantasia of the Unconscious* and *Psychoanalysis and the Unconscious* (1923: Harmondsworth: Penguin Books, 1971), pp. 102–3.

23 Willa Muir, *Women: An Inquiry* (1925) in *Imagined Selves* (Edinburgh: Canongate, 1996), pp. 2, 6, 8.

24 For a fuller discussion of this aspect of Muir's *Women: An Inquiry*, see Margery Palmer McCulloch, *Scottish Modernism and its Contexts*, pp. 79–82.

25 Carswell, *Lying Awake*, p. 200.

26 Lawrence, *Letters* vol. 3, p. 302.

27 Carswell, *Lying Awake*, pp. 123–4. For comment on West, see letter to F. Marian McNeill, Sunday [1930?], National Library of Scotland, MS 26195.

28 West, 'Reply to D. H. Lawrence's "Good Boy Husbands!"', *Gender of Modernism*, p. 584.

29 Edward Moore [Edwin Muir], 'What is Modern?', *We Moderns: Enigmas and Guesses* (London: Allen & Unwin, 1918), p. 91.

30 Glendinning, pp. 28, 35.

31 Carswell, quoted by West, *D. H. Lawrence*, pp. 41–4.

From *Portrait of a Young Scotsman* to the *Birth of Venus*: Edward Baird in 1930s Montrose

JONATHAN BLACKWOOD

Visual Art Modernism and the Interwar Scottish Renaissance

Art History records the beginnings of an interest in modernism – particularly French modernism – in Scotland, from the late 1870s onward. Alexander Reid, the Glasgow art dealer, had branches of his operation in London and in Glasgow, and was important in stimulating an interest in Impressionism, and Post-Impressionism, amongst consumers of art. The Glasgow Boys, in the 1880s, looked carefully at French realist painters such as Bastien Lepage, and the French-inspired William Stott of Oldham, in responding both to urbanisation and the isolation of East Lothian and the Borders.

However, as the twentieth century dawned, a new generation of artists began to respond to French art in a different way. John Duncan Fergusson and Samuel John Peploe both spent significant time in Paris in the first decade of the century, and were amongst the best-connected artists, from any part of the British Isles, in the French capital in the period before World War One. Fergusson was a *sociétaire* of the Salon d'Automne and counted Picasso, the Dutch Fauve Kees van Dongen, and several of the Puteaux Cubists amongst his friends. Both these artists were to act as a conduit for the latest ideas from Paris. Peploe returned to live in Edinburgh, permanently, in 1912, and worked through the ideas he had encountered from Matisse, Gauguin and Picasso in a series of still lives. Fergusson returned to London in 1914, and sporadically spent time in Edinburgh. In association with Margaret Morris, he found himself at the centre of the remains of London's pre-war avant-garde in Chelsea from c. 1918 onwards. He returned to France at the end of the 1920s, and did not return to Scotland permanently until 1939.

Fergusson was amongst the first Scots to set out his views on art purely from a Scottish, rather than British, point of view. In his extraordinary *Modern Scottish Painting*, completed in 1939 but not published, owing to wartime shortages, until 1943[1], Fergusson called for the renewal of the 'Auld Alliance' with France, not in political, but in cultural terms. Citing Scottish Presbyterianism as a baleful influence on contemporary culture, Fergusson called on his fellow artists to be much bolder in their use of colour, and experience its liberating power. By the time that Fergusson's book appeared, however, debates concerning the identification and development of a Scottish, rather than British, relationship with European culture, had been an ongoing debate for over twenty years. On the other hand, the origins of this debate were couched in political as well as in Fergusson's aesthetic terms.

Hugh MacDiarmid, the poetic *alter ego* of Christopher Murray Grieve, had established himself in Montrose in the 1920s, and used his editorship of the *Montrose Review* to proselytise ceaselessly for what was to become known as the 'Scottish Renaissance'. This was primarily a literary, rather than a visual phenomenon, although, as we shall see, visual art was to play a part as Renaissance ideas developed. In addition to its primary objective of revitalising writing in all three of Scotland's languages – Scots, Gaelic, and Scottish-English – and thus regaining a distinctive Scottish cultural identity, the aims of the Renaissance movement included the debunking of popular 'kailyard' stereotypes which, in McDiarmid's view, infantilised Scottish culture; the use of the forms of an industrialised, urbanised Scotland as the basis for a revivified Scottish literature and art; and, significantly, the re-establishment of direct cultural relationships between Scotland and Europe, without recourse to London and the rest of the United Kingdom.

MacDiarmid addressed these themes directly in a series of small edited publications in the early 1920s including *The Scottish Chapbook* and *The Scottish Nation*, while the culmination of his ideas in his creative writing in the 1920s was the long, modernist, Scots-language poem *A Drunk Man Looks at the Thistle*, published in 1926. Although the early high profile interventions of the revival movement were literary, MacDiarmid had also taken care to try and provide evidence of a Renaissance sentiment in the other arts. In music, the work of Francis George Scott, MacDiarmid's erstwhile schoolteacher, was held up as an example of the new ideas. In visual art, the painter, lithographer and critic William McCance became central to the project in the second half of the 1920s. A conscientious objector during the war, McCance had spent time in London after the end of the conflict, establishing a friendship with the ex-Vorticist painter William Roberts. McCance's work, such as the early *Heavy Structures in a Landscape Setting*, relate strongly to Vorticist ideas, and also to an awareness of the potential that the angular forms of heavy industry could have for the contemporary artist. As Tom Normand has shown, McCance's work from 1925–28 functioned as a concentrated exploration of

Scottish Renaissance ideas. In particular, pieces such as *The Engineer, His Wife and Family* and *From Another Window in Thrums* address the growing identification of Scotland with heavy industry, and the consequent irrelevance of what was referred to as the 'kailyard' ('cabbage patch' culture).[2] Whilst such images would have provoked debate within Scotland's art world, their impact outwith those national circles is hard to gauge, and is unlikely to have been more than slight.

McCance's severe geometry certainly made no impact whatever on the young Edward Baird, who was finishing a final year at Glasgow School of Art in session 1927–28. Based in Glasgow, Baird's awareness of Scottish Renaissance ideas is much more likely to have been stimulated by R. B. Cunninghame Graham's candidature for the post of rector at Glasgow University. Graham's campaign was sponsored by the Glasgow University Student Nationalist Association, and was mounted as a high profile platform for developing political ideas on Scottish nationalism. Although Cunninghame Graham was unsuccessful, he ran the incumbent Prime Minister, Stanley Baldwin, very close, and gained nationwide exposure for nationalist ideas. Partly as a consequence of this successful campaign, the National Party of Scotland was founded in late 1928, as a result of the merger of three smaller nationalist pressure groups, to work through the political implications of the ideas suggested by the writers and artists associated with the Scottish Renaissance. For Baird, the local branch of the new party was to provide an important focal point in the next four years of his life.

Edward Baird, Art and Politics in the 1930s

In April 1932, at the annual Royal Academy exhibition in London, a small portrait, in muted tones, was among the exhibits. This painting was by the young Montrose artist Edward Baird, and it stimulated a brief series of media interviews and appearances in the first part of that decade. The subject of the work was Fionn MacColla, a schoolboy friend of the painter, and a subsequent fellow traveller, politically, in the early years of the National Party of Scotland. In the same year, MacColla's first novel, *The Albannach*, was published in London, and what reviews the novel received were generally positive. Aside from personal friendship, the motivation for the painting seems to have been to record the appearance of a new generation of Scottish intellectuals, who would answer Hugh MacDiarmid's call for the redefinition of Scottish culture on its own terms, rather than remaining content to be a splash of provincial colour on a standardised British canvas. MacDiarmid had used his editorship of the *Montrose Review*, in the 1920s, as a platform to propagate such ideas. Whilst it remains uncertain whether Baird and the poet ever met, the painter would certainly have been fully aware of MacDiarmid's ideas, not least through his friendship with MacColla. Recognising the 'honour' of being 'hung on the line' at the London Royal Academy, the *Angus and Mearns Herald* interviewed Baird in the spring of 1932, and its readers were given a rare insight into his ideas. Baird speaks here through the words of an anonymous journalist:

> It is an attempt to paint a modern and distinctively Scottish portrait [...] to make a synthesis between an acquired technique, partly from sources, an actively involved sense of being part of a re-vivified Scottish culture [...] he felt that Scots art wanted to make a new start, because the national idioms of Scots art had been overlaid by the false products of the 'kailyard' school, or its equivalent in art [...] The Italian primitives and the French School showed the way to develop an art which was characteristically Scottish.[3]

Until very recently, these words from the newspaper report were all that scholars of Baird and the Scottish Renaissance had to go on in regard to information about this *Portrait of a Young Scotsman* painting. The painting itself was bought by the nationalist and cultural entrepreneur James H. Whyte, in St. Andrews, in the mid-1930s and hung for a brief period at the Scottish National Party headquarters in Edinburgh. From the beginning of World War Two, however, the image disappeared completely and was assumed either to have returned with Whyte to America, or to have been lost altogether. The recent re-emergence of the painting at auction in Sussex, and subsequent exhibition at Abbott and Holder in London, gives us a new opportunity to understand Baird's methods and ideas in the 1930s period of the Scottish Renaissance.

Typically, the picture makes no appeal to the viewer's senses, instead offering a direct challenge to the intellect. The colour palette is restricted to muted greens, greys and browns, with only the scarlet of the lion rampant, and tartan thread, offering any relief from the monochrome palette. The figure of MacColla is instantly recognisable from contemporary photographs, and he meets our gaze with an unflinching and determined stare. The background, featuring the sea and a generic rocky landscape, is probably based on the cliffs near to Montrose at Scurdieness, whilst the green curtains – oddly frozen in the middle distance behind the sitter – give evidence of a knowledge of the contemporary output of the painter James Cowie, whom Baird and James McIntosh Patrick had both admired while students at Glasgow School of Art from 1924–28.

Edward Baird: *Portrait of a Young Scotsman*, 1932
© Graham Stephen

The most extraordinary feature of this portrait, however, is MacColla's attire in pseudo-military uniform. The tunic and sash he wears is based in part on contemporary uniforms of the British army, but the tartan and lion detail perhaps suggest discussions regarding the formation of a separate Scottish army, or indeed recall the Jacobite armies of Bonnie Prince Charlie. In 1932, the idea of a 'political' uniform would not have been unfamiliar, with the emergence of Sir Oswald Mosley's Blackshirts (an active unit of the British Union of Fascists existed in nearby Aberdeen) and Major C. H. Douglas's 'Greenshirt' movement, which sought to agitate for theories of Social Credit. Some of the more extreme fringes of the early National Party of Scotland flirted with the idea of a paramilitary 'Clann Albainn' formation, but this idea seems to have had little traction beyond the fevered imaginings of a very few.[4] Although Baird was later to become very sceptical about the implications of radical cultural nationalism, he seems to have considered it in detail for this particular image.

This, then, is a stark statement of Baird's intellectual and political engagement with the Scottish Renaissance in early 1932. On another level, it demonstrates the closenesss of his friendship with MacColla at that time, as part of a larger circle of Montrosians who were interested in both the Renaissance and the political birth pangs of the National Party of Scotland. These included individuals such as the architect George Fairweather, whom Baird was to paint in 1935 (this portrait is currently in the Scottish National Portrait Gallery collection), the newsagent Andrew Dalgetty, secretary of the Montrose branch of the National Party of Scotland, Allan Ogilvie, a chartered accountant (Baird painted Ogilvie's wife, Susan, in 1932), and Peter Machir, a factory worker. Other occasional members of this circle included the sculptor William Lamb, although he and Baird were never close. This group of friends was the driving force in an early by-election in late summer 1932, when the Nationalists fielded a candidate in the town for the first time, and performed creditably enough. Baird's contribution was the design of one of the first logos for the National Party of Scotland.

Ultimately, however, the painter was to drift away from nationalist circles after this very busy year of involvement. MacColla left Montrose not long after the publication of *The Albannach*, and whilst Baird's friendship with Fairweather and Machir was to endure throughout his short life, the local branch of the National Party of Scotland imploded in the wake of the by-election campaign in a series of petty disputes with party headquarters. More broadly, the momentum behind the ideas of a Scottish Renaissance had begun to dissipate in the context of growing economic and political problems within and beyond Scotland, and, in response, Baird moved away from nationalism towards a more communitarian socialist position as the 1930s went on.

Baird spent a good deal of time in St. Andrews in 1933, where he enjoyed the patronage and support of James H. Whyte, editor of *The Modern Scot*. The American, having purchased *Portrait of a Young Scotsman*, also played a role in the commissioning of a portrait of the university lecturer William McCausland Stewart in 1933. Both pieces were exhibited sporadically in St Andrews between 1933 and 1936, at Whyte's gallery premises on North Street. However, Baird's most significant commission – and, in many ways, his most unusual work from this period – arose as a result of the engagement of his close friend, the painter McIntosh Patrick. Patrick married in 1934, and Baird gave him his painting *Birth of Venus* (now in the collection of the Scottish National Galleries – see the front cover of this book) as a wedding present. Typically, the painting was not finished for several months after the wedding ceremony, and was returned to Montrose during the war for safekeeping when McIntosh Patrick entered military service.

The motivations for this painting were clearly much more personal than for the earlier *Portrait of a Young Scotsman*, and Baird took the opportunity to develop his ideas on aesthetics, rather than politics. The work takes its inspiration from Sandro di Botticelli's painting of the same name, completed in 1485, which Baird had seen at the Uffizi Gallery in Florence, during a four month study trip to Italy in 1928–29. As in the Botticelli, Baird's *Birth of Venus* features a young woman at the centre of the composition, emerging from the sea, but bounded in the foreground of Baird's composition by a remarkable range of still life objects – marine ferns, buoys, navigational aides, shells and a plaster bust of a male head. In many ways, the painting is as much about Baird's relationship to his own fiancée, Ann Fairweather, as it is concerning his friendship with McIntosh Patrick. Certainly, the decision to depict Baird's fiancée in the nude, in a picture given to a friend as a wedding present, is extraordinary, and the completed work caused some scandal in Montrose when Ann Fairweather was recognised, during an exhibition of the work in a town gallery in September 1935.

Looking at *Birth of Venus* from a biographical point of view, we see it as a subtle, layered image, with each of the still life elements from Baird's past, foregrounding his fiancée at the centre of his present. The beach setting is at Montrose, whilst two of the still life elements – the shell in the immediate foreground to the right, and the plaster head – have their roots in microscopically accurate pencil drawings completed by Baird as a schoolboy at Montrose Academy. The open, super-sized shell to the left has a clear sexual connotation, set against a backdrop of driftwood and maritime odds and ends, presumably making reference to Baird's love of the sea, and his descent from a seafaring family. At the centre, the marine fern is an exotic, near hallucinatory detail, seducing the viewer through its soft violet hue. In fact, this colour caused much of the delay in the delivery of the painting to McIntosh Patrick; Baird had not used it before, and it caused him a great deal of trouble in the finishing of the painting. The figure of Ann at the centre links Baird's affinity with early Renaissance painting with the personal happiness he was experiencing in the present. Ann stands not only as an exemplar of female beauty, but also of love. Read in this way, the painting stands as a celebration of love and, by extension, a celebration of McIntosh's Patrick's love for his new wife.

Birth of Venus is unique in Baird's *oeuvre*, and certainly has received rather hesitant responses from art historians. Most have tended to tentatively place the work as a Surrealist experiment, noting the closeness of the work to contemporary paintings by Edward Wadsworth and Paul Nash. Any such similarities are, however, likely to be incidental. Baird was famously sceptical of many of the theories that underpinned modernism, and whilst he would have found Surrealism of interest, it is extremely unlikely that he would have set out on an experiment with its methodology in a painting of such personal significance. Rather, thanks to the reclamation of the circumstances surrounding this painting, and by referring to earlier work and events in his life, we can read it as an intense and meticulously planned documentation of close friendships, and of love.

Whilst *Birth of Venus* stands as a deeply personal anomaly within Baird's body of work, his development away from the nationalist concerns of the early 1930s seems to be confirmed by a painting of 1936, *Distressed Area*.[5] Painted from the vantage point of Rossie Island, a small islet in the River South Esk, this image offers a view of an abandoned hut, in the middle ground, with empty docks and the eerily depopulated village of Ferryden to the right, on the opposite bank of the river to Montrose. The inclusion of the Scurdiness lighthouse and the buildings of the harbour give this painting an identifiable local impetus but, more broadly, it offers an implicit condemnation of the policies of the then National Government led by Ramsay MacDonald and the impact of these policies outwith the South East of England. The empty river and buildings suggest the heavy absence of trade and commerce; only a line of washing, hung outside one of the Ferryden houses, gives any indication that the town has not been abandoned to its fate by a jobless population. The hut in the foreground also had personal significance for Baird. He had envisaged it as a space for cultural events for local unemployed people; it was also thought of as a possible meeting space for a new artist's colony on Rossie Island. Events were held at this venue for local children, but nothing was to become of Baird's vision of Rossie Island as a community for artists. The placing of this building at the centre of the image is further evidence of his move away from a fairly crude cultural nationalism, towards a communitarian, socialist outlook by the end of the 1930s. This political trajectory was strengthened during the years of World War Two, when Baird was appointed as an Official War Artist, and was also a key figure in exhibitions in Montrose, organised by the Committee for the Encouragement of Music and the Arts.

In a broader sense, *Birth of Venus* acted as a bridge between a period where the painter was working closely with the ideas of the Scottish Renaissance, and the section of his career that began with the portrait of George Fairweather in 1935, and continued until the penultimate year of the war, 1944. Baird, in these years, concentrated largely on documentary portraits, giving contemporary viewers and subsequent generations the opportunity to understand Montrose during that period of time, through some of its people. The artist's work, from this later period, saw him explore the role that art could play in a communitarian, socialist-inclined society, and as such set aside the fiery ideals which had driven his work in the years immediately following his return to Montrose from Glasgow, via Italy, in his immediate post-graduation years.

Notes

This paper is based on a presentation given at the University of Stirling in July 2009, and has been updated since the rediscovery of *Portrait of a Young Scotsman* in the summer of 2010 to take account of this painting. It has unfortunately not been possible to reproduce for this written paper all the images shown on screen in the original visual presentation.

1   J. D. Fergusson, *Modern Scottish Painting* (Glasgow: Maclellan, 1943).
2   For further information on such Scottish artists see Tom Normand, *The Modern Scot: Modernism and Nationalism in Scottish Art 1928–1955* (Aldershot: Ashgate, 2000). See in particular chapters 3 and 4.

3 *Angus & Mearns Herald*, 'Montrose Artist's Royal Academy Picture – First Attempt Accepted – Mr. Baird Talks Art', n.s, probably late April 1932.

4 For MacDiarmid and his 'Clann Albain' project, see Alan Bold, *MacDiarmid: Christopher Murray Grieve: A Critical Biography* (London: John Murray, 1988), pp. 244–5.

5 This painting is now in a private collection. It is illustrated in my book *Portrait of a Young Scotsman: A Life of Edward Baird 1904–49* (London: Fleming-Wyfold Art Foundation, 2004), cat. No. 51, and p. 53.

Modernism and Music in Scotland between the Wars

JOHN PURSER

This discussion of music in Scotland between the wars will refer to four modernist composers: F. G. Scott (1880–1958), Cecil Gray (1895–1951), Ronald Center (1913–1973), and Erik Chisholm (1904–1965), but will concentrate predominantly on Erik Chisholm.[1] It will also draw attention to the way in which Scottish modernist music is often connected with story and verse, and how the West – the Gaelic-speaking West – is represented in modernist music from Scotland. Sorley MacLean's poem *Hallaig* gives testimony to a broken community in that Gaelic-speaking west:

> Tha bùird is tàirnean air an uinneig
> troimh 'm faca mi an Aird an Iar –
>
> *The window is nailed and boarded*
> *through which I saw the West.*[2]

What we find in the music is the attempt to hear as well as see what lay and still lies beyond the window. Musically speaking, the window was opened for non-Gaels by the work of many collectors and researchers. In particular, Joseph and Patrick MacDonald, Daniel Dow, Simon Fraser, Keith Norman MacDonald, Angus MacKay, Major-General Thomason, Frances Tolmie and Lucy Broadwood; and, drawing substantially on Frances Tolmie's work, Marjory Kennedy-Fraser who popularised Gaelic music and song in the drawing-rooms of several continents.[3] Chisholm and Scott both show respect to the impressive inheritance of Scotland's music – and our Highland music in particular. Nor were the artists of the time insensible to music. William McCance compared Epstein's 1937 piece on *Consummatum Est* to *piobaireachd*, and J. D. Fergusson incorporated musical symbols into his illustrations for MacDiarmid's *In Memoriam James Joyce* (1955).

Yet it is not always easy to incorporate elements of another art form or culture into one's own creative work. In the music of F. G. Scott, for example, there is no question that we encounter here a wonderful composer of songs, fully in command of a complex idiom which responds magnificently to the poetry, whether it be by MacDiarmid or another Scottish poet. F. G. Scott's talents did not lie in large-scale forms, but his claim to a distinguished place in the history of Scottish music and, indeed, in the history of song, should be undisputed. If the reputation of Henri Duparc can survive on a mere dozen or so songs, then Scott is assured of permanence on the basis of many more of equal beauty and mastery.[4] However, in relation to the attempt to absorb the Highland tradition into music, it is interesting to note that Scott's response to *piobaireachd* is much more conservative than that of Chisholm. Scott's setting of Jean Lang's 'St Brendan's Graveyard' matches her evocation of the windswept cemetery on Barra. He reproduces the sense of timelessness with a vocal line floating in disembodied beauty and simplicity over a piano part which subtly varies the drone effect which is part of his overall intention of imitating *piobaireachd*. The score is marked 'Like a pibroch – impersonal and without nuance'.[5] However, this attitude to *piobaireachd* is wholly misplaced; *piobaireachd* should be anything but impersonal, and performances are highly nuanced. Moreover, many *piobaireachd* were composed in praise of or lament for specific persons. If Scott truly thought that, for example, *The Lament for the Children* was impersonal, then he had no understanding of it whatever. That said, the song itself is so indisputably beautiful, that we can ignore Scott's misdirection which is, after all, words only – if a musician may be excused expressing himself thus. 'St Brendan's Graveyard' also benefited from the impressionistic evocations of Marjory Kennedy-Fraser whose work Scott studied as part of his investigation of his native music roots. Although Kennedy-Fraser comes in for much criticism as having been a romanticiser, a dispassionate study of her accompaniments and harmonisations shows that she was ready to incorporate the kind of early modernist freedoms initiated by Debussy, and in this she no doubt also influenced Chisholm. From the same period comes the bulk of the output of Sir John Blackwood McEwen, a pioneer of post-impressionist writing, both in his French and Scottish-influenced works. He is still grossly undervalued in his native country, never mind abroad, and he too influenced Chisholm. In other words, neither Scott nor Chisholm emerged out of a total vacuum in terms of awareness of new idioms and experimental scoring, harmonising and accommodating tradition within those parameters.

Neither Scott nor Chisholm, on the other hand, would have been likely to have heard a single note of the music of Cecil Coles (1888–1918), whose settings of Verlaine and de Musset have a strange knowingness about them that is almost disturbing, even premonitory. As for Coles' magnificent setting of the nineteenth-century Robert Buchanan's 'Fra Giacomo', it realises that remarkable dramatic quality of the Buchanan, hovering between Browning and the great ballad tradition, but with a sense also of *grand guignol* which cannot be taken lightly, for, at times, Coles' music is positively terrifying. It may not be modernist in idiom, but modernist in outlook it most certainly is, inhabiting much the same psychological world as does Berg's *Wozzeck*. Coles' ability to sustain a religious calm in the face of the hideous story of deception and murder which is unfolding, is dramatic irony at its finest, especially in the setting of the following passage:

> In her beautiful sweet simplicity,
> With that pensive grey expression,
> She sighfully knelt at confession,
> While I bit my lips till they bled,
> And dug my nails in my palm.
> As I heard, with averted head
> The horrible words come calm.
> Each was a serpent's sting;
> But, wrapt in my gloomy gown,
> I sat like a marble thing
> As she uttered your name.
> Sit down!
> More wine. Fra Giacomo?[6]

The poisoned Fra Giacomo is finally also knifed to death, and Coles creates a climax as blood-drenched in its sound as the equally horrific conclusion of *Wozzeck*.

A much-neglected composer, is Ronald Center (1913–1973) whose major cantata, *Dona Nobis Pacem* and impressive post-Bartókian *Piano Sonata* are among the few works of his that have been recorded.[7] The cantata is a work of arresting spiritual uncertainty – a kind of harbinger of Britten's *War Requiem* in its mixture of texts and dramatic musical insistences. The *Piano Sonata* has many similarities with aspects of Chisholm's own *Sonatine Écossaise*, for all that the Center only employs Scottish idioms in its last movement. The music is taut, uncompromising and rhythmically vital, unafraid of dissonance, but equally unafraid of the past. The same applies to the *Six Bagatelles* which are beautifully crafted and anything but playthings. Just as with the Coles' setting, there is a depth of psychological insight that is striking in this music, especially notable in *Children at Play*, parts of which might have made a chilling appearance in a musical score for *Lord of the Flies*, and other parts of which would equally grace the knowing innocence of Stevenson's *Child's Garden of Verses*.

This theme of psychological insight can be readily identified in the work of Cecil Gray (1895–1951), who was one of the most vital and entertaining artistic commentators of his age.[8] Classified as English by Groves Dictionary, he himself wrote: The fact remains that this *echt* Scottish nationality is strongly characteristic and in high degree determinative of whatever qualities I may possess, both good and bad.[9]

This is important to stress, for one might see emerging in some of the works discussed here a parallel in music with a Scottish literary tradition of psychological self-examination which perhaps has its first manifestation in the diaries of Boswell, but reaches a maturity in Hogg's *Confessions*; is sustained by Stevenson and even by the much-maligned Barrie, whose profoundly ironic and disturbing vision in *Peter Pan* seems to be determinedly avoided by critics, in favour of criticising the author himself. As a young man, Chisholm composed a little suite called *Peter Pan* but has, I think, missed its ironies, not at the time having reached that 'enviable condition' known as marriage, never mind parenthood. Gray's contribution to this 'genre' if I may so call it, was a major opera, *The Temptation of St Anthony* based upon Flaubert's original. It would make a wonderful television opera (was indeed envisaged as such), focused as it is upon spectacular visual effects, called for in the score in Gray's own sensual translation of Flaubert's equally lush original. Particularly effective is the obsessive writing expressing the searching sexual desire of the Queen of Sheba.[10] Other works of Gray's include *Deirdre* and *The Women of Troy*, but as a composer he has been almost totally neglected.

Finally to Erik Chisholm, who explored the idiom of Highland instrumental and dance music more profoundly than virtually anyone before or since, acquiring the confidence to treat his originals with breathtaking freedom. He alone represents the full range of modernist music in Scotland in virtually every conceivable genre, from opera and ballet, symphony and concerto, to solo piano music and songs. (And here, for a Scottish modernist readership, I must sadly, in what follows, set the record straight.)

When Sir Arnold Bax wrote of Erik Chisholm that he was probably the most progressive composer that Scotland has produced,[11] I am certain he was unaware of MacDiarmid's opinion that F. G. Scott was

the only Scottish composer technically abreast of the highest developments of modern music in Europe, and the only composer today who
is endeavouring to establish a Scottish national idiom – who, in other
words, has got beyond kailyairdism .[12]

Bax was writing in 1938 and MacDiarmid in 1924. One might then reasonably forgive MacDiarmid had he but found the grace to modify his opinion
later in the face of the overwhelming evidence that accumulated against it.
But when Chisholm died in 1965 MacDiarmid wrote: 'alas, I felt about him,
even more than about Stevenson and Ogdon, what I have said above about
mere rabbit – or – caterpillar nibbling'.[13]

What this comment refers to is his statement earlier in the same letter
that the composer Ronald Stevenson and pianist John Ogdon 'have no background' and tackle any subject like 'a rabbit or a caterpillar nibbling at the
fringe of a cabbage leaf'. Comparing them with Sorabji's 'well-stocked mind',
he declares 'they have no depth in their minds'.[14] These are casual opinions, but
they are published without editorial comment and are influential in Scottish
modernist studies. Stevenson can defend himself. The late John Ogdon is still
internationally lauded, but there are few to defend Chisholm because there are
few who know anything much about him. Of those three, Chisholm's background as a musician could scarcely have been more widely informed, and he
was deeply experienced in all aspects of music-making from an early age. As
for MacDiarmid's writing thus to Sorabji, it would be interesting to know if
he received a reply. Sorabji worshipped Chisholm, performed for him when
he would perform for no-one else, and around 1938 Chisholm published an
essay on Sorabji.[15]

As a young virtuoso pianist, living and studying with the great Russian
pianist Pouishnoff, Erik Chisholm tackled a vast repertoire which he learnt by
heart. As a concert promoter, he brought some of Europe's greatest musicians
to Glasgow and performed alongside them or conducted their music. As a
conductor, he gave first British performances of Mozart and Gluck operas and
the world premiere of the complete *Trojans* by Berlioz, with ballet, two wind
bands and only an hour interval between parts I and II on the final day. As a

composer he studied his own nation's music closely (for which I will person-
ally vouch), as well as that of Hindustan (for which the Hindustani singer
Prakritti Dutta will vouch). As for his fitness for the Chair of Music at Cape
Town University, Donald Tovey wrote:

> I hope that the high praise which is the least that I find due to Dr
> Erik Chisholm may not be discounted as the language of 'testimonio-
> lese'. [. . .] His own musical resources are very extensive and of a high
> order. [. . .] I have not met any person who dislikes him, and my own
> acquaintance with him entitles me to form a poor opinion of any such
> person.[16]

William Walton's support was equally enthusiastic:

> It is, I think, hardly necessary to say he is an excellent composer and
> that he combines a modernistic outlook with scholarly foundations.
> He is also most enterprising in other branches of music.[17]

We need to understand this magnificent achievement on its own terms: not
in the terms laid down for us by a poet who was stated by George Bruce to be
'tone deaf' (MacDiarmid himself would appear to have had no appreciation
of music)[18]; or on the terms of a somewhat embittered fellow composer, F. G.
Scott, according at least to information given by Maurice Lindsay in his book
on Scott and the Scottish Renaissance. Lindsay writes:

> Scott, however, had the notion (rightly as it turned out) 'that
> Chisholm hopes to push through some symphony of his own, eating
> up a good £150 of the fund, and is prepared to spend a paltry £50
> on me as a blind. He is a real snake in the grass, is Erik, and I get on
> guard whenever he makes a move in my direction'. The Chisholm
> volume eventually published in piano score was his ballet *The Forsaken
> Messiah*, [*sic*] and the Dunedin Society had, indeed, no funds thereaf-
> ter to publish the promised volume of Scott's songs.[19]

Such an attack on Chisholm cannot be allowed to pass without comment.
Chisholm, (whose £25 prize money had gone into the Dunedin Association's
music publishing fund) had championed Scott's music in print and in the

programmes of both the Active Society and the Dunedin Association. He had had little enough of his own music in print by 1940, whereas Scott had already published five volumes of songs with Bayley & Ferguson. MacDiarmid, writing from Whalsay, described it as 'the Chisholm-Dunedin Society-MMM-Celtic Ballet-Willa Muir racket'.[20] But a more likely explanation for Scott's disparaging comment is that he was probably smarting a good deal from the results of the Dunedin composition competition. In the second category thereof, he had come third with his *Overture Renaissance* to Stewart Findlay's *Violin Sonata* and Malcolm MacDonald's *Overture to Youth*. In the song category, where he might reasonably have expected to do well, neither Bax, Tovey nor Buesst (the judges of the competition) thought any entry merited the prize, though Scott's *Guid E'en to you Kimmer* got an honourable mention.[21] One wonders whether Lindsay's extraordinary alteration of the title of *The Forsaken Mermaid* to *The Forsaken Messiah* (in the passage from his book quoted previously) was not a Freudian slip, favouring his own champion. It is worth pointing out that in 1962 Chisholm 'caused Scott's entire archive to be photostatted'[22] for the Mitchell Library, as Lindsay himself admits. Not the work of a snake – nor yet a rabbit or a caterpillar.

Let us then lay aside partial opinion and move on to the facts of the matter – namely Chisholm's music. There are three phases to Chisholm's modernism. First, his engagement with and extension of Scottish traditional music – primarily of Gaelic origin: secondly, his study of Hindustani music, which led to the composition of several major works: and thirdly, the modernist operas, which include settings of Strindberg, O'Neill and Brecht. Unfortunately, there is a tendency to regard modernism and traditional music as being polar opposites. In literature, the gap is bridged by Joyce who, not content with localising the *Odyssey*, then writes *Finnegan's Wake*, which relies fundamentally on Gaelic mythology and has no need of the Greeks. In music, however, few are allowed to bridge that gap, and one of the few is Bela Bartók. Bartók twice came to Scotland at Chisholm's invitation. He was Chisholm's senior by twenty-four years, but for those who would wish to stick with the description of Chisholm as 'MacBartók', it is worth pointing out that what Chisholm had been doing with Hebridean music, from as early as 1929,[23] pre-dates the bulk of Bartók's *Mikrokosmos*.

Chisholm's *Straloch Suite* dates from 1933 and is based upon airs from the lost *Robert Gordon of Straloch Lute Book* of 1627 which survives in a copy made in 1847. This interest in Scotland's early music was a Scottish response to the antiquarianism of the European modernists such as Stravinsky and Hindemith, who were exploring neoclassical and earlier idioms. But the quintessential modernist who was also deeply involved in traditional music was undoubtedly Bartók. Chisholm knew Bartók's music well. Indeed in 1929 or 1930 he gave what must have been one of the very first performances of Bartók's *Piano Concerto No. 1* – a work demanding virtuosic pianism and establishing a new, almost brutal, language that few were ready to grasp. Chisholm was only in his mid-twenties when he played it, accompanied by the St Matthew's United Free Church organ – there was absolutely no hope whatever of a Scottish orchestra performing such a work at that time. But Chisholm did more than perform. Besides twice hosting Bartók in Glasgow, Chisholm discussed music of all sorts with him, and introduced him to *piobaireachd*, to Bartók's absolute delight. Chisholm has frequently been dubbed 'MacBartók'. This may be fair enough, but let me caution you just a little when you listen to *Galua Tom* and *I Long for thy Virginitie* both from his *Straloch Suite*. You might be forgiven for thinking that the off-beat rhythms accompanying *Galua Tom* are derived from Bartók's Bulgarian influences, but they are actually derived directly from the original seventeenth-century lute piece.[24] This music was composed in 1933. It is now nearly eighty years later and I do not believe that any Scottish composer has done anything better in this line. Chisholm was happy to compose for children also, and in this he was paralleling, with equal brilliance, the didactic folkloristic arrangements of Bartók's *Mikrokosmos*. For example, Chisholm's version of the *piobaireachd MacKintosh's Lament* is beautifully conceived for children, not too difficult, varied in mood and technique, yet true to the idiom. It is a perfect miniature easily as good as anything in the *Mikrokosmos*.[25] It is traditional, but modern, with its beautifully judged modal bi-tonalism, sharpening the edges of the lament.

However, neither Chisholm nor Scott can be accused of subservience to the tradition, and both reflect MacDiarmid's reaction to William Johnstone's painting:

> Our task is not to reproduce Nature
> But to create and enrich it
> By method like musical notes, mathematical tables, geometry
> Of which Nature knows nothing,
> Artificially constructed by man
> For the manifestation of his knowledge
> And his creative will.[26]

For musicians, the connections between nature and mathematics and geometry were as old as Pythagoras and had been passed down as such and pursued by the greatest scientific and artistic minds from Boethius to Newton, with Kepler and a few others in between. In painting, sculpture and architecture the same was true – art was derived from nature, not creating it (*pace* MacDiarmid). Geometry and mathematics were inherent in it. Thus, if we take the structure of a piece of *ceòl mòr* (*piobaireachd*), we can analyse it with much the same kind of structural intensity as can be applied to early Gaelic poetry. William Johnstone's fine portrait of F. G. Scott (c. 1933), draws upon similar structural interests.

Modernist structures, then, were not antipathetic to traditions, be they those of 'native' music, or of formal portraiture. But to find examples of the depth of Chisholm's ability to probe human psychology, one has to reach out from such Scottish works as the first movement of the *Pictures from Dante* and the profoundly thoughtful *Night Song of the Bards*, (about both of which I have written extensively elsewhere), to those influenced by Hindustani music, or by modernist drama.[27]

Night Song of the Bards demonstrates what might very well elude the literary critic: namely that even in MacPherson there can be discovered matter of profound philosophical import. I have argued, unsuccessfully, with some philosophers, that music can be philosophy. Sadly, the notion that philosophy is only to be expressed in words and numbers appears to prevail in academic philosophical circles, and the supremely beautiful logic of the discourse of a fugue, be it by Shostakovich or Bach, eludes them. The reason is, of course, quite simple: in most cases they do not know the language and might be as well trying to study their philosophy in proto-Indo-European.

Likewise, there is frequently a failing among literary critics to appreciate the significance of the lyric gift. Wilhelm Müller is much denigrated as a very minor German romantic poet – but he always said his poems were written for music. It took a Schubert to understand them, not just in their simplicity, but in their profundity. Schubert could not have composed *Winterreise* and *Schöne Müllerin* without Müller, because Müller's was a unique vision. As with MacPherson's footnote in *Croma*, there is no logical discourse, nor any obvious poetic 'argument'. What there is, is pointed observation and careful insistence, coupled with very simple storytelling. If only Müller could have heard Schubert's settings, and if only MacPherson could have heard Chisholm's, they would have known that they had not laboured in vain.

Although essentially Scottish, *Night Song of the Bards* was also influenced by Chisholm's encounter with Hindustani music. In his Hindustani works, Chisholm explores a very different psychology from that of the west. There is a colourful extravagance as well as a sensual intensity, the latter most seductively obvious in the second movement of the *Hindustani Piano* Concerto. This is how I have described it elsewhere:

> It is an *Andante*: a set of seven variations on a theme based on *Râg Shri*. It is associated with the months of December and January and with the early evening. The image that goes with it is of a youth of such beauty that women become infatuated, and anger is soothed. But it can also be spiritual in its effect, like a call to evening prayer.[28] In Chisholm's opening statement, the notes of the *Aroha* (ascent) and *Avaroha* (descent) are combined, and accompany a melodic line similarly derived. The movement is a wonderfully compelling exploration of mystery, sensuousness and allure. In particular, the fifth variation draws close to the mood and the mode of *Râg Shri*, extruding a sinuous line against a rippling ostinato that breaks upon the shores of this exotic music in gentle but urgent waves. One critic found this overdone,[29] but its seduction is not for one moment over-prolonged, and the beauty with which Chisholm embellishes the line, with subtle use of repeated notes and tremolo, would surely have created sensations down Sorabji's spine. Sorabji might well have preferred to receive the dedication of this work, rather than the heavenly purity of Beatrice as envisioned in *Pictures from Dante*; but Chisholm's true musical homage is here, for it is in passages such as this that the scent-laden sensuality of Sorabji's own *Djâmi* drifts into the more austere world of Chisholm and, as the *Song of Solomon* would have it, steals like little foxes into the heart of the beloved.[30]

But Chisholm was not so seduced by oriental sensuality as to ignore the realities of occidental angst. The two come together in his astonishing operatic setting of Strindberg's *Simoon*, which I have been able to study only from the orchestral score. That was, however, sufficient to show that this is a riveting drama, and a composition of unearthly and magically varied sounds and textures, both vocal and instrumental. Along with *Simoon*, Chisholm's equally astonishing opera based upon Eugene O'Neill's *Before Breakfast* was given in

New York. With O'Neill's agreement, Chisholm changed the title to *Dark Sonnet* and structured the whole work in sonnet form, while adhering word for word to the O'Neill text, as he also did for the English translation of the Strindberg. Chisholm's insight into the state of mind of Mrs Roland brings to O'Neill's stark kitchen-sink tragedy a depth of feeling, both aggressive and wounded and as full of longing as it is of hatred, that is more hinted at than realised in the text itself. *Dark Sonnet* has been produced with great success on several occasions – televised in the 1950s and, most recently performed in Cape Town. *Simoon* has yet to be heard in its full orchestral dress, although it was performed in New York with piano accompaniment. I do not want to die without having heard it as Chisholm intended, for it is, in my view, a modernist masterpiece.

Finally, it is one of the major problems in assessing Scottish music from the nineteenth century onwards, that the bulk of the major works is unavailable in print or, indeed on recording. Chisholm might be considered to be a fortunate exception, in that two of his orchestral works are available on CD and two of his concertos are forthcoming on the Hyperion label. But not one of his operas is commercially available in any form – and the same applies to the operas of MacCunn and Mackenzie, never mind their oratorios. It was into such major works that these composers put some of their best efforts, but it is hard enough for researchers to assess complex material from manuscript scores and parts, never mind others to appreciate the major roles their works should play in the story of our cultural development. There remains much to be done.

Notes

1 The present chapter is adapted from a spoken paper, illustrated by contextual visual and musical examples, given at the Association for Scottish Literary Studies conference on Scottish and International Modernism, held at the University of Stirling in June 2009. Inevitably, it has not been possible to reproduce it fully in its original illustrated form in this print-based publication. References to available recordings will be given in the endnotes where relevant. The original presentation was part of a five-year joint research project between Sabhal Mòr Ostaig and the University of Dundee called *Uinneag Dhan Àird an Iar* – Window to the West.

2 Somhairle MacGill-Eain (Sorley MacLean), 'Hallaig', *Spring Tide and Neap Tide: Selected Poems 1932–72* (Edinburgh: Canongate, 1977), p. 142.

3 For more information on these collectors and their publications, see John Purser, *Scotland's Music* (1992: Edinburgh: Mainstream Publishing, 2009).

4 See Purser, *Scotland's Music*, 2009, pp. 298–300.

5 'St Brendan's Graveyard', *Songs of Francis George Scott 1880–1958*, selected and edited by Neil Mackay (Aylesbury: Roberton Publications, 1980), p. 107.

6   Buchanan's poem is reproduced in its entirety in the liner notes for the CD *Cecil Coles – Music from Behind the Lines*, Hyperion CDA67293. The Coles score itself is only available in ms. in the NLS and the Scottish Music Centre. The poem was first published in Buchanan's complete works, published in 1901.

7   Ronald Center, Altarus Records AIR-2-9100. The *Piano Sonata* is recorded on *Piano Music from Scotland*, Olympia OCD 264, Tracks 9–12.

8   See Cecil Gray, *Musical Chairs* (London: Thames Publishing, 1985), and Pauline Gray, *Cecil Gray his Life and Notebooks* (London: Thames Publishing, 1989).

9   Gray, *Musical Chairs*, p. 17.

10 See Cecil Gray, *The Temptation of St Anthony*, vocal score (London: Chappell & Co, 1954) p.47 et seq.

11 Copy of Testimonial partly dated and addressed from Sir Arnold Bax, London, 1938, University of Cape Town University Archives, Chair of Music 1939–1945, Box 12.1.5.

12 Hugh MacDiarmid, writing under the pseudonym of Isobel Guthrie, 'Mr Scott and Scottish Music', *Northern Review* August 1924; reprinted in Calder, Murray and Riach (eds) *Hugh MacDiarmid: The Raucle Tongue Volume I* (Manchester: Carcanet, 1996), pp. 218–19.

13 Hugh MacDiarmid, letter to Khaikhosru Shapurji Sorabji 27 June 1965, Grieve, Edwards and Riach (eds) *Hugh MacDiarmid: New Selected Letters*, (Manchester: Carcanet, 2001), p. 409.

14 Ibid, pp. 408–9.

15 Erik Chisholm, *Kaikhosru Sorabji: An essay by Erik Chisholm, with a Descriptive Catalogue of his Works* (London, c. 1938), reprinted privately c. 1964.

16 Undated copy of Testimonial from Donald Tovey, Hedenham Lodge, Bungay, Suffolk. University of Cape Town University Archives, Chisholm personal file.

17 Partly dated copy of letter from William Walton, Ashby St. Ledgers, Rugby. 1938. University Archives, Chair of Music 1939–1945, Box 12.1.5

18 Personal communications from George Bruce and Maurice Lindsay.

19 Maurice Lindsay, *Francis George Scott and The Scottish Renaissance* (Edinburgh: Paul Harris, 1980), p. 208. *The Forsaken Messiah* should of course have been titled *The Forsaken Mermaid*.

20 MacDiarmid, Letter to F. G. Scott, 28 August 1940, *New Selected Letters*, p. 185.

21 Anon, 'Scots Composers', *Evening Dispatch*, 20.3.1940. Morag Chisholm Papers, Press Cuttings, Scotland 1939–1940.

22 Quoted in Lindsay, *Francis George Scott and the Scottish Renaissance*, p. 152

23 Purser, *Erik Chisholm, Scottish Modernist*, 2009, p. 41. It is not known who first coined this nickname, but it has been passed on via a kind of 'oral tradition'.

24 See Ronn MacFarlane, *The Scottish Lute*, Dorian DOR-90129, Track 22: *Erik Chisholm Music for Piano* Volume 1, Dunelm Records DRD0222, Track 3: Purser, *Erik Chisholm, Scottish Modernist*, p. 9.

25 *Erik Chisholm Music for Piano* Volume 1, Dunelm Records DRD0222, Track 13.

26 Hugh MacDiarmid, 'Ode to the North Wind', *Complete Poems 1920–1976* (London: Martin Brian & O'Keefe, 1978), II, p. 1075.

27 Purser, pp. 102–121. Also liner notes for *Erik Chisholm Piano Music* Volume 6, diversions dvd 24149, tracks 33–38. *Pictures from Dante* can be heard on Dutton Epoch CDLX 7239, Tracks 6–7. See also for *Night Song of the Bards*, John Purser, *Scottish Studies Review* 6.1, Spring 2005, pp. 43–58.

28 The characteristics associated with the various râgas are derived from the relevant comments in *Sangit Bhava* and from Alain Daniélou's *The Râgas of Northern Indian Music*, London, 1968, Part II.

29 Ernest Fleischman, in an otherwise thoroughly laudatory review, wrote that 'The insistent
    ground of the sixth [variation] (for piano solo) tended to pall somewhat, though.' 'E. F.',
    'First Performance of Chisholm Concerto', In: *The Cape Times*, 23.11.1949.
30 Purser, *Erik Chisholm, Scottish Modernist*, pp. 142–145. The two Chisholm piano concertos
    are due out on the Hyperion label by 2012.

Prismatic Modernities: Towards a Recontextualisation of Scottish Modernism

CARLA SASSI

Introductory

It is appropriate to open the present discussion with a terminological remark of no small consequence: the notion of a Scottish modernism (privileged in the present essay), by now fully established among critics,[1] is in fact a relatively recent one. Its first (tentative) usage possibly dates back to a 1987 study on T. S. Eliot by Angus Calder, who mentions Hugh MacDiarmid's *Drunk Man* as one of the works influenced by *The Waste Land* and defines it as 'the masterwork of Scottish "modernism".'[2] Calder's use of inverted commas signals here what has been a long-standing insecurity regarding the appropriateness of such a phrase. On the other hand, the much more established term 'Scottish Renaissance', whose chronological span largely coincides with the conventional periodisation of Euro-American modernism, was for a long time perceived and described both within and without Scotland as a primarily vernacular/nationalist movement, which related modernism exclusively through MacDiarmid – its most visible and charismatic representative. As Margery Palmer McCulloch has observed, 'studies of early twentieth century writing in Scotland seldom have the word "modernism" in their indexes'.[3] In fact, as recent criticism has brought to light, while MacDiarmid was ostensibly the only writer within the Renaissance explicitly engaging with avant-garde and metropolitan modernist practices, his many contemporary colleagues and fellow country(wo)men worked on an equally radical agenda of modernisation of Scottish literary expressions and, in their own different ways, by breaking away from the insular boundaries of an Anglo-centrically defined Scottishness, promoted a trans/national revision of their cultural identity. Even by quite narrowly canonical standards, and irrespective of MacDiarmid's kinship with the metropolitan avant-garde, the Scottish Renaissance is then a modernist expression in its own right. The choice of the term Scottish modernism for the present discussion, therefore, is not to be taken as a negation of the Scottish Renaissance's essentially modernist stance, but rather as an indication of the need for a broader and more inclusive perspective, both in terms of aesthetic modes and thematic/ideological concerns. No matter how amply conceived, in fact, an affiliation with the Scottish Renaissance always implied that nationalist/localist agenda, which was being embraced by more and more people as the twentieth century progressed, as recalled by Helen Cruickshank:

> In Scotland many felt that even in our own country there was not enough knowledge of our cultural heritage, and there is no doubt that the rising tide of national Scottish sentiment brought many members into the movement.[4]

While such 'national sentiment' remains no doubt a conspicuous feature of modernist expressions in Scotland, it can only provide a partial account of the contribution of some of its most significant and internationally renowned exponents, such as the poet and translator Edwin Muir, or even of relevant sections of the work of ostensibly 'nationalist' writers who entertained extra-Scottish affiliations and interests (Lewis Grassic Gibbon or Catherine Carswell), and ultimately deprives us of the possibility of articulating a comprehensively objective picture of this historical/cultural period. Finally, our terminological choice points in the direction of a timely re-contextualisation of this chapter of Scotland's cultural history within the contemporary debate on global modernism(s) and modernities. The main aim of the present essay is indeed to attempt to provide a theoretical framework for such re-contextualisation, as well as to foster comparative dialogue among and across theoretical/empirical areas of academic investigation within the expanding field of modernist studies. Before doing so, however, it is necessary to survey briefly some of the well-known problems, identified in recent years mainly by postcolonial and feminist critics, relating to early definitions of modernism as a timebound, Euro-American avant-garde movement and as an experimental literary/artistic expression, located approximately between the turn of the century and the Second World War.

A first problem area may be identified in the ideological climate of the 1950s and 1960s, when the first theories of modernity and modernism were shaped and deployed. Indeed, as David Slater has pointed out, the post-World War Two decades were marked by the establishment and subliminal diffusion of the binary distinction between 'modern' and 'traditional' social systems:

The modern was defined in relation to a series of ostensibly primary attributes of Western societies – the scientific, secular, rational, innovative, democratic, open, plural, urban-industrial, achievement-oriented, and universally relevant – to be distinguished from the traditional, which was defined in relation to characteristics such as the particular, the religious, backwardness, the predominance of the rural, undeveloped divisions of labour, pre-democratic institutions, over-population.[5]

It was largely within this hegemonic perspective, on the one side conflating modernity with progress, on the other gauging the social/cultural value of communities on the ground of their alignment with Western/metropolitan practices, that the first modernist canon was exclusively constructed – both in terms of representative authors and texts and in terms of 'authorised' readings of canonical texts. The first definitions of modernism marginalised or excluded, largely on the grounds of gender, race/ethnic prejudice, even many of those who had been indisputably at the forefront of the Euro-American cosmopolitan experimental avant-garde, or who networked with modernist artists/circles in the great metropolitan centres – a pivotal figure such as Virginia Woolf, for example, was excluded from the *Modern British Literature* volume of the 1973 *Oxford Anthology of English Literature* (which nonetheless included Edwin Muir and MacDiarmid, presented however through a limited number of poems and somewhat patronisingly defined as eccentric and 'remote'[6]). The Harlem Renaissance, 'frequently faulted for its "failure" to produce *vital, original, effective,* or "modern" art',[7] was also excluded along similar ideological lines, until very recent times, from canonical representations of Anglo-American modernism.

A second problem area is represented by the history of the reception of modernism, inextricably bound to the history of the academic study and teaching of literature: this is especially true of the Anglo-American context, where English Literature became an established academic discipline between the turn of the century and the early decades of the twentieth century. The diffusion and appreciation of modernist texts, therefore, has notoriously depended in a larger measure than that of, say, Romantic or Victorian texts on institutional/authorised readings. The 'radical' agenda of modernist expressions has then, interestingly, run parallel to the 'institutional incorporation' of literature, described by Peter Childs as a gradual strengthening of its normative function within a growingly centralised and patriarchal-oriented British state:

Previously, literary study had been considered suitable for women and not for men, but in the early 1900s it was more and more thought that [...] literature could teach codes of behaviour and define national identity. Consequently the literary 'world' became colonised by various benign commercial and didactic interests: the *Times Literary Supplement,* the Oxford University Press series of World's Classics and the Everyman imprint [...] and the creation of the English Association (1907) to establish the essential role English literature should play in British culture.[8]

There is then a high degree of collusion between the modernist revolution and the 'second revolution' (in Charles Newman's definition) represented by the coming of age of academic criticism: modernism is indeed 'transmitted through criticism, to the extent that the two revolutions have become indistinguishable',[9] and it is such collusion that largely accounts for canonical definitions of modernism that conflate Ezra Pound's 'Make it New' with a cult of the difficult and obscure, and that exclude writers/artists not conforming (in terms of gender, race and/or cultural affiliation) to the powerful norm of the newly defined 'English' canon.

A third and final problem which is worthwhile to refer to briefly is the aporia generated by the academic-centred transmission of modernism, promoted as a cosmopolitan/transnational expression and yet taught and studied within the essentially national structure of academic institutions and programmes. The contradictory outcome of this conflicting pull has been on the one hand the establishment of the study of modernism within nationally defined disciplinary areas (subtly undermining its transnationalist radical agenda); and on the other the reinforcement of the prestige of 'major' national traditions through their allegedly 'superior' stance of metropolitan cosmopolitanism – that supposed capacity to espouse multiple cultures and multiple languages which is still seen as incompatible with peripheral or 'vernacular' traditions. What is often referred to as 'English modernism' is a case in point: largely constructed around charismatic and yet non-native and/or non resident/non-English identified figures such as Joyce, Eliot or Pound, it has been received and transmitted by academic scholarship as a cosmopolitan and yet (more cryptically) also as a specifically 'national' expression.

The impact of these three problem areas on both the reception and the transmission of Scottish modernism in general and of the Scottish

Renaissance in particular cannot be overestimated: Scottish writers of this period (arguably to a higher degree than their eighteenth or nineteenth-century colleagues) have been framed as a 'vernacular' or local expression by an overarching academic discourse which thrived on the binary opposition between local and cosmopolitan, and therefore deemed incompatible with metropolitan modernism. An authoritative reference work such as *The Oxford Critical and Cultural History of Modernist Magazines* (2009), albeit recuperating 'regional' modernisms, still conveniently revolves around (and thus reinforces) the binary opposition between 'metropolis' (England) and a vaguely named 'beyond' (Wales, Scotland, Ireland – about one ninth of the whole volume),[10] defined only through its distance from London, thus reinforcing both its centrality as well as the hegemonic relation between the two terms. Their frequent affiliation with popular/vernacular culture, their practice of experimentalism within a markedly traditional framework (as in the case of Lewis Grassic Gibbon or Nan Shepherd), their 'remoteness' from the hubs of Euro-American modernism, their concern with issues of national identity have been seen for a long time as features which automatically excluded them from the modernist practice or located them at its margins.

Re-mapping Modernisms

Re-definitions of modernism starting from the 1980s have largely clustered around two strategic lines: a) expanding and problematising the modernist canon and therefore drawing a larger and more detailed cultural map by retrieving silenced/marginalised voices/regions (we might describe this as an 'archaeological' phase); and b) opening up to a radical re-vision of modernist studies by questioning the very principles of traditional 'cartography' and radically rethinking central issues like periodisation, genealogies, affiliations, and forms/genres. In both cases re-visions have been largely fuelled and shaped by the two great revolutions of thought of the twentieth century – feminism and postcolonialism – and have led to a gradual redefinition of both the modernist canon and eventually of the modernist paradigm. Postcolonial theories, in particular, have encouraged a re-evaluation of the centrality of Empire and hence of culture-clash, displacement, otherness in modernist expressions. Indeed modernism, as Stephen Slemon claims: 'would have been unthinkable had it not been for the assimilative power of Empire to appropriate the cultural work of a heterogeneous world "out there" and to reproduce it for its own social and discursive ends'.[11] Postcolonial theories have taught us to transcend the narrow limits of Euro-American expressions and to envisage a global history of modernism. As Edward Said, for example, has reminded us:

> In the interwar period students from India, Senegal, Vietnam and the Caribbean flocked to London and Paris; journals, reviews, and political associations formed — one thinks of the pan-African congresses in England, magazines like *Cri des nègres*, parties like the *Union des Travailleurs Nègres* established by expatriates, dissidents, exiles and refugees, who paradoxically work better in the heart of empire than its far-flung domains, or of the invigoration provided African movements by the Harlem Renaissance. A common anti-imperialist experience was felt, with new associations between Europeans, Americans and non-Europeans, and they transformed disciplines and gave voice to new ideas that unalterably changed that structure of attitude and reference which had endured for generations within European culture.[12]

To borrow Said's phrase, metropolitan modernism is as much a voyage out as a 'voyage in': it involves that encounter with other cultures and places which nineteenth-century imperialism fostered and enforced, but also the productive force of 'peripheral, off-centre work that gradually enters the West and then requires acknowledgement'.[13] Far from being a purely Western expression, modernism is born out of colonial hybridisation and cultural syncretism/ clash, articulated as either a celebration (as in Matisse or Picasso's 'primitive' art) or as a threatening event (as in Joseph Conrad's journey into the 'Heart of Darkness'). Modernism is therefore about 'worlding'/transcending national borders as much as it is about the periphery's resisting homogenisation to the centre, holding onto its own 'local' specificity. It is largely through postcolonialism that we have learned to look at modernism as both a local *and* a global phenomenon. Elleke Bohemer, for example, has called for 'an expanded picture of a globalised and constellated modernism' taking into account the various modernist and nationalist expressions of the non-metropolitan and non-white writers of this period, including:

> the eclecticism of the 1900s Bengal art movement pioneered by E. B. Havell, Abanindranath Tagore, and Sister Nivedita; the Jamaican Claude McKay's 1910s articulations both in Caribbean patois and standard English; the atmospheric 1920s poetry of the Australian Ken

Slessor or the Fauvist paintings of his compatriot Margaret Preston; and the Eliot-influenced progressive Hindi poetry of Ajneya and Gajanan Madhav Muktibodh in the 1940s and 1950s.[14]

The gradual revelation of a complex network of different and yet related modernisms across the globe has also generated new, challenging paradigmatic frames. For Schedler, for example:

> modernism does look surprisingly different when one leaves the metropolis and stands not in the province [...] but on the border – that marginal space (the frontier, the colonial periphery, the border-lands) beyond the metropolitan center, where distinct cultural groups come into contact and conflict.[15]

He thus introduces the notion of a 'border modernism', sharing 'with its metropolitan kin the modernist predicament (the question of subjectivity and the problem of epistemology) and likewise the search of representational devices to respond to it',[16] and yet conveying quite a different type of response to modernity:

> In border modernism, the external world is seen as constitutive of the self, and identity is explored through association with those defined as culturally, racially, or linguistically 'other'. [...] The conception of identity as constituted in relation to the external world and through association with others is represented in border modernism through an emphasis on historical context, oral forms of expression, and simplification.[17]

While it is beyond the scope of this chapter to provide an exhaustive survey of recent re-figurations of modernism, it is worthwhile to stress here their potentially radical impact on a re-vision of Scottish modernism: the emphasis on the border rather than on the metropolis (here deployed in a North American context), for example, is indeed a case in point. This is in fact a paradigm that may be seen as capable of articulating at least in part the specificity of the Scottish context[18] – similarly retaining a privileged relation to the external world (both in terms of political commitment and/or – in a strictly literary perspective – closeness to the tenets of realism), similarly affected by the 'history' (underlying the very notion of a Scottish 'Renaissance') and engaging/experimenting with oral forms and genre (as for example in Lewis Grassic Gibbon's classic, *A Scots Quair*).

European-centred scholarship has also, in the past two decades, shifted its focus on the investigation of modernism as a local/vernacular expression as well as a transnational one. Recent studies have highlighted how in many European countries, such as Hungary, Poland, Romania, Italy and Greece, modernist expressions went indeed hand in hand with a quest for a national style, as elements of modernity blended in with notions of tradition, of 'high' and 'low'/popular/folk culture and art. Even at a theoretical level, the 'local geographies' of modernism have gained growing recognition in the academia alongside critical work on regionalism in literature:[19] as Marjorie Pryse has put it, 'regionalism allows modernism to be understood as a crisis of definition'[20] and has become a crucial term of reference 'in the larger conversation concerning [. . .] modernism, cosmopolitanism, and transnationalism'.[21] Possibly as a partial response to such wide re-evaluation of the local/traditional within and outwith modernist studies, several scholars have, in recent years and from different perspectives, traced the provincial roots of 'British' modernisms, not just in relation to Wales, Scotland or Ireland, but to England itself. Scottish scholar Robert Crawford has pioneered such an approach by presenting Eliot and Pound as the most eloquent examples of 'provincials' who brought their native strength to the metropolis.[22] Crawford, furthermore, has observed that 'even among English writers, the culminating voice of the Victorian novel is not metropolitan but resolutely provincial', and that 'there are hidden currents between these provincial voices and their twentieth-century inheritors which have yet to be fully explored'.[23] Unwittingly responding to Crawford's call for an investigation of the intimate connections between the late nineteenth century and the early decades of the twentieth century, Alexandra Harris, among others, has very recently revealed the important 'Romantic', nostalgic and localised strain of England's modernism – a 'desire to invoke tradition' as a response to the crisis triggered by modernity.[24] Her study, awarded the Guardian First Book Award in 2010, goes also a long way to highlight the impact of the rural and the provincial in the construction of English modernist imagination.

Finally, it is worthwhile remembering that if, within the 'Atlantic Archipelago', England's vernacular modernism has only been recently re-evaluated as an important alternative to the canonical London-centred, cosmopolitan depiction of an elitist and avant-gardist movement, issues of nationalism/regionalism have been amply investigated in relation to Irish modernism, where, very much as in Scotland, 'nationalism's valorisation of a perceived traditional identity can be seen as a rejection of the anxieties of modern existence'.[25]

This deeply changed and continually evolving theoretical/empirical scenario, locating modernism at the confluence of globality and locality, depicting it as a prismatic structure that involves relatedness and connectedness among different regions, rather than as a homogeneous event with a centre and peripheries, allows today for a radical re-evaluation of Scotland's nationalist and vernacular modernist expressions, rescuing them from accusations of eccentricity or unaccountability, and presenting them as akin to or interdependent of different modernisms across the globe.

Networking (Scottish) Modernism

If there is no doubt that the little critical consideration that Scottish modernism has received so far outside Scotland is largely grounded on the limitations implied in canonical definitions of modernism, it is also true that such definitions have colluded with twentieth-century constructions of the Scottish canon, according to which features such as cosmopolitanism or elitism were incompatible with the national, vernacular, 'democratic' focus of the Scottish tradition. This is a perspective that infiltrates, for example, Tom Normand's stance, when he claims that even though it cannot be argued that 'the modernist project failed in Scotland', it appears that 'where it succeeded it was under conditions quite unpropitious to its sustained growth'.[26] The biased approach of canonical representations of modernism has been then introjected rather than resisted, preventing Scottish Studies critics, until very recent times, from addressing some of the specifically radical aspects of Scottish modernism literature. Margery Palmer McCulloch's recent critical work in this field[27] has invaluably opened the path to further theoretical and empirical investigations in a field that still appears as extraordinarily under-investigated. With the single exception of Hugh MacDiarmid, most of the protagonists of the Scottish Renaissance, women especially (such as Willa Muir or Nan Shepherd), are still awaiting a full re-evaluation as 'vernacular modernists' – a re-evaluation which should be carried out in view not only of a sounder articulation of Scotland's literary history but, as importantly, of a re-visioning of modernism as a global event. As Chana Kronfeld contends, 'only if we construct the major through the minor, not – as current wisdom has it – the minor through the major, can we begin to discern the regionalism, contextual diversity, and interdependence of even the most highly canonical forms of modernism',[28] and indeed 'theories of modernism that are modelled on belated, decentered or linguistically minor practices may provide some insight into the processes that have become automatised or rendered imperceptible in the canonical center'.[29]

As a conclusion to this theoretical overview, it is appropriate to deal briefly with an empirical example of re-contextualisation of Scottish modernism and of the potential of an exchange between different academic discourses and practices. An Italian Government-funded international research project on 'Networking Women: Subjects, Places, Links Europe–America, 1890–1939 – towards a Rewriting of Cultural History'[30] between 1999 and 2004 developed a re-vision of the modernist paradigm focussing on the key image of the modernist 'network,' with reference to both the role often covered by modernist women (letter-writers, editors of journals, hostesses of literary salons etc.) and to a specific feature of modernist cultural production.[31] That networking was central to modernist practices is well-known: individual artists and writers often worked together in magazines, referenced each other, met at conferences and exhibitions – networking was both a political gesture and a practical solution for overcoming local isolation by creating a common space for communication, debate and experimentation within social/national contexts in which they were not infrequently marginalised or stigmatised. The Networking Women project, however, deployed this well-known infrastructural feature as a powerful conceptual tool, along the lines of feminist and postcolonial theories. As Susan Friedman, one of the participants, highlighted:

> The project [...] has used the metaphor of networking to track the crossroads of intersecting influences, the dynamism of exchange and change, and the relationality of production in the cultural sphere. Instead of focusing on single authors, movements, genders, or national traditions, the project has foregrounded connectivity across national, continental, ethnic, and gender borders.[32]

Equally central to the Networking Women project was Friedman's 'locational' approach, developed in the course of several publications, which gives new significance to site-specificity, emphasising multiple centres and points of origin for the study of modernism. Friedman has in fact called for 'a new spatial orientation for writing literary history' and 'a *situated* approach to Modernism worldwide', based on the 'assumption that each location on the globe has a geographically specific engagement with modernity that results in distinct forms of cultural expression.'[33] Such an approach develops along the lines of her theorisation of a 'locational feminism' paying 'attention to the specificities of time and space, but unlike fundamentalist identity politics [. . .] not parochially limited to a single feminist formation and [taking] as its founding principle the multiplicity of heterogeneous feminist movements.'[34]

It was against this theoretical background that the author of the present article, as a participating member of the project, worked on a re-reading of Catherine Carswell as a modernist networker – a letter-writer, a freelance journalist and reviewer, a 'life-writer' – as well as a leading representative of the Scottish Renaissance.[35] This was an opportunity not only to retrieve and discuss the work of a long marginalised writer, but also, by demonstrating the centrality of her literary practices to such revised modernist paradigm, and hence to both Scottish and global modernisms, to open up the construction of the Scottish Renaissance as a male/MacDiarmid dominated movement to a fruitful process of revision.

Carswell was a writer who was devoted to the local, but who was also deeply concerned with the global issues of her time – socialism, feminism, pacifism. Militantly Scottish but also a 'nomad' who travelled extensively in Europe and spent the greater part of her life in England, an experimental writer who yet practised traditional modes of expression and who described herself as not being a 'Modern',[36] she is indeed a quintessentially modernist networker, who 'travelled not only between different regions/nations but also between different genres of writing, privileging either hybrid forms of expression and/or anonymous and "ephemeral" ones.'[37] An attentive investigation of her heterogeneous and fragmentary body of work reveals a writer who might indeed be described (as she defined herself) as a 'tramp' or a 'scatter-brain' – someone who is 'not adept at excluding or concentrating', but is instead joyously caught in 'the multiplicity of [her] interests',[38] a writer who consciously chose to locate herself in a borderland, famously evoked in the title of her autobiography – *Lying Awake* – describing a balanced and somewhat harmonious suspension between sleep and wake, death and life. Carswell's work, often articulating a nationalist agenda and yet subtly undermining the discourse of the nation, creates a liminal space between assimilation and alterity, between local and global transcending 'the binary opposition province/metropolis, around which (high) Modernist discourse was constructed'[39] and thus brings 'into visibility [that] diasporic modernity and modernist expression based in a dialectic of "aller retour", of going and returning, of homelessness and homecoming'.[40]

By way of conclusion: in the context of an ongoing, wide-ranging re-vision of the meaning and scope of modernism as a global phenomenon, as a 'prismatic singularity', we can indeed discard the negative representation of Scottish modernism as a belated and minor offshoot of the normative metropolitan centre, and embrace instead the positive notion of a cultural expression in its own right, a 'local' search for the representational devices to respond to the global predicament of modernity, with its own set of concerns and features, in dialogue with other (world) modernisms. This new perspective also frees us from the obligation to focus exclusively on MacDiarmid and allows us to extend our investigation to include all Scottish writers who engaged with modernity, irrespective of their gender, their national(istic) concerns, or their 'rural' focus and distance from the metropolis or their reluctance to engage with avant-garde formal practices. Only such an inclusive approach will at last reveal the local specificity of Scottish modernism – refracted through the local–global dialectic of inside and outside, of belonging and exile – along with its global relevance.

Notes

1   See for example Peter Brooker et al (eds), *The Oxford Handbook of Modernisms* (Oxford: Oxford University Press, 2010), pp. 765–81, in which Margery Palmer McCulloch's 'Scottish Modernism' is presented alongside 'Irish Modernism' and other 'National and Transnational Modernisms'.

2   Calder, Angus, *T. S. Eliot* (Sussex: Harvester Press, 1987), p. 47. Margery [Palmer] McCulloch's use of modernism related to a Scottish text is even earlier. See her 'Modernism and the Scottish Tradition: The Duality of *A Drunk Man Looks at the Thistle*', Chapman 25, Autumn 1979, pp. 50–6.

3   Margery Palmer McCulloch, *Scottish Modernism and Its Contexts, 1918–1959: Literature, National Identity and Cultural Exchange* (Edinburgh: Edinburgh University Press, 2009), p. 1.

4   Helen Cruickshank, *Octobiography* (Montrose: Standard Press, 1976), p. 68.

5   Slater, David. *Geopolitics and the Post-Colonial: Rethinking North-South Relations* (Malden, Mass: Blackwell, 2004), pp. 60–1.

6   Frank Kermode and John Hollander (eds), *The Oxford Anthology of English Literature: Modern British Literature* (New York: Oxford University Press, 1973), pp. 559–67.

7   Houston A. Baker, *Modernism and the Harlem Renaissance* (Chicago: University of Chicago Press, 1987), p. xiii.

8   Peter Childs, *Modernism* (London: Routledge, 2008), p. 23.

9   Charles Newman, *The Post-Modern Aura: The Act of Fiction in an Age of Inflation* (Evanston: Northwestern University Press, 1985), p. 27.

10   Brooker, Peter, and Andrew Thacker (eds), *The Oxford Critical and Cultural History of Modernist Magazines*. Vol. 1 (Oxford: Oxford University Press, 2009).

11   Stephen Slemon, 'Modernism's Last Post' in Ian Adam and Helen Tiffin (eds), *Past the Last Post: Theorizing Post-Colonialism and Post-Modernism* (New York: Harvester Wheatsheaf, 1991), p. 1.

12   Edward W. Said, *Culture and Imperialism* (New York: Knopf, 1993), pp. 241–2.

13   Ibid, p. 216.

14   Elleke Boehmer, *Empire, the National, and the Postcolonial, 1890–1920: Resistance in Interaction* (Oxford: Oxford University Press, 2002), p. 175.

15   Christopher Schedler, *Border Modernism: Intercultural Readings in American Literary Modernism. Literary Criticism and Cultural Theory* (New York: Routledge, 2002), p. xi.

16   Ibid, p. xiv.

17   Ibid.

18   See Carla Sassi, 'The (B)order in Modern Scottish Literature' in Ian Brown, Alan Riach (eds), *The Edinburgh Companion to Twentieth-Century Scottish Literature* (Edinburgh: Edinburgh University Press, 2009), pp. 145–55.

19   See *MFS Modern Fiction Studies*, 55:1 (2009). (Special issues on 'Regional Modernism', ed. Scott Herring).

20   Marjorie Pryse, 'Afterword: Regional Modernism and Transnational Regionalism' in *MFS Modern Fiction Studies*, 55:1 (2009), 189.

21   Ibid, 190.

22   Ibid, 216–70.

23   Robert Crawford, 'Modernism as Provincialism', *Devolving English Literature*. (Oxford: Clarendon Press, 1992), pp. 216, 217.

24   Alexandra Harris, *Romantic Moderns: English Writers, Artists and the Imagination from Virginia Woolf to John Piper* (London: Thames & Hudson, 2010), pp. 10–11.

25   Anne Markey, 'Modernism, Maunsel and the Irish Short Story' in Edwina Keown and Carol Taaffe (eds), *Irish Modernism: Origins, Contexts, Public*. (Oxford: Peter Lang, 2010), p. 52.

26   Tom Normand, *The Modern Scot: Modernism and Nationalism in Scottish Art, 1928–1955* (Aldershot: Ashgate, 2000), p. 5.

27   In addition to *Scottish Modernism and Its Contexts, 1918–1959: Literature, National Identity and Cultural Exchange*, previously cited, see *Modernism and Nationalism: Literature and Society in Scotland, 1918–1939 : Source Documents for the Scottish Renaissance* (Glasgow: Association for Scottish Literary Studies, 2004).

28   Chana Kronfeld, *On the Margins of Modernism: Decentering Literary Dynamics* (Berkeley: University of California Press, 1996), p. 5.

29   Ibid.

30   The project was funded by the Italian Department of Research (MIUR), coordinated by Marina Camboni (Università di Macerata) and articulated in two parts (1999–2000 and 2001–2002). It involved over forty researchers from different Italian universities and from different disciplinary areas, as well as non-Italian scholars of international renown.

31   See Marina Camboni, 'Networking Women: A Research Project and a Relational Model of the Cultural Sphere' in Marina Camboni (ed.), *Networking Women: Subjects, Places, Links*

Europe–America : Towards a Re-Writing of Cultural History, 1890–1939 : Proceedings of the International Conference, Macerata, March 25–27, 2002 (Roma: Edizioni di storia e letteratura, 2004), pp. 1–26.

32 Susan Stanford Friedman, 'Networking Women on a Transnational Landscape: Globalism, Modernism, and Gender' in Giovanna Covi (ed.), *Modernist Women Race Nation: Networking Women 1890–1950* (London: Mango Publishing, 2005), p. 33.

33 Susan Stanford Friedman, 'Modernism in a Transnational Landscape: Spatial Poetics, Postcolonialism, and Gender in Cesaire's Cahier/Notebook and Cha's *Dictee*'. *Paideuma* 32: 1/2/3 (Spring/Fall/Winter 2003), 41–42.

34 Susan Standford Friedman, *Mappings: Feminism and the Cultural Geographies of Encounter* (Princeton, N.J: Princeton University Press, 1998), p. 5.

35 See Carla Sassi, 'Relating Art to Life: Catherine's Carswell's Literary Biographies and Letters' in Marina Camboni (ed.), *Networking Women*, pp. 429–40.

36 Catherine Carswell, Letter to 'Flo' Marian McNeil, [?1930], National Library of Scotland, Manuscript Division, MS 26195.

37 Carla Sassi, '"I want to abolish Burns Nicht": Catherine Carswell's Transnational Re-definition of Scottish Identity', in Giovanna Covi (ed.), *Modernist Women Race Nation*, p. 63.

38 Catherine Carswell, *Lying Awake: An Unfinished Autobiography and Other Posthumous Papers,* ed. John Carswell (Edinburgh: Canongate Books, 1997), p. 175.

39 Sassi, '"I want to abolish Burns Nicht"', p. 62.

40 Friedman, 'Networking Women on a Transnational Landscape', p. 33.

Notes on Contributors

Jonathan Blackwood studied Art History at the University of St Andrews and the Courtauld Institute of Art, University of London. He is a freelance art historian and an honorary research associate of the University of Dundee. As well as research interests in modern and contemporary Scottish art, he has recently been working on the art history of the former Yugoslavia.

Aileen Christianson is a Senior Editor of *The Collected Letters of Thomas and Jane Welsh Carlyle*. Her publications include critical essays on Jane Welsh Carlyle, Muriel Spark, and Willa Muir, together with her most recent monograph *Moving in Circles: Willa Muir's Writings* (2007). She is an Honorary Fellow in the School of Literatures, Languages and Cultures, University of Edinburgh, and is currently writing *Jane Welsh Carlyle: Writing Volumes*.

Alexander J. Cuthbert is completing his doctoral thesis on the writings of Edwin Muir in the School of Critical Studies, University of Glasgow. His other research interests include European modernisms and the sixteenth-century poet and dramatist David Lyndsay. He contributes an annual bibliography of the previous year's publications to *Scottish Literary Review*.

Emma Dymock is a Post-doctoral Fellow in the Department of Celtic and Scottish Studies, University of Edinburgh. She gained a First Class Honours degree in Celtic Studies and a doctorate based on Sorley MacLean's *An Cuilithionn*. She has recently co-edited a new collected edition of MacLean's poetry with Christopher Whyte and is currently editing the Sorley MacLean–Douglas Young correspondence.

Mark Gaipa has a doctorate in Modern Literature from Brown University, has published on modernism, rhetoric and writing pedagogy, and has taught at Brown and Harvard Universities as well as at the Universities of Freiburg and Stuttgart in Germany. He has been Project Manager at the Modernist Journals Project since 2008.

Scott Lyall is Lecturer in Modern Literature at Edinburgh Napier University, having taught previously at Trinity College, Dublin, and the University of Exeter. He is the author of *Hugh MacDiarmid's Poetry and Politics of Place: Imagining a Scottish Republic*, published by Edinburgh University Press in 2006 and co-editor of *The Edinburgh Companion to Hugh MacDiarmid* (2011).

Alistair McCleery is Professor of Literature and Culture and Director of the Scottish Centre for the Book at Edinburgh Napier University. He has published widely on Scottish and Irish literature, particularly on Neil M. Gunn and James Joyce. He is co-author of *An Introduction to Book History* and *The Book History Reader*, and co-editor of *The History of the Book in Scotland 1880–2000*.

Margery Palmer McCulloch is the author of monographs on Neil M. Gunn and Edwin Muir, and co-editor of a collection of essays on Lewis Grassic Gibbon. Her most recent books are *Modernism and Nationalism* (2004), *Scottish Modernism and its Contexts* (2009), and, as co-editor, *The Edinburgh Companion to Hugh MacDiarmid* (2011). She is Senior Research Fellow at Glasgow University and co-editor of *Scottish Literary Review*.

John Purser is a composer, musicologist, poet and playwright, and author of the award-winning *Scotland's Music: A History of the Traditional and Classical Music of Scotland from Early Times to the Present Day*, published in 1992 with a new edition in 2007. His most recent book is *Erik Chisholm, Scottish Modernist 1904–1965* (2009). Dr Purser is also a Research Fellow at Sabhal mòr Ostaig, Isle of Skye.

Alan Riach is Professor of Scottish Literature at Glasgow University, General Editor of the *Collected Works of Hugh MacDiarmid*, and author of *Hugh MacDiarmid's Epic Poetry* (1991), *The Poetry of Hugh MacDiarmid* (1999), *Representing Scotland in Literature, Popular Culture and Iconography* (2005) and *Homecoming* (2009). He co-authored *Arts of Resistance: Poets, Portraits and Landscapes of Modern Scotland* (2008).

Ritchie Robertson is a graduate of Edinburgh and Oxford Universities and is currently Taylor Professor of German at Oxford University. His books include

Kafka: Judaism, Politics, and Literature (1985), *The 'Jewish Question' in German Literature, 1749–1939* (1999), *Kafka: A Very Short Introduction* (2004), and *Mock-Epic Poetry from Pope to Heine* (2009). In 2004 he became a Fellow of the British Academy. He is a Director of the Oxford Kafka Research Centre.

Carla Sassi is Associate Professor of English Literature at the University of Verona and specialises in Scottish and Postcolonial studies. Among her publications are *Why Scottish Literature Matters* (2005) and, as co-author, *Caribbean–Scottish Relations* (2007). She was a Royal Society of Edinburgh Visiting Research Fellow in 2008 and Visiting Research Fellow at Glasgow University in 2011.

Andrew J. Sneddon's doctorate from the University of Stirling focused on discourses of race, place and nationalism in the fiction and journalism of Neil M. Gunn. He has published several articles on the broadly political aspects of Gunn's oeuvre, has co-edited a book on poetry and sexuality, and has had a number of his own poems published.

Roderick Watson was educated at Aberdeen University and Peterhouse, Cambridge, and is Professor Emeritus at the University of Stirling. He has lectured and published very widely on the poetry of Hugh MacDiarmid, Scottish literature and culture, modernism, language and identity. He currently co-edits the *Journal of Stevenson Studies*.

Index

Lightning Source UK Ltd.
Milton Keynes UK
UKOW021128031011

179685UK00004B/4/P

9 781906 841072